Boundaries of Journalism

The concept of boundaries has become a central theme in the study of journalism. In recent years, the decline of legacy news organizations and the rise of new interactive media tools have thrust such questions as "what is journalism?" and "who is a journalist?" into the limelight.

Struggles over journalism are often struggles over boundaries. These symbolic contests for control over definition also mark a material struggle over resources. In short: boundaries have consequences. Yet there is a lack of conceptual cohesiveness in what scholars mean by the term "boundaries" or in how we should think about specific boundaries of journalism.

This book addresses boundaries head-on by bringing together a global array of authors asking similar questions about boundaries and journalism from a diverse range of perspectives, methodologies, and theoretical backgrounds.

Boundaries of Journalism assembles the most current research on this topic in one place, thus providing a touchstone for future research within communication, media and journalism studies on journalism and its boundaries.

Matt Carlson is associate professor of communication at Saint Louis University. His work examines the contested cultural construction of journalism. He is author of *On the Condition of Anonymity: Unnamed Sources and the Battle for Journalism* and co-editor of *Journalism, Sources, and Credibility: New Perspectives.*

Seth C. Lewis is an assistant professor and the Mitchell V. Charnley Fellow in the School of Journalism and Mass Communication at the University of Minnesota. He studies the changing nature of journalism amid the rise of sociotechnical phenomena such as big data, social media, and digital audience analytics.

Shaping Inquiry in Culture, Communication and Media Studies

Series Editor: Barbie Zelizer

Dedicated to bringing to the foreground the central impulses by which we engage in inquiry, the *Shaping Inquiry in Culture, Communication and Media Studies* series attempts to make explicit the ways in which we craft our intellectual grasp of the world.

Boundaries of Journalism

Professionalism, Practices and Participation

Edited by
Matt Carlson and Seth C. Lewis

Routledge
Taylor & Francis Group

LONDON AND NEW YORK

First published 2015
by Routledge
2 Park Square, Milton Park, Abingdon, Oxon, OX14 4RN

and by Routledge
711 Third Avenue, New York, NY 10017

Routledge is an imprint of the Taylor & Francis Group, an informa business

© 2015 Matt Carlson and Seth C. Lewis, editorial selection and material;
individual chapters, the contributors

The right of Matt Carlson and Seth C. Lewis to be identified as the authors
of the editiorial material and the individual authors for their chapters has
been asserted in accordance with sections 77 and 78 of the Copyright,
Designs and Patents Act 1988.

British Library Cataloguing in Publication Data
A catalogue record for this book is available from the British Library

Library of Congress Cataloging in Publication Data
Boundaries of journalism : professionalism, practices and participation / edited
by Matt Carlson and Seth C. Lewis.
pages cm. -- (Explorations in communication and history)
Includes bibliographical references and index.
1. Journalistic ethics. 2. Journalism--Objectivity. I. Carlson, Matt, 1977- editor.
II. Lewis, Seth C.
PN4756.B665 2015
070.4--dc23
2014032191

ISBN: 978-1-138-01784-9 (hbk)
ISBN: 978-1-138-02067-2 (pbk)
ISBN: 978-1-315-72768-4 (ebk)

Typeset in Sabon
by Taylor & Francis Books

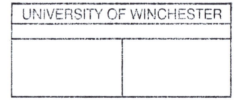

Printed and bound in Great Britain by Ashford Colour Press Ltd.

MIX
Paper from
responsible sources
FSC
www.fsc.org   FSC® C011748

From Matt Carlson:
For Claire, with boundless love

From Seth C. Lewis:
For Jackson, Addison, Preston, and Asher—the four happy hobbits in my life

Contents

List of contributors

Adriana Amado is Professor of Communication Theories at the University UNLAM, Argentina. She holds a PhD in Social Sciences from Flacso. She teaches, researches, and has written extensively about media, public communication and journalism. Her latest book is the co-edited volume *La palabra empeñada.*

Mike Ananny is an Assistant Professor at the University of Southern California's Annenberg School for Communication & Journalism, and a Faculty Associate at Harvard's Berkman Center for Internet & Society. He studies public significances of networked news systems.

C.W. Anderson is an Assistant Professor of Media Culture at the College of Staten Island (CUNY) and the author of *Rebuilding the News: Metropolitan Journalism in the Digital Age.*

Matt Carlson is associate professor of communication at Saint Louis University. His work examines the contested cultural construction of journalism. He is author of *On the Condition of Anonymity: Unnamed Sources and the Battle for Journalism* and co-editor of *Journalism, Sources, and Credibility: New Perspectives.*

Mark Coddington is a doctoral student in the School of Journalism at the University of Texas at Austin. His research centers on professional journalistic values and networked journalism. He writes regularly for the Nieman Journalism Lab at Harvard University.

David Domingo is Chair of Journalism at the Department of Information and Communication Sciences at Université Libre de Bruxelles. Previously, he was visiting assistant professor at the University of Iowa and senior lecturer at Universitat Rovira i Virgili. He has also been a doctoral fellow and visiting researcher at the University of Tampere. His research focuses on innovation processes in online communication. He is coauthor of *Participatory Journalism: Guarding Open Gates at Online Newspapers.*

Alfred Hermida is an associate professor at the University of British Columbia, Canada. A former BBC journalist, his research focuses on changes in journalistic practices, social media, and emerging genres of journalism. His latest book is *Tell Everyone: Why People Share and Why It Matters*.

Florence Le Cam is Chair of Journalism at the Department of Information and Communication Sciences at Université Libre de Bruxelles (Brussels). Previously she was assistant professor at Université de Rennes 1 and also was a post-doctoral researcher at the National Archive in Quebec. Her research interests are the socialization of journalists and the historical construction of the profession. She is the author of *Le journalisme imaginé*, and co-editor of the multilingual scientific journal *Sur le journalisme / About journalism / Sobre jornalismo*.

Seth C. Lewis is an assistant professor and the Mitchell V. Charnley Fellow in the School of Journalism and Mass Communication at the University of Minnesota. He studies the changing nature of journalism amid the rise of sociotechnical phenomena such as big data, social media, and digital audience analytics.

Matthew Powers is Assistant Professor in the Department of Communication at the University of Washington. He is currently writing a book on the information work of humanitarian and human rights NGOs and their place in the changing media landscape.

Sue Robinson is an associate professor at the University of Wisconsin-Madison's School of Journalism & Mass Communication where she researches how digital technology is being used to evolve journalism and shift patterns of information flow.

Jane B. Singer is Professor of Journalism Innovation at City University London. Her research explores digital journalism, including changing roles, perceptions, norms, and practices. She is co-author of *Participatory Journalism* and *Online Journalism Ethics*.

Helle Sjøvaag is Post Doctor at the University of Bergen, Norway. She has published widely on the issues of journalistic ideology, online news, media ownership and regulation, and methodology.

Karin Wahl-Jorgensen is Professor and Director of Research Development and Environment at the Cardiff School of Journalism, Media and Cultural Studies. She does research on the relationship between media practices and citizenship, and has written or edited five books, including, most recently, *Disasters and the Media* with Mervi Pantti and Simon Cottle. She is currently completing *Emotions, Media and Politics*.

Silvio Waisbord is Professor of Media and Public Affairs at George Washington University. His latest books are *Reinventing Professionalism: Journalism* *and News in Global Perspective*, and the edited volume *Media Sociology: A Reappraisal*. He is the editor-in-chief of the *Journal of Communication*.

Jenny Wiik works at the Department of Journalism, Media and Communication (JMG) at the University of Gothenburg in Sweden. Her main area of interest is journalism as a profession, and the challenges of this profession when conditions are changing rapidly.

Acknowledgements

This book grew out of our mutual realization that there was something of value in applying the concept of boundaries and boundary work to journalism. Yet aside from a few disconnected pieces of scholarship – including our own work – there still lacked a definitive effort to work out what this approach meant. So, we took it upon ourselves to do so through this volume. Of course, we did not do it alone. We thank the authors for their wonderful contributions that made this book a reality. Their immediate enthusiasm for this project confirmed for us the need for this book. At Routledge, Natalie Foster and Sheni Kruger helped us get this project into shape from proposal to finished product. Our universities helped in important ways as well: We both enjoyed research leaves during the 2013–14 academic year that gave us additional time for this work; and we acknowledge graduate students Samir Adrissi, Corinne Gibson and Meilin Shen (Saint Louis University) and Casey Carmody (University of Minnesota) for their help as research assistants. Most especially, we thank Barbie Zelizer for seeing the value of this project and encouraging it to completion.

Finally, we appreciate the constant patience and support of our families.

Matt Carlson
Saint Louis University
Seth C. Lewis
University of Minnesota

Introduction

The many boundaries of journalism

Matt Carlson

"I'm 61 ... I can't believe I would be one of the people who's changing the world of media." These words were spoken in April 2008 by a little-known citizen journalist named Mayhill Fowler to the *New York Times*,[1] one of the world's most venerated and recognizable news organizations. Fowler had been covering a tight U.S. presidential primary race between Democratic senators Barack Obama and Hillary Clinton – at her own expense – for the *Huffington Post* online news site. She was not on the site's paid editorial staff, but one of an army of citizens following the heated primary battle as part of its OffTheBus project. The idea of the project was to draw from Fowler and others like her to break away from the stultifying coverage of pack journalism epitomized decades earlier in *The Boys on the Bus*.[2] Wary of the endless, homogenous flow of news from journalistic insiders following the campaigns across the country, the *Huffington Post* sought fresh perspectives on the race.

Fowler's big moment came when she made it into an Obama fundraiser in California. It was a closed-door event, understood to be off-limits to journalists, and Fowler merely had to turn on her tape recorder to catch what became one of the better-known gaffes of the entire election: Barack Obama, speaking openly to a room full of supporters, opining that rural Americans "cling to guns or religion or antipathy to people who aren't like them."[3] The sound bite ricocheted throughout election coverage, dogging the frontrunner Obama. His primary loss in Pennsylvania a few weeks later kept the primary challenge from Clinton alive for another two months. Eventually, Obama went on to win the nomination and then the presidency; Fowler receded from public view; and professional journalists continued to cover the news.

What, then, does this episode mean for journalism? One way to view its impact is by asking what it tells us about journalism's boundaries. This was a moment – one of an increasing number – in which the borders of something assumed to be concrete called "journalism" appeared flimsy and malleable. Fowler's scoop made news, but did this make it journalism?

Looking at this incident with an eye toward boundaries invites a torrent of questions about where to place – or erase – journalism's edges. Is Mayhill Fowler, a self-described "teacher, editor, and writer," a journalist? In most

Western nations, with no entrusted body declaring "you are a journalist" or "you are *not* a journalist," the question of what makes someone a journalist hangs in the air. Did Fowler's open support for Obama and her criticisms of Clinton disqualify her from obeying the norms of neutrality at the heart of objective U.S. journalism? Did being an unpaid volunteer matter? Was what Fowler did journalism? In an age of camera-equipped smart phones, mediated witnessing has become the norm,[4] but does this equate to journalism? Finally, was what Fowler did journalistically *appropriate*? How much respect was owed to the Obama campaign's efforts to wall off the event from professional journalists? Should Fowler have identified herself *as a journalist*? Was she being journalistically *ethical*? In all these questions we see a blurring of boundaries – boundaries involving people, practices, and places. What was assumed to be a division between journalists and the public could no longer be assumed. The world was different.

This book is about the boundaries of journalism. It begins with the simple question of how journalism comes to be demarcated from non-journalism. This division is already deeply contested and cannot be readily resolved by falling back on some agreed-upon formal parameters or a functionalist accounting of who qualifies as a journalist or what qualifies as journalism. There are no such checklists, nor do we offer any here. Instead, this book sets out by promoting a view of journalism as a varied cultural practice embedded within a complicated social landscape. Journalism is not a solid, stable *thing* to point to, but a constantly shifting denotation applied differently depending on context. Whatever is distinct about journalism must be continuously constructed.

Struggles over journalism are often struggles over boundaries. Basic questions of definition – who counts as a journalist, what counts as journalism, what is appropriate journalistic behavior, and what is deviant – are all matters that can be comprehended through the perspective of "boundary work." Focusing on the domain of science, Thomas Gieryn defines boundary work as the "attribution of selected characteristics to the institution of science (i.e., to its practitioners, methods, stock of knowledge, values and work organization) for purposes of constructing a social boundary that distinguishes some intellectual activities as 'non-science.'"[5] Substituting "journalism" for "science" in the previous quote moves us to questions of how boundaries are constructed, challenged, reinforced, or erased about who should rightfully gather and disseminate the news – and who should not.

Contests over journalism's boundaries are symbolic contests in which different actors vie for definitional control to apply or remove the label of journalism. Yet this symbolic struggle has tangible consequences as well. Gains in symbolic resources translate into material rewards. Being deemed a "legitimate" journalist accords prestige and credibility, but also access to news sources, audiences, funding, legal rights, and other institutionalized perquisites. Also, struggles over what is appropriate journalism bear on the actual news products as some practices are held to be worthy while others are rejected. Objectivity norms, pack journalism, and citizen witnessing are all part of this picture.

Boundary work does not have a strong foothold in studies of journalism. Some notable exceptions are sprinkled throughout the corpus of journalism studies, but for a richer conceptualization of boundaries it is necessary to turn elsewhere in the social sciences. The sections below trace the development of boundaries within the sociology of knowledge and science and technology studies (STS). The long history of attending to boundaries provides frameworks for considering how boundaries are constructed around journalism.

The study of boundaries in the social sciences

How do some groups attain authority and control in performing various social functions? How are other groups excluded? Whose knowledge of the world is correct? The notion of boundaries is intuitive when we think of complex social systems. Society is marked by difference, whether with regard to notions of deviance, geography, gender, or professions. Yet how social boundaries are erected reveals a complex relationship between cultural understandings and social structures. In their review of studies of boundaries across the social sciences, Lamont and Molnár note the common emphasis on "understanding the role of symbolic resources (e.g., conceptual distinctions, interpretive strategies, cultural traditions) in creating, maintaining, contesting, or even dissolving institutionalized social differences."[6] In this constructionist view, the emphasis falls on how social actors actively shape boundaries through a variety of expressive practices bent on inclusion and exclusion and how such implied differences structure the social world of these actors. Placement inside or outside a boundary – whether concerning racial groupings, a legitimate profession, or deviant behavior – has real material consequences.

While research on boundaries remains prevalent in many corners of social sciences,[7] it has been a particularly useful concept within the sociology of knowledge and the study of knowledge producers. Questions as to who may possess – and act on – legitimate knowledge have long been at the forefront of the sociology of knowledge and its concern for the conditions in which a group claims the right to present the truth about the world. Of particular interest to this volume is the work of sociologist Thomas Gieryn.[8] Addressing the problem of demarcation between science and non-science, Gieryn looks past functionalist or trait-based explanations to instead highlight public struggles among groups seeking social recognition to rightfully perform an action or occupy a social space. It is through rhetorical means that various groups engage in "boundary-work" to compete publicly for "epistemic authority" – "the legitimate power to define, describe, and explain bounded domains of reality."[9] Epistemic authority binds knowledge and power together as authority carries concomitant rewards of prestige, autonomy, and material benefits. After all, epistemic authority draws from its exclusivity[10] – authority only matters if it is somehow restricted, available only to some and not others at a particular time.

Gieryn positions boundary-work as anti-essentialist, placing it in direct contrast with earlier efforts by Merton, Popper, and Kuhn to locate universal traits or rules for identifying science.[11] He removes the selection of attributes that make science *science* away from the analyst to instead privilege how actors themselves argue with each other, or "how people in society negotiate and provisionally settle for themselves the borders and territories of science."[12] In this view, scientific objectivity, to take one example, is not an essential scientific trait on its own but one accorded to science by those vying for epistemic authority against competing ways of understanding the world.

Without fixed traits to fall back on, where are we to find the boundaries of epistemic authority? On this point, Gieryn avoids locating epistemic authority as something possessed, asserting rather that it should be understood as "perpetually contested terrain" present in specific moments and places.[13] In adopting a constructivist perspective on boundaries, Gieryn directs attention away from sweeping generalizations to instead focus on specific, context-bound struggles that he labels "credibility contests."[14] Following the work of anthropologist Clifford Geertz, Gieryn advocates grounding the study of boundary work in specific incidents:

> One must look into the contingencies of each local and episodic contest for credibility in order to find out what science becomes then and there, to discover the many places it can be located on the cultural maps that become interpretive grounds for extending or denying epistemic authority.[15]

This pinpointing of specific examples underscores both a conceptualization of boundary work connected to epistemic authority and a method for analyzing boundary work that is applicable both historically and for contemporary credibility contests.

Three primary components comprise boundary work.[16] First, Gieryn populates credibility contests with "players and stakeholders," broadly construed to include actors laying claim to the mantle of science and those affected by such claims. Second, boundary work involves the "goals and interests" of all those involved in credibility contests, which gets to the stakes involved in their outcome. However, this is not a purely instrumentalist view that reduces boundary struggles to a cabal of conniving, power-hungry plotters. To do so would be to shortchange the range of motives among players and stakeholders. Egos notwithstanding, scientists and journalists identify their work as socially important beyond their individual recognition. Finally, we have the "arenas" where contestation occurs, from academic conferences to courtrooms to the news media. Gieryn also identifies three broad genres of boundary-work that take place around science[17]: *expulsion*, in which rivals strive to be branded authoritative in the same terrain; *expansion*, or struggles to expand the domain of science into other spheres; and *protection of autonomy*, in which scientists erect "interpretive walls" to prevent non-scientists (e.g., government or business interests) from co-opting scientists' epistemic authority.

While Gieryn sets his sights on science, other work in the sociology of the professions dovetails in productive ways.[18] Most notably, Andrew Abbott's seminal *The System of the Professions,* like Gieryn, privileges social context in understandings of professionalism.[19] Rather than isolate individual professions, Abbott places them in a shared social space in which they compete for *jurisdiction* over various domains. Similar to epistemic authority posited above, in Abbott's conceptualization "a profession asks society to recognize its cognitive structure through exclusive rights" to its jurisdiction.[20] In this competition for cultural legitimacy, members of professions seek the right to do a particular kind of work while excluding others from it. Thus, Abbott goes beyond Gieryn in emphasizing how the work of various professions supports arguments for epistemic authority. The resulting jurisdictional contests produce outcomes with winners and losers.

Another view connecting boundaries, epistemic authority, and professionalism can be found in the work of Paul Starr on the history of medicine.[21] Starr accentuates the power of professional dependence in the cultural conferral of authority; a profession gains power as it comes to be relied on by those outside of it. Again, the contextualization of professions within a complex cultural landscape underscores attempts to think about boundaries. Starr then asserts that medicine's authority lies in its control over particular domains of knowledge. He defines this not as political power but as "cultural authority" – "the probability that particular definitions of reality and judgments of meaning and value will prevail as valid and true."[22] This view echoes Gieryn's "epistemic authority" by pointing to boundaries regarding the production and possession of specialized knowledge, be it science or medicine.

To the spatial metaphors of boundaries and jurisdictions we must add Pierre Bourdieu's influential field theory.[23] For Bourdieu, society is structured into distinct but overlapping *fields* – a term he uses to move beyond the more limited denotations of "profession" or "institution." Fields have complex internal structures, marked by contests to establish *doxa* and secure legitimacy. But what is of interest to this book is how fields create social boundaries. Exclusivity lies at the heart of field theory – as Bourdieu notes: "To exist in a field … is to differentiate oneself."[24] Internally, actors compete to "impose the dominant definition" within the field by shaping its boundaries.[25] For Bourdieu, "The *boundary* of the field is the stake of struggles," which requires inquiry grounded in actors' own understandings of such struggles: "the social scientist's task is not to draw a dividing line between the agents involved in it by imposing a so-called operational definition … but to describe a *state* … of these struggles … by the competing agents."[26] Fields only ever achieve relative autonomy, which varies by field. In keeping with Bourdieu's relational view, specific fields are to be understood within a complex universe populated with other fields.

In looking past their differences to find similarities, it is clear that Starr, Abbott, and Bourdieu share with Gieryn an emphasis on the role of knowledge in demarcating social space. Claims to expertise are at once solidifying while differentiating; the authorized knowers are held up against those who do know (or whose knowledge claims are not recognized as legitimate) – and the boundary in between becomes a site of tension. In this way, epistemic/cultural authority, fields, and jurisdictions all emphasize the need to consider the interactions between insiders and outsiders. While all authors recognize what Starr calls "a kind of solidarity" associated with professionalism,[27] it is not enough to look internally at a group, but instead necessary to conceive of any social group as embedded within a shifting set of allegiances with the larger society. This line drawn between insiders and outsiders, with its mix of variability and firmness, is the stuff of boundaries.

These authors, in their different ways, also call attention to the relationship between structural and rhetorical resources. For Bourdieu, the unequal distribution of various capitals – economic, educational, social – contributes to disparities among and within fields. Abbott too highlights how jurisdictional claims are not merely rhetorical but involve, in some measure, the structural resources of competing forces seeking jurisdiction over a particular domain of work. Gieryn stresses the rhetorical side of boundary work, but his case studies call attention to the importance of social structure in settling credibility contests. Starr looks at institution-building in the ascendant authority of medicine. Thus, attempts to understand boundary work must be attuned to both the rhetorical and material resources marshaled by competing groups in their efforts to establish boundaries.

Before turning to how the boundaries concept can aid studies of journalism, it is important to offer a competing view situating boundaries not as divisive, but as meeting points for distinct groups. The authors above cast boundaries as sites of struggle over authority for a variety of different activities – science, medicine, etc. However, other work challenges the inherent antagonism embedded in boundary work to instead stress how boundaries can act as a "means of communication, as opposed to division."[28] In particular, Starr and Griesemer take as a starting assumption the necessary heterogeneity of scientific work, and then ask how disparate communities are able to cooperate.[29] They pursue this question by adopting an anti-reductionist perspective accounting for the different interests of a variety of actors, which in their study of the Museum of Vertebrate Zoology at the University of California ranges beyond scientists to include everyone from university administrators and benefactors to trappers and even animals. With all of these "allies" involved, how do they communicate?

Star and Griesemer explain the coordination of heterogeneous groups through the concept of "boundary objects" – a class of objects that have different meanings for different groups, but act as shared objects "maintaining coherence across intersecting social worlds."[30] These objects straddle social domains, allowing different groups to protect their identity and autonomy while allowing for shared communication. For example, in their study, Star and Griesemer show how the creation of certain specimen-recording conventions formed a boundary object connecting scientists and trappers. The scientists, concerned with the meticulous collection of data about animal habitats, crafted a protocol that allowed them to communicate with trappers and conservationists working in the field according to their own interests. As a boundary object, this protocol allowed an evolutionary biologist and an avid conservationist to coordinate the production of information, even as each one draws different meanings from the information. Another example that Star and Griesemer offer is a map of California. Although the boundaries of the state are fixed and shared, the collectors and conservationists emphasized maps with roads and trails for navigating the physical terrain in contrast to the scientists' map of abstract ecological zones. As these examples illustrate, boundary objects are at once something shared among disparate groups while holding sometimes radically different meanings.

Taking up the idea of "boundary objects" shifts attention from discursive battles over control to material connections involved in coordination. Although Star and Griesemer prefer to think of their perspective as "ecological," treating boundary objects as common meeting points among allies suggests a different spatial metaphor: the network. In science and technology studies, the work of actor-network theory (ANT) by Latour and others looks past the discursive emphasis of boundary work to highlight how various human and nonhuman *actants* form connections, sometimes in unexpected ways.[31] Whereas boundaries stress limits, networks accentuate connections. This serves as a reminder to think beyond how boundaries come to be established, contested, or even demolished to include how groups form allegiances that work across boundaries.

Placing journalism's boundaries

It is tempting to simply insert journalism into the boundaries framework put forth by Gieryn and others. Generically, journalism provides one more site of struggle in which parties compete for authority through defining – and contesting – its cultural boundaries. But to do so haphazardly ignores the peculiarities of journalism as a cultural practice and as form of knowledge production. This section begins by proffering a nuanced view of journalistic boundaries in the hopes of contextualizing the chapters that follow and laying a foundation for future research.

In translating boundary work to journalism, the first stumbling block is the inherent porousness of journalistic work. Even for the authors above, Abbott labels journalism "a very permeable occupation"[32] while Bourdieu emphasizes the "heteronomy" of journalism due to its status as "a very weakly autonomous field."[33] The reasons for this are well known.[34] Journalism has long had an uneasy relationship with the trappings of professionalism that help other groups – doctors, for example – construct boundaries around their work. Journalism, at least in North America and much of Europe, lacks the formal barriers commonly associated with a profession, such as licensing, educational requirements, or trade association membership. To be a plumber requires a license; to be a journalist requires, in 2015, an Internet connection.

Translating the study of boundaries into journalism is further complicated by journalism's continuous technological shifts. Long before *Huffington Post*, journalism quite uneasily had to confront the rise of radio[35] and television[36] as legitimate media for news. Cable news and talk radio continue to be marginalized by many within journalism, and new media have only exacerbated questions of what should be under journalism's umbrella. Changes in news-gathering have led journalists to integrate new "technologically specific forms of work"[37] such as photojournalism and, later, computer-assisted reporting in their news practices. Taking the long view, it is clear that journalism is an unstable referent, deployed differently by different actors. Ryfe asserts that journalism is "unraveling" to the point where there is no longer a stable entity to label as journalism.[38] This uncertainty portends an uptick in boundary work in the vacuum created by a lack of settled boundaries, but it is unclear whether this will ever result in the re-establishment of recognized boundaries in the future.

Journalism's lack of firm borders has not stopped scholars from conceptualizing how it maintains a semblance of cohesiveness. Soloski sidesteps debates regarding what to label journalism – profession, occupation, craft, etc. – to instead question what it means for journalists to consider themselves as a profession.[39] Another approach has been to appropriate the idea of "interpretive community" from literary theory to examine how journalists establish common interpretive strategies.[40] Even if journalism cannot be treated as a profession in the classic sense, it strives for the benefits of professional status – internal cohesion and the right to enforce its own exclusivity.[41] This is only possible through boundary work.

There is another difference between journalism and the other professions described in the previous section that has received less attention but is no less important. To take Gieryn's domain – science – it is clear that much of the knowledge work produced by scientists takes the form of specialized reports meant for other scientists. Scientific discourse, and more broadly legalistic and medical discourses, are all contained within textual communities possessing the requisite training to comprehend and produce such discourse.[42] Of course, scientists, lawyers, and doctors do interact with the public outside their boundaries, as Starr makes clear in asserting the role of patient dependence in the case of medicine. But when they do, they translate internally comprehensible texts to external audiences ill-equipped to follow a scientific conference paper, court ruling, or medical journal article. By contrast, aside from perhaps the rare insider trade journal, journalistic discourse is not contained to an exclusive group. It is gathered from non-journalists and generated for a non-journalistic public.[43] Journalistic discourse is explanatory, requiring clear language capable of being understood by a broad, unspecialized audience with varying educational aptitudes. This is not to dismiss journalism's own expertise in newsgathering and its own internally understood discourses as unimportant.[44] After all, journalism education more than ever stresses the development of a wide range of skills. But it is crucial to draw a distinction between journalism and other knowledge-producing professions. Although this further complicates the application of boundary work and its attendant concepts to journalism, it does encourage attention to the peculiarities of journalism.

In spite of the looseness of journalism as a distinct activity, journalists very much view their work as a practice of great social importance and defend it against incursions from non-journalists. This belief stems from a basic ideological commitment to professionalism[45] – or what we may call the "professional logic"[46] – as the mark of distinction. Yet in recent years, economic, techno-logical, and cultural changes have altered the media landscape in ways that make boundary work explicit and inescapable. Professional journalists' claims to exclusivity over news production and distribution have weakened, forcing them to confront how it is they differ from other social actors – if it all. Understanding various responses to this environment requires careful attention to how questions of boundaries shape the future of news.

Conceptualizing boundaries in journalism

A review of how the concept of boundaries has been used in journalism studies reveals a growing body of research seeking to understand the demarcation of journalism norms, practices, and participants. For the most part, studies have explored the nuances of boundary work taking place within individual cases. What is clear from these efforts is the stubborn lack of cohesion plaguing the practice of journalism.[47] It is also clear that it is time to look across studies taking up the mantle of boundary work to identify common themes and propose future research. This section takes up this task, although with the caveat that categorizing patterns within journalism studies requires its own cartographic intervention.

From the existing work on journalism's boundaries reviewed in this section, it is clear that there cannot be a single, one-dimensional understanding of boundary work and journalism. Instead, what is needed is a broader frame-work capable of encompassing different types of boundaries while relating these types within a cohesive structure. This section proposes such a matrix to situate individual studies of boundary work and journalism alongside one another in a systematic way. The main components of this matrix, presented as rows in Table 0.1, are Gieryn's three generic types of boundary work – expansion, expulsion, and protection of autonomy – and, as columns, three areas of journalism around which boundary work occurs – participants, practices, and professionalism.

Table 0.1 Forms of boundary work in journalism

	Participants	*Practices*	*Professionalism*
Expansion	Incorporating non-traditional journalists	Taking over new media practices as acceptable	Absorbing new media as acceptable journalism
	Example: Citizen journalists	*Example:* Tweeting as journalistic form	*Example:* Television and blogging gain entry into professional journalism
Expulsion	Expelling deviant actors	Expelling deviant practices	Expelling deviant forms and values
	Example: Jayson Blair being fired from the *New York Times*	*Example:* Dismissing paparazzi photographers	*Example:* Defining partisan news or tabloid news as not journalism
Protection of autonomy	Keeping out non-journalistic informational actors	Defense of ability to define correct practices	Defense from non-professional outsiders
	Example: Public relations agents, advertising departments, citizens	*Example:* The Leveson Inquiry, the legality of classified leaks	*Example:* Keeping management away from editorial control

Beginning with the columns, at its most basic, boundary work surrounding "Participants" involves placing lines separating journalists from non-journalists. But it also points to complex efforts to stratify actors both inside and outside of news. If the question at the heart of participants-based boundary work is "who is appropriate?" then the basic question for the second column, "Practices," concerns "what is appropriate?" It is here that the boundaries of acceptable newsgathering or distribution methods are set. Finally, the area of "Professionalism" includes efforts by journalists to establish themselves as a distinct community with specialized knowledge. Certainly this involves both participants and practices, but it is situated as its own column because of the close connection between professionalism and epistemic authority.

The rows in Table 0.1 correspond to Gieryn's[48] generic boundary-work typology. Although expansion, expulsion, and protection of anonymity are not specific to journalism, these types can be adapted to fit journalistic boundary work. "Expansion" denotes efforts by journalists to extend the borders of what may be considered journalism into new domains. Here Gieryn dovetails with Abbott's concept of jurisdictional claims in which different groups (or occupations) compete to rightfully control an area of knowledge production.[49] With journalism, expansion can be seen in the spread of journalism from print to electronic formats beginning with radio and later encompassing television, and online formats like blogs.[50]

"Expulsion," by contrast, relates to struggles to erect or strengthen boundaries within journalistic practice to reposition something or someone as being outside of acceptable journalism. Expulsion acts as a "means of social control" in which "borders get placed and policed."[51] The classic example is the expulsion of those actors branded to be deviant.[52] Their exile provides the journalistic community with an opportunity to publicly set the "boundaries of the permissible."[53] For example, when reporter Jayson Blair was fired from the *New York Times* after being caught fabricating and plagiarizing stories, the newspaper – and the larger journalistic community – reacted by reaffirming core norms and practices.[54] Another example of expulsion in journalistic boundary work would be a contest over whether some new form laying claim to "journalism" – or encroaching on journalism's jurisdiction – is actually journalism.

Expulsion-based boundary occupies much of the research on the boundaries of journalism. Winch put Gieryn's framework to use regarding professionalism with his study of how journalists draw sharp distinctions between tabloid-style journalism and hard news.[55] Other scholars have studied the expulsion of specific practices, including paparazzi style photography following the 1997 death of Princess Diana,[56] pack journalism by political reporters,[57] constructed quotations,[58] earnestness,[59] and questionable newsgathering practices.[60] Efforts to establish boundaries also occur through memory work.[61]

Much of the recent work on boundaries concerning participants examines the limits and forms of non-journalistic participation. The "professional-participatory tension" arises as outsiders assume an ever-larger role in the creation and circulation of news and information.[62] For example, Örnebring's interviews with journalists reveal ingrained cognitive efforts to define and differentiate news professionals from amateurs.[63] Even in admitting the value of amateurs, a solid wall was still constructed around professional journalism. In studying how a news organization handled reader comments online, Robinson shows how different boundaries emerged between and among journalists and audiences, resulting in a "grand identity complex" as the institutional hierarchy of professional journalism is challenged in digital spaces.[64] Taking the "boundary-crossing" metaphor as their point of departure for describing the inclusion of audiences in the news-making process, Beckett and Mansell argue that as journalism becomes networked – the journalist situated more as facilitator of a public debate rather than mere broadcaster of information – it enables a potentially new set of cultures, values, and viewpoints to be expressed in the public arena, for good or ill.[65] Meanwhile, the boundaries between journalists and their information sources have become contested terrain as well, perhaps most notably in the case of WikiLeaks. For example, even while collaborating with the international nonprofit website to reveal government secrets, the *New York Times* was careful to hold the group at arm's length as just another "source" that lacked objectivity, thereby pushing WikiLeaks "outside journalism's professional boundaries while reaffirming its own place inside those boundaries, as an established, trusted institution worthy of the social authority to monitor other important institutions."[66]

Both expansion and expulsion boundary work involve the extension or contraction of what qualifies as journalism. By contrast, the category of "Protection of autonomy" involves fending off incursions by non-journalists seeking to control or shape journalism. It is not that these outsiders wish to be labeled as journalists. Instead, they seek to influence journalism in what journalists perceive as a threat to autonomy. For example, the protection of autonomy can be seen in efforts to oppose advertisers from manipulating editorial content. Or, in the UK, journalists have opposed efforts by the government to enact regulatory statutes over news in the wake of the *News of the World* scandal and the Leveson Inquiry. The protection of autonomy is deeply ingrained within journalism, as Revers's study of U.S. statehouse reporters uncovered.[67] The journalists he studied displayed internalized boundary performances of journalism through their eagerness to act professionally and avoid non-journalistic behavior. Future work will hopefully go beyond rhetoric to connect boundaries with performativity.[68]

A few words of warning are needed at this point. First, like any model, the bounded space of a matrix appears more orderly than actual boundary work practices – or the studies of such practices. Journalistic boundary work certainly spills over across the cells of this matrix, which are by no means mutually exclusive – nor should they be. In placing studies within this matrix, what is important is where the *emphasis* of the boundary work taking place falls among participants, practices, and professional norms. What do the actors involve *accent* in their arguments for establishing – or erasing – divisions? At the same time, the different combinations that occur deserve attention for what they indicate about the nature of journalistic boundary work.

Second, the matrix appears to freeze time, locking journalism into place. However, the boundaries that develop should not be construed as temporally static. Instead, different participants, norms, or practices move across the cells over time. For example, where blogging was once largely expulsed from journalism as the work of amateurs, in recent years the boundaries of journalism have expanded to encompass blogging as an acceptable form for disseminating news. Such movement is not a failure of the matrix but rather an indicator of the malleability of journalism's borders over time. Longitudinal investigations of expulsion and expansion should be encouraged.

Finally, this matrix is not some natural entity with immutable laws but a constructed representation aiming to shed light on boundary work. That is, to *explain* boundaries, this matrix *creates* boundaries. Like all representations, it is open to challenge and alteration. Therefore this matrix should not, by itself, crystallize a conception of what constitutes journalism. To do so would be counterproductive. Rather, this matrix provides a model sensitive to the many directions from which journalism comes to be constructed or contested – the task to which this book is dedicated.

Plan of the book

By now it should be clear that there is no single route for examining the boundaries of journalism. The ways in which journalism becomes a socially distinct type of work pursued by a distinct class of workers are complex and multi-faceted. No single study of boundaries could provide all the answers. What's more, the changing media terrain complicates the question of boundaries. Previously rigid boundaries between producer and audience and between news and not-news have given way to more fluid positions shifting with each new context. Perhaps it is at this point of transition that the study of journalism's boundaries is most needed to bring to light how the news is situated as a cultural activity. To this end, the chapters in this book provide a multiplicity of entry points for thinking about boundaries.

The chapters in Part I (Professionalism, norms, and values) trace the relationship between how journalism is thought about and the types of work practices and outputs that emerge. In Chapter 1, Jane Singer examines how, in a media environment in which anyone can publish, journalistic norms become important boundary markers allowing journalists to distinguish themselves from non-journalists. Such core notions as independence, verification, and accountability not only guide journalists' work and shape their identity; they also provide a wedge between other voices. However, the pervasiveness of social media and rise of entrepreneurial journalism complicate this boundary work, leading to a stress on such emergent values as transparency.

These themes carry on into Chapter 2 in Alfred Hermida's close inspection of the state of verification in journalism today. Journalists have long touted their ability to verify information as a key part of the boundary separating them from other actors. Yet, increasingly, citizens who act as eyewitnesses to breaking news are able to share their images and stories to the public faster than journalists can verify them. This has led to the renewal of verification in a media world with weakened boundaries, including an emphasis on transparency and collaboration with the audience. Both Hermida and Singer stress the growing importance of transparency as opening up journalistic processes to the outside.

In Chapter 3, Adriana Amado and Silvio Waisbord look at the state of journalism in Argentina to shed light on boundary practices outside of North America and Western Europe. They find a far less cohesive professional situation, as journalists remain hampered by intrusive state policies that divide the field. Debates play out among the Argentine press over its ideal political and social role, but a pervading weak sense of professionalism undercuts attempts at journalistic boundary work and leaves journalists vulnerable to influence by powerful actors outside of news.

Chapter 4 moves us from the state to the economics of news. Mark Coddington examines the status of the "Chinese Wall" dividing journalists from advertising. This division has long been at the forefront of journalists' understanding of their autonomy as producing and distributing the news unencumbered by external forces. This has always been an idealistic expression, as journalism has long been buffeted about by market forces. But the digital era presents new challenges to the advertising–editorial division, with such developments as entrepreneurial journalism and native advertising offering alternatives to the absolute model of editorial independence. What this chapter identifies is stress over journalism's core ideals in the face of a trying economic situation.

The next three chapters take us inside journalism to look at internal boundaries. In Chapter 5, Mike Ananny examines the intersection of news norms and technology through a study of Google Glass and journalistic witnessing. Witnessing lies at the heart of journalistic practice, and journalists work to maintain what Roger Silverstone labels "proper distance" from their subjects. But journalistic witnessing is inherently technological, and each new recording technology alters the conditions of witnessing. The development of Google Glass is the latest technology to alter our conceptions of witnessing. As the harbinger of wearable computing, Google Glass drastically alters ideas of proximity and harm.

In Chapter 6, Helle Sjøvaag looks at how the categories of hard and soft news structure labor and prestige within newspapers. Through a content analysis of Norwegian newspapers, she identifies the protection of hard news as the essence of legitimate news, which is therefore more likely to be showcased in print. Meanwhile, soft news is more likely to be syndicated across newspapers and online. This chapter shows that even when produced by journalists, not all news is treated the same, with a small section of hard journalism being used to create boundaries between journalists and the economic pressures that bear on them.

Finally, in Chapter 7, Jenny Wiik also looks inward, using survey data from Sweden to examine the hierarchy of working conditions. Wiik challenges views of the newsroom as a homogenous place and asks whether newsrooms are becoming more stratified. On the one hand, journalists express a high degree of commonality regarding their ideological commitments – a unity that helps form a boundary between journalists and non-journalists. Yet, on the other hand, the actual work practices and increasingly precarious job prospects of certain journalists reveal some important fractures, indicating a lessening of cohesion in the newsroom. This includes new tensions arising between veterans and young journalists fresh from school.

The chapters in Part II (Encountering non-journalistic actors in news-making) shift the focus to the role that boundaries play in the interactions between different types of journalistic and non-journalistic actors. Even the title of this section presupposes that such boundaries exist, and the authors are quick to examine both the rigidity and fragility of such divisions.

In Chapter 8, David Domingo and Florence Le Cam dive into the question of the audience–journalist boundary through a case study of a struggle over multiculturalism in Belgium. They push for a wider perspective that looks across boundaries to ask instead about the networks necessary for newsmaking to occur. Using a combination of actor-network theory and dialogism, they trace the contingency of news practices through such networks, showing how boundaries are constantly crossed and re-crossed in the production of news.

In Chapter 9, Sue Robinson examines how the emergence of online commentators on news sites alters notions of boundaries between journalistic and non-journalistic actors. Non-journalists have found room for their voices in the very space of news through comments. Robinson invokes Bourdieu's field theory to question how the community of commenters functions and what this means for journalism to be inviting non-journalists into the space of news.

Following on the heels of these chapters, in Chapter 10 Karin Wahl-Jorgensen interrogates a point where non-journalists and journalists interact: the case of user-generated content (UGC) in news texts. While digital technologies promise to obscure the boundaries between audience and author, journalists have expressed reluctance at giving up too much control. This has resulted in boundary work strategies of cooptation and segregation. However, a study of the *Guardian* newspaper's UGC platform, GuardianWitness, reveals the complex negotiation of boundaries between journalists and their active consumers, raising larger questions about journalistic epistemology.

In Chapter 11, Matthew Powers introduces a different kind of actor by exploring the growing work of NGOs in foreign news coverage. Groups like Amnesty International and Human Rights Watch play increasingly prominent roles in the provision of information from abroad, complementing a domain that previously was reserved for journalists. All of this takes place in a context of diminished resources for journalism, especially as it pertains to costly international coverage. The increased role of these NGOs raises questions about the boundaries of who should be creating and distributing news from places far out of sight to most news consumers.

Finally, in Chapter 12, C. W. Anderson takes a longer view of the boundaries between sociology and journalism. A century ago, these boundaries were quite fluid, with many in sociology viewing journalism as a vehicle for distributing social science-informed research for mass consumption. Both journalists and sociologists sought to provide empirical evidence about the world, but in ways that became increasingly divergent as the twentieth century went on. After early hybridity, a thick boundary between sociology and journalism formed by mid-century, with journalism only returning to the attention of sociologists as an object of analysis for a brief moment in the 1970s. A century after being collaborators, journalists and sociologists find themselves as distinct actors.

The book concludes with an epilogue by Seth Lewis. He argues that it's not enough to demonstrate the importance of boundaries and their study in journalism; we need to take seriously the project of conceptual innovation, lest boundaries, as a concept, loses its analytical utility amid duplicative work. He asks: which particular elements of boundaries deserve special consideration as researchers take up the concept generally and in journalism studies specifically? Lewis argues for refining our approach to the *social* and the *material* – and the interplay between them – and then building upon that refinement to develop a more supple, expansive, and cross-disciplinary approach, one that is better suited for studying the emerging technologies that dominate contemporary news work.

Notes

1 Katharine Seelye, "Blogger is Surprised by Uproar Over Obama Story, But Not Bitter," *New York Times*, 16 April 2008.
2 Timothy Crouse, *The Boys On The Bus* (New York: Random House, 1972).
3 Seelye, "Blogger is Surprised."
4 Stuart Allan, *Citizen Witnessing* (Cambridge, UK: Polity, 2013).
5 Thomas Gieryn, "Boundary-Work and the Demarcation of Science from Non-Science: Strains And Interests In Professional Ideologies Of Scientists," *American Sociological Review* 48, no. 6 (1983): 782.
6 Michéle Lamont and Virág Molnár, "The Study of Boundaries in the Social Sciences," *Annual Review of Sociology* 28, no. 1 (2002): 168.
7 Lamont and Molnar, "The Study of Boundaries."; Mark Pachucki, Sabrina Pendergrass, and Michéle Lamont, "Boundary Processes: Recent Theoretical Developments And New Contributions," *Poetics* 35, no. 6 (2007): 331–51.
8 Gieryn, "Boundary-Work"; Thomas Gieryn, "Boundaries of Science," in *Handbook of Science and Technology Studies,* eds Shelia Jasanoff, Gerald Markle, James Peterson and Trevor Pinch (Newbury Park, CA: Sage, 1995), 393–443. Thomas Gieryn, *Cultural Boundaries of Science* (Chicago: University of Chicago Press, 2001).
9 Gieryn, *Cultural Boundaries of Science,* 1.
10 Gieryn, *Cultural Boundaries of Science,* 14.
11 Gieryn, "Boundaries of Science."
12 Gieryn, *Cultural Boundaries of Science,* 27.
13 Gieryn, *Cultural Boundaries of Science,* 15.
14 Gieryn, *Cultural Boundaries of Science,* 1.
15 Gieryn, *Cultural Boundaries of Science,* 21.
16 Gieryn, *Cultural Boundaries of Science,* 21–24.
17 Gieryn, *Cultural Boundaries of Science,* 15–17.
18 Chris Anderson, "Journalism: Expertise, Authority, and Power in Democratic Life," in *The Media and Social Theory*, eds David Hesmondhalgh and Jason Toynbee (London: Routledge, 2008), 248–64; Seth C. Lewis, "The Tension Between Professional Control and Open Participation: Journalism and its Boundaries," *Information, Communication & Society* 15 no. 6 (2012): 836–66.
19 Andrew Abbott, *The System of Professions* (Chicago: University of Chicago Press, 1988).
20 Abbott, *The System of Professions,* 59.
21 Paul Starr, *The Social Transformation of American Medicine* (New York: Basic Books, 1982).
22 Starr, *The Social Transformation,*13.
23 Pierre Bourdieu, *The Field of Cultural Production* (New York: Columbia University Press, 1993). See also Rodney Benson and Erik Neveu, eds, *Bourdieu and the Journalistic Field* (Cambridge, UK: Polity, 2005).
24 Pierre Bourdieu, "The Political Field, the Social Science Field, and the Journalistic Field," in *The Field of Cultural Production,* eds Rodney Benson and Erik Neveu, (Cambridge, UK: Polity, 2005), 39.

25 Bourdieu, "The Political Field, the Social Science Field, and the Journalistic Field," 42.

26 Bourdieu, "The Political Field, the Social Science Field, and the Journalistic Field," 42–43, original emphasis.

27 Starr, *The Social Transformation*, 16.

28 Lamont and Molnár, "The Study of Boundaries," 177.

29 Susan Star and James Griesemer, "Institutional Ecology, 'Translations' and Boundary Objects: Amateurs and Professionals in Berkeley's Museum of Vertebrate Zoology, 1907–39," *Social Studies of Science* 19, no. 3 (1989): 387–420.

30 Star and Griesemer, "Institutional Ecology," 393.

31 Bruno Latour, *Reassembling the Social* (Oxford, UK: Oxford University Press, 2005).

32 Abbott, *The System of Professions*, 225.

33 Bourdieu, "The Political Field," 33.

34 See Silvio Waisbord, *Reinventing Professionalism* (Cambridge, UK: Polity, 2013).

35 Gwenyth Jackaway, *Media at War* (Westport, CT: Greenwood Publishing Group, 2005).

36 Barbie Zelizer, *Covering the Body* (Chicago: University of Chicago Press, 1992)

37 Matthew Powers, "'In Forms That Are Familiar and Yet-to-Be Invented:' American Journalism and the Discourse of Technologically Specific Work," *Journal of Communication Inquiry* 36, no. 1 (2012): 24–43.

38 David Ryfe, *Can Journalism Survive?* (Cambridge, UK: Polity, 2012), 140.

39 John Soloski, "News Reporting and Professionalism: Some Constraints on the Reporting of the News," *Media, Culture & Society* 11, no. 2 (1989): 207–28.

40 Stanley Fish, *Is there a text in this class?* (Cambridge, MA: Harvard University Press, 1980); Barbie Zelizer, "Journalists as Interpretive Communities," *Critical Studies in Media Communication* 10, no. 3 (1993): 219–37. Dan Berkowitz and James TerKeurst, "Community as Interpretive Community: Rethinking the Journalist-Source Relationship," *Journal of Communication* 49, no. 3 (1999): 125–36; Sue Robinson and Cathy DeShano, "'Anyone Can Know': Citizen Journalism and the Interpretive Community of the Mainstream Press," *Journalism* 12, no. 8 (2011): 963–82.

41 Lewis, "The Tension Between Professional Control and Open Participation"; Wiasbord, *Reinventing Professionalism*; Michael Schudson and Chris Anderson. "Objectivity, Professionalism, and Truth Seeking in Journalism," in *The Handbook of Journalism Studies*, eds Karin Wahl-Jorgensen and Thomas Hanitzsch (New York: Routledge, 2009), 88–101.

42 Carolyn Marvin, *When Old Technologies Were New* (New York: Oxford University Press, 1988).

43 See Zvi Reich, "Journalism as Bipolar Interactional Expertise," *Communication Theory* 22, no. 4 (2012): 339–58.

44 See Anderson, "Journalism: Expertise, Authority, and Power in Democratic Life."

45 Mark Deuze, "What is Journalism? Professional Identity and Ideology of Journalists Reconsidered," *Journalism* 6, no. 4 (2005): 442–64.

46 Lewis, "The Tension Between Professional Control and Open Participation"

47 Lewis, "The Tension Between Professional Control and Open Participation"; Schudson and Anderson, "Objectivity, Professionalism, and Truth Seeking in Journalism."

48 Gieryn, *Cultural Boundaries of Science,* 15–17.

49 Abbott, *The System of Professions*, 88.

50 Jane Singer, "The Political J-blogger 'Normalizing' a New Media Form to Fit Old Norms and Practices," *Journalism* 6, no. 2 (2005): 173–98.

51 Gieryn, *Cultural Boundaries of Science,* 16.

52 Matt Carlson, "Gone, But Not Forgotten: Memories of Journalistic Deviance as Metajournalistic Discourse," *Journalism Studies*, forthcoming (2014).

53 David Eason, "On Journalistic Authority: The Janet Cooke Scandal," *Critical Studies in Mass Communication* 3, no. 4 (1986): 429–47.

54 Elizabeth Hindman, "Jayson Blair, *The New York Times*, and Paradigm Repair," *Journal of Communication* 55, no. 2 (2005): 225–41.
55 Samuel Winch, *Mapping the Cultural Space of Journalism: How Journalists Distinguish News From Entertainment* (Westport, CT: Praeger, 1997).
56 Dan Berkowitz, "Doing Double Duty Paradigm Repair and the Princess Diana What-a-story," *Journalism* 1, no. 2 (2000): 125–43; Ronald Bishop, "From Behind the Walls: Boundary Work by News Organizations in their Coverage of Princess Diana's Death," *Journal of Communication Inquiry* 23, no. 1 (1999): 90–112.
57 Russell Frank, "These Crowded Circumstances: When Pack Journalists Bash Pack Journalism," *Journalism* 4, no. 4 (2003): 441–58.
58 Elizabeth Fakazis, "Janet Malcolm Constructing Boundaries of Journalism," *Journalism* 7, no. 1 (2006): 5–24.
59 Matt Carlson and Jason Peifer, "The Impudence of Being Earnest: Jon Stewart and the Boundaries of Discursive Responsibility," *Journal of Communication* 63, no. 2 (2013): 333–50.
60 Matt Carlson and Dan Berkowitz, "'The Emperor Lost His Clothes': Rupert Murdoch, News of the World and Journalistic Boundary Work in the UK and USA," *Journalism* 15, no. 4 (2014): 389–406.
61 Dan Berkowitz and Robert Gutsche, "Drawing Lines in the Journalistic Sand; Jon Stewart, Edward R. Murrow, and Memory of News Gone By," *Journalism & Mass Communication Quarterly* 89, no. 4 (2012): 643–56.
62 Lewis, "The Tension Between Professional Control and Open Participation," 838.
63 Henrik Örnebring, "Anything You Can Do, I Can Do Better? Professional Journalists on Citizen Journalism in Six European Countries," *International Communication Gazette* 75, no. 1 (2013): 35–53.
64 Sue Robinson, "Traditionalists vs. Convergers: Textual Privilege, Boundary Work, and the Journalist–Audience Relationship in the Commenting Policies of Online News Sites," *Convergence* 16, no.1 (2010): 125–43.
65 Charlie Beckett and Robin Mansell, "Crossing Boundaries: New Media and Networked Journalism," *Communication, Culture & Critique* 1, no. 1(2008): 93. See also Marie-Claire Shanahan, "Science Blogs as Boundary Layers: Creating and Understanding New Writer and Reader Interactions Through Science Blogging," *Journalism* 12, no. 7 (2011): 903–19.
66 Mark Coddington, "Defending a Paradigm by Patrolling a Boundary: Two Global Newspapers' Approach to WikiLeaks," *Journalism & Mass Communication Quarterly* 89, no. 3 (2012): 389. See also Scott Eldridge, "Boundary Maintenance and Inter-loper Media Reaction: Differentiating Between Journalism's Discursive Enforcement Processes," *Journalism Studies* 15, no. 1 (2014): 1–16.
67 Matthias Revers, "Journalistic Professionalism as Performance and Boundary Work: Source Relations at the State House," *Journalism* 15, no. 1 (2014): 37–52.
68 Jo Bogaerts, "On the Performativity of Journalistic Identity" *Journalism Practice* 5, no. 4 (2011): 399–413. Marcel Broersma, "Journalism as Performative Discourse: The Importance of Form and Style in Journalism," in *Journalism and Meaning-making: Reading the Newspaper*, ed. Verica Rupar (Cresskill, NJ: Hampton Press, 2010), 15–35.

Part I

Professionalism, norms and boundaries

Chapter 1

Out of bounds

Professional norms as boundary markers

Jane B. Singer

In times of relative media stability, journalists use normative standards and ethical principles to distinguish between "good" and "bad" members of their own profession. But in times of media instability, they also – even primarily – use ethics to distinguish between insiders and outsiders: who is or is not a journalist at all.

This chapter suggests that in an open media environment that presents no limits on who can publish, journalists cite norms not only as identity markers of the professional news worker ("Who I am") but also as boundary markers between professionals and non-professionals ("Who I am not"/"Who is not me"). The distinctions they draw rest on ethical practices such as verification (getting information right vs. getting it out as quickly as possible), principles such as independence (serving the public vs. serving commercial or other vested interests), and promises such as accountability for the consequences of their actions. After outlining journalists' evocation of normative concepts in response to "new" media forms in the past, two evolving hallmarks of contemporary journalism are used to illustrate how this boundary marking works, as well as the ways in which the boundaries are being redefined.

First, as social media have become pervasive over the past decade, normative principles that initially formed the basis of resistance subsequently have helped guide journalists toward productive use of material originating outside the newsroom. The boundary related to social media – considered here in the more specific context of "social journalism" – is an outward-facing one, involving relationships between journalists, sources, and publics.[1]

Second, the newer phenomenon of "entrepreneurial journalism" offers an example of the use of professional norms to delineate a different and still-salient obstacle. Here we see the norms still being applied to define and articulate resistance. The clearest boundary is a more "internal" one; it involves the need for journalists themselves to wear multiple hats within an emerging enterprise, typically involving both content-production and revenue-production roles.

In discussions of both social and entrepreneurial journalism, the professional norm of accountability, often translated as "transparency" in a networked media environment, is being evoked with increasing vigor. Less than 20 years ago, accountability was a controversial addition to professional ethics codes such as those of the U.S. Society of Professional Journalists: "I don't think that journalists should be accountable to anything but the truth," one practitioner-turned-professor declared in response.[2] Now linked to the professionally desirable trait of honesty, it is emerging as a definitive norm of digital journalism.[3]

Professional norms as boundary devices: Response to "new" media

The survival of journalism as an occupation depends on its credibility, which is gained through the collective behavior of its practitioners.[4] The right to wield internal oversight over that behavior is typically fiercely protected; in democratic societies, journalists see it as a far more appropriate form of control than external or formal oversight, such as by government or another regulatory entity. Particularly in the United States, where legal structures provide enormous room for journalistic autonomy, practitioners tend to view the professional norms that they themselves develop, articulate, and (perhaps) enforce as forming the only acceptable boundaries around occupational behavior.

More broadly, journalists use normative concepts as definitional devices – and have done so at least since they began to see their occupation as a fledgling profession more than a century ago.[5] Successive iterations of their own evolving identity as "real" journalists (as opposed not so much to "fake" ones as to "bad" ones) have, over time, created a professional ideology based in large part on broadly accepted and widely shared values.[6] Although structural differences lead to variations in how journalists in democratic societies see their role, there are widespread commonalities in the articulation of fundamental professional norms. For example, the provision of reliable, factual information by impartial social watchdogs is seen almost universally as a central journalistic function, and Western journalists are markedly wary about active promotion of particular values or ideas.[7]

Within the United States, where a pervasive "ethos of autonomy" means even European-style press councils are seen as anathema to constitutionally protected press freedom, various professional entities have developed guidelines to codify these shared occupational norms.[8] From the "Journalist's Creed" articulated 100 years ago by the founding dean of the Missouri School of Journalism – who declared the journalism that "best deserves success" to be "stoutly independent" and to convey only what the journalist "holds in his heart to be true"[9] – to extended debates about whether professional codes should be updated to reflect digital exigencies, the fundamental norms have remained stable. The largest such organization, the Society of Professional Journalists, identifies four of them in its widely cited Code of Ethics: commitment to truth-telling, minimization of harm, independence, and accountability and transparency, that last norm added only in September 2014. Codes and guidelines from other professional organizations and news outlets are in much the same vein.

Us and them

Such normative guidelines arguably have served multiple purposes over the past century, but one consistent purpose has been a boundary-setting one: journalists and the organizations that employ them need to be perceived by the public (aka their audience) as crucial to the provision of factual, reliable, timely, and meaningful information.[10] They therefore have an interest in positioning other entities as less crucial, and an excellent way to make the point is to brand them as less ethical – that is, less committed to norms that engender factualness, reliability, and so on. Although digital media have accelerated the pace of change, the successive emergence and growth of "new" media forms throughout the twentieth century and into the twenty-first repeatedly generated defensive responses, couched in normative terms, from many of the established practitioners of the day. Over and over, attempts to delineate and safeguard occupational turf drew on eloquent evocation of ethical standards and a declaration that the "traditional" journalist would uphold them against challenges from poseurs.

Despite the intertwined early history of newspapers and radio, for example, publishers were soon protesting that radio risked becoming a propaganda instrument because of its ties to government, offered only superficial news that created public confusion if not downright ignorance; and was in any case more interested in making money than serving citizens.[11] Entertainment programming was a focus of press criticism of early television – whose "lapses in taste and judgment" made it dubious for family viewing, the *New York Times* pronounced[12] – but the medium in general was soon depicted as sullied by commercial motivations that undermined its ostensible devotion to the public interest. On it has gone into the 2000s, when popular "fake" news comedy shows such as *The Daily Show with Jon Stewart* were determined to be "interesting because sometimes they do a better job performing the functions of journalism than journalists themselves" but ultimately to fall short because presenters do not share "journalists' moral commitments".[13]

The rise of the Internet as a journalistic platform in the late 1990s and early 2000s ushered in a new and intense round of paradigm repair, a boundary-setting tactic used by journalists to separate appropriate from inappropriate media logic and activity.[14] Rather than abating as the medium has taken root in Western society, this delineation of boundaries has become something of a perpetual professional activity. In contrast to the relative stability of broadcast media over time, the Internet has continued to mutate into newly challenging forms, and a sizable contingent of traditional journalists – certainly not all but many, especially in newspaper newsrooms – have responded each time by protesting that the ethics of their online counterparts are not quite up to snuff, or at best that they can far too easily go astray.

In the Internet's earliest days as a news medium, concerns focused on the ethical use of online sources. The perceived difficulty of verifying facts was seen as a major problem, compounded by a perception that the Internet was a free-for-all containing unreliable, badly sourced, and generally dubious information and, just as bad, that its emphasis on speed would trump attempts at accuracy.[15] "In print, we've always had the luxury of, well, let's see if what we have immediately is actually true and the whole story and can be verified," a newspaper editor fretted way back in 1995. "The old adage was, you know, 'Get it first, but first, get it right.' Well, now it's just 'get it first.'"[16]

In addition to concerns about accuracy, journalists in the first decade of widespread online use articulated a host of other normatively desirable activities under threat, from doing original reporting, to protecting the privacy of content and the individuals behind it, to certifying the provenance of anonymous sources.[17] Ruggiero found that, at least up to the time of his research, many journalists viewed the Internet as housing bogus and otherwise untrustworthy news, and operating well outside the objectivity-driven norms of conventional news gathering and presentation. In response, practitioners erected cultural boundaries by applying such exclusionary characterizations as "unprofessional" and "unreliable".[18] A few years later, newspaper journalists were still rating online news overall as only moderately credible – defined as believable, accurate, and fair – though they seemed willing to admit that online news provided by traditional journalistic entities might be kind of OK.[19] In other words, as greater newsroom effort went into maintaining an affiliated website, the definitional boundary shifted to encompass those online journalists employed by a "real" news outlet while continuing to exclude everyone else.

Concerns expressed in ethical terms also have greeted changes in newsroom structures or practices in connection with new technological affordances and economic demands. In the early 2000s, as news organizations explored cross-platform production under the then-trendy label of "newsroom convergence," journalists protested about perceived threats to accuracy from an emphasis on speed (again), the subversion of "news values" to "entertainment values" (again), and compromised journalistic autonomy, primarily through a blending of promotion with news delivery.[20] Journalists in converged newsrooms believed that new responsibilities or work practices left them less time to investigate and verify information and that in general, the public benefited far less than media companies (and journalists themselves far less again than either companies or audiences).[21]

The early 2000s also saw large-scale adoption of the blogging format – a form of social media – by online users from all walks of life. The reaction of many journalists will be no surprise: skepticism and suspicion of this "mutant breed" of self-absorbed and hyper-opinionated amateurs.[22] Attention was focused on such blogging breaches as plagiarism or even fabrication of information, misrepresentation of identity, and conflicts of interest created by bloggers taking money from vested interests in return for favorable posts.[23] A survey in the mid-2000s found that sizable numbers of journalists believed blogs were neither trustworthy, credible, factual, nor well-written, with newspaper journalists more likely that those in other media to see blogs as threatening the profession.[24] In short, as bloggers came to personify the growing challenge to journalists' power as society's authoritative storytellers,[25] journalists responded largely by focusing on bloggers' perceived ethical shortcomings, notably in relation to the crucial journalistic task of monitoring political actors.[26] More broadly, the presence of bloggers as rivals on journalists' occupational turf encouraged those journalists to redefine their own practices and processes – for instance, to emphasize normative strengths such as a professed commitment to fact-checking – as a protective strategy or boundary-setting device.[27]

For nearly a century, then, journalists have greeted each emerging news platform with concerns framed in normative terms. Moreover, they have applied those terms, consistently and explicitly, to distinguish themselves and their news-generating activities from those outside the magic circle that encompasses newsroom professionals. The rest of this chapter looks at how these efforts are playing out in relation to the rise of social media in the late 2000s and the more recent emergence of the "entrepreneurial journalist."

Social journalism

Journalists' increasing use of social media to engage with audiences demonstrates not only their go-to reliance on normative principles as a boundary marker but also how both principles and boundaries have been reconceptualized over a fairly short period of time. This section considers two related aspects of social journalism that initially prompted journalists to declare their professional distance but that increasingly have come to be seen as at least potentially compatible with practitioner norms. The first involves content from outside the newsroom, and the second involves journalists' own activities in social media spaces.

User-generated content

By the early 2000s – after the Internet was in widespread use in U.S. newsrooms but before social media had taken root – more than two-thirds of U.S. journalists claimed to believe it was very important to include ordinary citizens as sources.[28] But when news organizations opened their digital doors to so-called "user-generated content" (UGC), information produced outside the newsroom and housed on media websites, many journalists again reacted with alarm over perceived ethical (and legal) implications. UGC was described as unethical in its own right and as subverting practitioners' normative standards. Comments to researchers about the perils of online populism, while never unanimous, were nonetheless ubiquitous and unambiguous. Here are just a few examples:

- Users are "a bunch of bigots" shouting at each other "without ever bothering to listen. ... If someone did try to put a reasonable, balanced view, it was an exception."[29]

- Because of the relative anonymity afforded by comment posts and the associated lack of accountability, "people feel licensed to say things in content and style that they wouldn't own if publishing as themselves."[30]
- The value of UGC is "disproportionate to the excessive amount of management time which is taken up with trying to ensure it is accurate, balanced, honest, fair and – most importantly – legally safe to publish."[31]
- "Things can be construed as fact when there's nothing to back them up as facts," and it would be "pretty labor-intensive" for journalists to check user contributions out.[32]

And more. Much more. The institutional response was to publish extensive codes of conduct for use of commenting spaces, in particular. *USA Today*, for instance, prohibits "threatening, abusive, libelous, defamatory, obscene, vulgar, pornographic, profane or indecent information of any kind"; in Britain, *The Times* bans "content or activity" that "promotes racism, terrorism, hatred or physical harm." Other news organizations all over the world have similar proscriptions.

Yet within a decade, not only have the boundaries around content become more porous but the emphasis on such boundaries has also become less prominent in journalists' discourse about UGC. As early as the mid-2000s, practitioners were acknowledging that audience members can be "very knowledgeable about certain areas"[33] and at least a "small number" can engage others in ways that "make it much more interesting for everyone else."[34] Perhaps, some even suggested, journalists should be "developing ways of allowing users to add more value to debate, rather than giving them a space that interpolates them as 'inferior'" journalists.[35] Over time, more journalists began expressing the view that while UGC might not conform to some normative goals, it contributed substantively to others, most notably goals related to diversity of information and information sources, and thus to the provision of a more multi-faceted truth. "I've seen the future," UK *Guardian* editor Alan Rusbridger declared, "and it's mutual."[36]

Particularly after the rise of Twitter in the late 2000s and its striking demonstration of journalistic utility during crises and disasters, the construction efforts of growing numbers of journalists shifted from fences to bridges. Though the immediate reaction in some quarters predictably sought to differentiate it from proper journalism – one veteran columnist described Twitter in 2009 as "a toy for bored celebrities and high-school girls," while another said using it to find information was "like searching for medical advice in an online world of quacks and cures" – many practitioners quickly saw its utility.[37]

They saw, too, its potential to revisit some long-standing normative practices. For instance, the use of live blogging formats to cover breaking news enables journalists to be far more transparent about their news-gathering practices, as discussed further below. Journalists now can tell users "'Look, this is out there, we can't verify it, but this is being talked about, this is part of the story.' We're letting you in on the workflow of the journalist in a way," as one reporter who helped pioneer live blogging at the *Guardian* explained.[38] Journalists also said they were more likely to confess to getting something wrong in a Live Blog and to apologize as well as fix the mistake promptly. In general, the transparency of the format was seen as fostering inclusivity of users in the news-making process, making the boundaries around journalistic work more porous than in even the recent past.

Other journalists have come to believe that, at least for some stories, getting information out quickly actually does trump getting it perfect the first time, particularly if users are aware of the process. In including unverified tweets in their breaking news coverage of the 2008 Mumbai bombings, BBC news executives said "monitoring, selecting and passing on the information we are getting as quickly as we can" was the right approach because "many people will want to know what we know and what we are still finding out."[39]

Indeed, social journalism can be seen as part of a larger conceptual shift to journalism as the creation of collective rather than exclusively individual intelligence, authority, and expertise[40] and, more broadly, from "journalism as product" to "journalism as process."[41] The overall effect of this shift is to make boundaries – plus the need to patrol them and to control their crossing – less important by lending normative legitimacy to participation.[42] Some of the reasons for the shift are, no doubt, rooted in resignation: If you can't beat 'em, join 'em. Users are highly unlikely to fold up their laptops, toss out their cell phones, and go away, so journalists have responded in part by rationalizing their role as desirable (which they certainly are financially, regardless of any editorial merit provided) and not merely inescapable. But it also is obvious that while some users are indeed rude, ridiculous, or wrong, much of the information generated outside the newsroom – from on-the-scene reports to news tips to cogent analysis – is proving invaluable.

Journalists' primary response, then, has shifted from disapprobation to accommodation, particularly as the dominant forms of UGC have expanded from post-publication commentary (which continues to attract ranters) to pre-publication alerts about both news and newsworthiness through newly prominent formats such as Twitter. Where a few years ago journalists were restricting user contributions to the final interpretation stage of the news-production process, users today are important in stages previously closed to them, including observation of news and selection of newsworthiness.[43] That is indeed a boundary-breaching change: Rather than trying to seal their ethical borders, practitioners are looking for ways to bring UGC within their own ethical sphere.

Journalists' use of social media

They have done so in two ways: in using UGC as source material, and in crafting their own social media presence. The growing reliance on material originating outside the newsroom has already been outlined, but its incorporation in journalists' stories as distinct from their own tweets, live blogs, or other transitory messages deserves a bit more attention.

Beyond using tweets from ordinary people as a digital *vox populi* to illustrate public opinion on a topic, journalists continue to maintain more rigid rules around full-fledged stories compared with social media flutters.[44] The Associated Press guidelines for the use of information derived from social media – which add a complex layer to existing verification procedures – are indicative. The AP's multi-faceted verification process includes, among other steps, checking the source's social history, comparing the content with AP reporting, running material past regional experts, and verifying the context. "Even if something is incredibly compelling and it doesn't pass one of our steps, then it doesn't go out," says AP social media and UGC editor Fergus Bell. "That's how we stop from being wrong."[45] The BBC responded to the explosion in UGC by setting up a special verification Hub, staffed by as many as 20 journalists, to sift through potentially newsworthy textual and visual material and assess its credibility using tools ranging from search engines to Twitter trend data to online discussions among trusted contacts.[46]

When information can't be definitively verified, however, disclosure again becomes key. The primary norm remains the long-standing one of truth-telling, but where supporting standards in a traditional environment might be independence or objectivity, the fallback principle in social spaces is transparency. Karlsson connects this shift to the nature of an interactive, participatory medium: "When more than one version of events is made public ... it becomes necessary to demonstrate why one version is better than another."[47] For journalists, "the barriers are broken down," as a *Guardian* editor said. "Users do expect more journalists to step out from behind articles, defend, and discuss them."[48]

The focus so far has been on journalists' use of material generated outside the newsroom. But, of course, journalists also actively use social media platforms to distribute their own work. Here, too, they and their employers have wrestled with where the lines should be drawn. In addition to concern about the potential to undermine credibility by posting bogus information – dealt with primarily through the verification processes already discussed – this practice raises another ethical issue: the threat to their status as impartial observers and reporters.

The neutrality norm offers a fresh aspect of ongoing boundary negotiation. Some news organizations, notably national "newspapers of record," have sought to maintain impermeable boundaries between journalists' private views and public voices. As the social media policy of South Africa's *Mail and Guardian* stated as of the early 2010s:

> The bedrock of our authority as a publication is our impartiality. ... Your profiles, retweets, likes and postings can reveal your political and

ideological affiliations. Be very sure that your audience either understands that you are professional enough to put those aside in the workplace, or that those affiliations will not be construed as having an effect on your ability to do objective journalism.

Similarly, the *New York Times* during the same period advises circumspection about online posts – at least on some topics. Its policy states:

> Bloggers may write lively commentary on their preferences in food, music, sports or other avocations, but as journalists, they must avoid taking stands on divisive public issues. ... A blog that takes a political stand is as far out of bounds as a letter to the editor supporting or opposing a candidate.

But journalists who work extensively with social media are coming to see that stance as unrealistic, even counterproductive. Researchers have been saying for some time that the shift to an interactive environment would necessarily challenge a traditional commitment to strict objectivity, and recent work has indicated at least some journalists now agree.[49] A study of journalists' use of Twitter, for example, found that their views about the normative importance of neutrality were shifting, with 43 percent of coded tweets containing an expression of opinion.[50] Vis found opinion to be a significant part of the Twitter coverage of the North London riots in 2011, suggesting "the watering down of an established journalistic norm, possibly giving rise to a new hybrid norm on Twitter."[51] And a 2012 study of U.S. online journalists by Agarwal and Barthel found that many interviewees "roundly rejected" norms of objectivity and neutrality, describing the need to get a point across "without first burying it in equivocations or false political stances and *New York Times*-y stuff."[52] They were more interested in getting at "the truth as you see it" rather than adhering to what many described as outdated rituals of objectivity.

Thus, unlike many journalists working primarily in traditional formats who continue to value a more impartial stance, the evidence suggests those embedded in social spaces are finding that traditional boundaries no longer function in the same ways they once did – if indeed they function at all.[53] The fluidity of information on platforms such as Twitter means that material produced by journalists intermingles in myriad ways with material produced by users, bringing to the fore an emphasis on verification and transparency while lessening the importance of traditional norms such as objectivity. The incorporation of social media practices in journalistic work and practitioners' understanding of that work has brought a rethinking of normative values, with norms that enable ongoing relationships emerging as more valuable than those that seek to distance journalists from the outside world.

Entrepreneurial journalism

If social journalism offers an exemplar of journalists' use of normative markers to establish their relationship with outsiders, the application of normative principles to entrepreneurial journalism suggests a more inward focus. The concern is primarily with how journalists do their own job, specifically how they maintain distinctions between roles that require loyalty to both audiences and advertisers or other sources of financial support. In other words, the boundary here is the vaunted "wall" separating editorial and commercial considerations. There has been far less academic or industry discourse to date about entrepreneurial journalism in comparison with the extensive and ongoing conversation about social media, but the point that successful innovation hinges on overlap among the needs of customers, content producers, and financiers explicitly calls into question the nature and viability of boundaries separating them.[54]

As suggested above, American journalists in particular have long seen autonomy, a fundamental norm of all professions,[55] as vital to the public service enterprise they seek to perform.[56] Pressures on that norm abound, and even before the rise of Web 2.0 interactivity, the Internet was recognized as posing particular pressures on journalistic autonomy because of its vulnerability to market influence.[57] The prevalence of sponsored content and the relatively close working relationships between online editorial and marketing departments have been among the causes for concern.[58]

Entrepreneurial journalism not only makes such pressures overt but also concentrates them in the activities of a single person or small team. Journalists who form a start-up business wear multiple hats every day, from the relatively familiar one of content producer to the far less familiar ones of marketer, advertising executive, and business manager. Issues of journalistic independence and conflicts of interest "will soon become the dominant theme in journalism ethics," media ethicist Stephen Ward predicts, necessitating construction of guidelines to safeguard norms and respond to public skepticism.[59] Ward urges rigorous editorial oversight combined with disclosure of any potential conflicts to address "the looming ethical problems of an entrepreneurial age." Similarly, Poynter Institute ethicist Kelly McBride cautions that "Money itself isn't tainted, but it comes with stipulations always."[60]

Nor are the concerns limited to for-profit enterprises. Scholars and other observers have asked whether sufficient boundaries exist between journalists and their foundation benefactors in the nonprofit start-ups that have gained traction in the twenty-first century – or, for that matter, whether foundations in general are subjected to the journalistic scrutiny they deserve as ideological institutions wielding considerable social and political power. "By what means would this become manifest in reporting, and how might such manifestations be detected?" Browne asks. "Interests come in many shapes and sizes, and operate on all sorts of potentially competing and hidden agendas."[61]

So whether the pressures are exerted by foundations and donors, as in many non-profit endeavors, or by commercial entities such as advertisers or sponsors, the rise of the content producer who doubles as revenue generator clearly suggests potential pitfalls. With social media, as we have seen, the primary ethical concerns have related to truth-telling (addressed by a re-engagement with the forms and functions of verification processes as boundary devices) and impartiality (addressed by an apparent willingness to reconsider the ongoing value of such a norm altogether). With entrepreneurial journalism, the norm of independence is the dominant one, and the tension so far seems unresolved. A recent study of media trade press coverage of entrepreneurial journalism[62] suggests that journalists are actually broadly supportive of the idea in general, but some trip over the ethical considerations, expressing concern about a potential "willingness to transgress time-honored barriers – for instance, by blurring the division between reporting and advertising."[63]

Entrepreneurial journalism demands a reconsideration of the value (or not) of independence from audiences as well as advertisers or sponsors. Although social media have created new relationships between journalists and audiences, the resulting ethical issues have mostly revolved around sourcing, as shown earlier. For the entrepreneur, the conception of an audience potentially shifts from "the public, the people who rely on me for credible information" to "my customers, the people whom I rely on to keep my journalistic enterprise going (and who also continue to rely on me for the credible information that forms the basis of my enterprise)." In a traditional news environment, keeping audiences happy was only indirectly the job of the journalist. The extent to which a start-up's audience-as-customer must be catered to in order to survive financially, balanced against the value of autonomous editorial judgment and the journalist's traditional norm of public service broadly defined, is another topic ripe for exploration from a normative perspective.

Considerably more work is needed on entrepreneurial journalism in order to understand how and whether normative boundaries are being reimagined, reconciled with new exigencies, or reified along traditional lines. As growing numbers of journalists, willingly or unwillingly, become independent operators, just what will that "independence" look like?

Transparency as the new norm(al)

The discussion above indicated the growing view of transparency, a somewhat undervalued and even contested norm in traditional media, as a prominent norm in social journalism. There is some evidence that it is being called upon in ethical considerations of entrepreneurial journalism, as well, whether involving a commercial or a nonprofit enterprise. "As important as having ethics is letting people know that you do," advises Briggs.[64] "A startup has no track record to establish its credibility. As a journalism entrepreneur, it's crucial to be open about the goals and standards of your site."

Transparency, of course, is all about communication across boundaries. The inherent function of the norm of truthful forthrightness is to make clear what otherwise might be hidden, from processes to beliefs to motives.[65] Although journalists have for some time been willing (reluctantly, in some cases) to acknowledge a need to be accountable for their decisions and actions, transparency involves a more proactive stance: a before-the-fact profession of goals or interests that supplements but also goes beyond an after-the-fact admission of responsibility. The fluidity and interactivity of a digital environment create both a need and an opportunity that seemed to most journalists considerably less self-evident in a traditional media world. Indeed, the nature and extent of disclosure facilitated by digital media was arguably not even feasible in the past;[66] its current use extends journalistic authority as well as credibility, providing a sound ethical foundation for the honest relationships on which both social journalism and entrepreneurial journalism rest.[67]

In addition to those just cited, a growing number of other scholars also have urged the adoption of this boundary-breaching norm. Phillips, for example, calls for an increased emphasis on transparency, especially about the origin of reported information, as a safeguard of truth. Particularly given the online emphasis on speed of delivery, she says, "accuracy and sincerity reside in transparency," with clear attribution and increased use of links making it "rather more difficult for journalists to quote selectively and in so doing completely distort the facts."[68] In their exploration of shifts in journalistic capital, Hellmueller and her colleagues connect the immediacy of networked online journalism to emerging forms of professional responsibility. Showing audiences where facts originated "shifts the responsibility from the journalist's judgment to its source of origin," with journalists and audiences collaborating as "mutually reliant tellers of the truth."[69] Van der Wurff and Schönbach see transparency as an overarching norm and "the major measure to secure the quality of modern-day journalism" without giving up professional autonomy in the process.[70]

In short, it appears that journalism's ideological commitment to control, rooted in an institutional instinct toward protecting legitimacy and boundaries, may be giving way to a hybrid logic of adaptability and openness: a willingness to see audiences more as peers, to appreciate their contributions, and to find normative purpose in transparency and participation.[71] Early indications are that audiences, in turn, see value in the change. For example, the provision of supporting evidence and other transparent attribution practices in the *Guardian*'s Live Blogs contributed to readers' assessment of these as a more objective form of journalism than the newspaper itself; they described the feeds as more factual, less opinion-based, and more balanced.[72]

When we begin to tear down the walls that separate us – including normative walls – our commonalities really do become clearer. In a social and entrepreneurial environment where the boundaries around journalists have become steadily more porous, those commonalities are arguably the key to the survival of a profession that can no longer thrive in splendid isolation.

Notes

1 Alfred Hermida, "Social journalism: Exploring how social media is shaping journalism" In *The Handbook of Global Online Journalism,* eds Eugenia Siapera and Andreas Veglis (Malden, MA: Wiley-Blackwell, 2012), 309–28.

2 David Noack, "Prof criticizes SPJ ethics code" *Editor & Publisher,* 23 January 1999, 13.

3 Michael Karlsson, "The immediacy of online news, the visibility of journalistic processes and a restructuring of journalistic authority," *Journalism* 12, no. 3 (2011): 279–95.

4 David Weaver, Randal Beam, Bonnie Brownlee, Paul Voakes, and Cleveland Wilhoit, *The American journalist in the 21st century: U.S. news people at the dawn of a new millennium* (Mahwah, NJ: Lawrence Erlbaum Associates, 2006).

5 Michael Schudson, *Discovering the news: A social history of American newspapers* (New York: Basic Books, 1981).

6 Mark Deuze, "What is journalism? Professional identity and ideology of journalists," *Journalism* 6, no. 4 (2005): 442–64.

7 Thomas Hanitzsch, Folker Hanusch, Claudia Mellado, Maria Anikina, Rosa Berganza, Incilay Cangoz and Mihai Coman, "Mapping journalism cultures across nations: A comparative study of 18 countries," *Journalism Studies* 12, no. 3 (2011): 273–93.

8 Erik Ugland, "The legitimacy and moral authority of the National News Council (USA)," *Journalism* 9, no. 3 (2008): 285–308.

9 Walter Williams, "The journalist's creed," School of Journalism, University of Missouri (1914), http://journalism.missouri.edu/jschool/#creed

10 Arthur Hayes, Jane Singer and Jerry Ceppos, "Shifting roles, enduring values: The credible journalist in a digital age," *Journal of Mass Media Ethics* 22, no. 4 (2007): 262–79.

11 George Lott, "The press-radio war of the 1930s," *Journal of Broadcasting* 14, no. 3 (1970): 275–86.

12 Matthew Murrary, "Television wipes its feet: The commercial and ethical considerations," *Journal of Popular Film & Television* 21, no. 3 (1993): 128–38.

13 Sandra Borden and Chad Tew, "The role of journalist and the performance of journalism: Ethical lessons from 'fake' news (seriously)," *Journal of Mass Media Ethics* 22, no.4 (2007): 300–314.

14 Lance Bennett, Lynne Gressett, and William Haltom, "Repairing the news: A case study of the news paradigm," *Journal of Communication* 35, no. 2 (1985): 50–68.

15 Bruce Garrison, "Journalists' perceptions of online information-gathering problems," *Journalism & Mass Communication Quarterly* 77, no. 3 (2000): 500–514.

16 Jane Singer, "Still guarding the gate? The newspaper journalist's role in an on-line world," *Convergence* 3, no. 1 (1997): 72–89.

17 Mark Deuze and Daphna Yeshua, "Online journalists face new ethical dilemmas: Lessons from the Netherlands," *Journal of Mass Media Ethics* 16, no. 4 (2001): 273–92; Singer, "Still guarding the gate? The newspaper journalist's role in an on-line world," 72–89.

18 Thomas Ruggiero, "Paradigm repair and changing journalistic perceptions of the internet as an objective news source," *Convergence* 10, no. 4 (2004): 99.

19 William Cassidy, "Online news credibility: An examination of the perceptions of newspaper journalists," *Journal of Computer-Mediated Communication* 12, no. 2 (2007): 478–98.

20 Jane Singer, "Partnerships and public service: Normative issues for journalists in converged newsrooms," *Journal of Mass Media Ethics* 21, no. 1 (2006): 30–53.

21 Laura Smith, Andrea Tanner, and Sonya Forte Duhe, "Convergence concerns in local television: Conflicting views from the newsroom," *Journal of Broadcasting &*

Electronic Media 51, no. 4 (2007): 555–74; Edgar Huang, Karen Davison, Stephanie Shreve, Twila Davis, Elizabeth Bettendorf and Anita Nair, "Facing the challenges of convergence: Media professionals' concerns of working across media platforms," *Convergence* 12, no. 1 (2006): 83–98.

22 Tom Regan, "Weblogs threaten and inform traditional journalism," *Nieman Reports* (2003), www.nieman.harvard.edu/reports/article/101041/Weblogs-Threaten-and-Inform-Traditional-Journalism.aspx

23 David Perlmutter and Mary Schoen, "'If I break a rule, what do I do, fire myself?' Ethics codes of independent blogs," *Journal of Mass Media Ethics* 22, no. 1 (2007): 37–48.

24 Deborah Chung, Eunseong Kim, Kaye Trammell and Lance Porter, "Uses and perceptions of blogs: A report on professional journalists and journalism educators," *Journalism & Mass Communication Educator* 62, no. 3 (2007): 305–22; Kaye Sweetser, Lance Porter, Deborah Chung, and Eunseong Kim, "Credibility and the use of blogs among professionals in the communication industry," *Journalism & Mass Communication Quarterly* 85, no. 1 (2008): 169–85.

25 Donald Matheson, "Weblogs and the epistemology of the news: Some trends in online journalism," *New Media & Society* 6, no. 4 (2004): 443–68.

26 Matt Carlson, "Blogs and journalistic authority: The role of blogs in US Election Day 2004 coverage," *Journalism Studies* 8, no. 2 (2007): 264–79.

27 Wilson Lowrey, "Mapping the journalism-blogging relationship," *Journalism* 7, no. 4 (2006): 477–500.

28 Weaver *et al.*, *The American Journalist in the 21st Century: U.S. news people at the dawn of a new millennium.*

29 Neil Thurman, "Forums for citizen journalists? Adoption of user generated content initiatives by online news media," *New Media & Society* 10, no. 1 (2008): 145.

30 Jane Singer and Ian Ashman, "Comment is free, but facts are sacred: User-generated content and ethical constructs at the *Guardian*," *Journal of Mass Media Ethics* 24, no. 1 (2009): 16.

31 Jane Singer, "Quality control: Perceived effects of user-generated content on newsroom norms, values and routines," *Journalism Practice* 4, no. 2 (2010): 134.

32 Seth C. Lewis, Kelly Kaufhold and Dominic Lasorsa, "Thinking about citizen journalism: The philosophical and practical challenges of user-generated content for community newspapers," *Journalism Practice* 4, no. 2 (2010): 170.

33 Alfred Hermida and Neil Thurman, "A clash of cultures: The integration of user-generated content within professional journalistic frameworks at British newspaper websites," *Journalism Practice* 2, no. 3 (2008): 349.

34 Hermida and Thurman, "A clash of cultures: The integration of user-generated content within professional journalistic frameworks at British newspaper websites," 353.

35 Singer and Ashman, "Comment is free, but facts are sacred," 33.

36 Singer and Ashman, "Comment is free, but facts are sacred."

37 Alfred Hermida, "Twittering the news: The emergence of ambient journalism," *Journalism Practice* 4, no. 3 (2010): 299–300.

38 Neil Thurman and Anna Walters, "Live blogging – digital journalism's pivotal platform? A case study of the production, consumption, and form of Live Blogs at Guardian.co.uk," *Digital Journalism* 1, no. 1 (2013): 93.

39 Hermida, "Twittering the news: The emergence of ambient journalism," 300.

40 Alfred Hermida, "Tweets and truth: Journalism as a discipline of collaborative verification," *Journalism Practice* 6, no 5/6 (2012): 659–68.

41 Sue Robinson, "Journalism as process: The labor implications of participatory content in news organizations," *Journalism & Communication Monographs* 13, no. 3 (2011): 138–210.

42 Seth C. Lewis, "The tension between professional control and open participation: Journalism and its boundaries," *Information, Communication & Society* 15, no. 6 (2012): 836–56.

43 David Domingo, Thorsten Quandt, Ari Heinonen, Steve Paulussen, Jane Singer, and Marina Vujnovic, "Participatory journalism practices in the media and beyond: An international comparative study of initiatives in online newspapers," *Journalism Practice* 2, no. 3 (2008): 326–42.

44 Marcel Broersma and Todd Graham, "Social media as beat: Tweets as a news source during the 2010 British and Dutch elections," *Journalism Practice* 6, no.3 (2012): 403–419.

45 Craig Silverman, "Editor Fergus Bell explains how AP verifies user-generated content from Sandy to Syria," *PoynterOnline*, 16 November 2012, www.poynter.org/ latest-news/regret-the-error/192540/new-editor-fergus-bell-explains-how-ap-verifies-user-generated-content-from-sandy-to-syria/

46 David Turner, "Inside the BBC's verification Hub," *Nieman Reports*, summer 2012, www.nieman.harvard.edu/reports/article/102764/Inside-the-BBCs-Verification-Hub.aspx

47 Karlsson, "The immediacy of online news, the visibility of journalistic processes and a restructuring of journalistic authority," 286.

48 Singer and Ashman, "Comment is free, but facts are sacred," 16.

49 Mark Deuze, "What is journalism? Professional identity and ideology of journalists," 442–64.

50 Dominic Lasorsa, Seth C. Lewis and Avery Holton, "Normalizing Twitter: Journalism practice in an emerging communication space," *Journalism Studies* 13, no. 1 (2012): 19–36.

51 Farida Vis, "Twitter as a reporting tool for breaking news: Journalists tweeting the 2011 UK riots," *Digital Journalism* 1, no. 1 (2013): 43–44.

52 Sheetal Agarwal and Michael Barthel, "The friendly barbarians: Professional norms and work routines of online journalists in the United States," *Journalism* (2013), http://jou.sagepub.com/content/early/2013/12/11/1464884913511565

53 Morten Skovsgaard, Erik Albaek, Peter Bro, and Claes de Vreese, "A reality check: How journalists' role perceptions impact their implementation of the objectivity norm," *Journalism* 14, no. 1 (2012): 22–42.

54 Robert Picard, "Changing business models of online content services: Their implications for multimedia and other content producers," *International Journal on Media Management* 2, no. 2 (2000): 60–68.

55 Magali Larson, *The rise of professionalism: A sociological analysis* (Berkeley: University of California Press, 1979).

56 Randal Beam, David Weaver, and Bonnie Brownlee, "Changes in professionalism of U.S. journalists in the turbulent twenty-first century," *Journalism & Mass Communication Quarterly* 86, no. 2 (2009): 277–98.

57 Elisia Cohen, "Online journalism as market-driven journalism," *Journal of Broadcasting & Electronic Media* 46, no. 4 (2002): 532–48.

58 Deuze and Yeshua, "Online journalists face new ethical dilemmas: Lessons from the Netherlands," 273–92.

59 Stephen Ward, "Journalism in the entrepreneurial age," *Center for Journalism Ethics, School of Journalism and Mass Communication*, University of Wisconsin-Madison, 15 September 2009, http://ethics.journalism.wisc.edu/2009/09/15/journalism-in-the-entrepreneurial-age/

60 Mark Briggs, *Ethics lessons for news entrepreneurs* (2010), www.journalism20.com/ blog/2010/07/14/ethics-lessons-for-news-entrepreneurs/

61 Harry Brown, "Foundation-funded journalism: Reasons to be wary of charitable support," *Journalism Studies* 11, no. 6 (2010): 901.

62 Tim Vos and Jane Singer, "Entrepreneurial journalism: Shifting journalistic capital?" Paper under consideration for presentation at the Association for Education in Journalism and Mass Communication annual convention, August 2014.

63 Andrew Rice, "Putting a price on words," *The New York Times Magazine*, 12 May 2010, www.nytimes.com/2010/05/16/magazine/16Journalism-t.html

64 Mark Briggs, *Entrepreneurial journalism: How to build what's next for news* (Thousand Oaks, CA: CQ Press, 2012), 54.

65 Patrick Plaisance, "Transparency: An assessment of the Kantian roots of a key element in media ethics practice," *Journal of Mass Media Ethics* 22, no. 2–3 (2007): 187–207.

66 Arthur Hayes, Jane Singer and Jerry Ceppos, "Shifting roles, enduring values: The credible journalist in a digital age," *Journal of Mass Media Ethics* 22, no. 4 (2007): 262–79.

67 Karlsson, "The immediacy of online news, the visibility of journalistic processes and a restructuring of journalistic authority," 279–95.

68 Phillips, "Transparency and the new ethics of journalism," 379–80.

69 Lea Hellmueller, Tim Vos, and Mark Poepsel, "Shifting journalistic capital? Transparency and objectivity in the twenty-first century," 301.

70 Richard Van Der Wurff and Kaus Schonbach, "Between profession and audience: Codes of conduct and transparency as quality instruments for off- and online journalism," *Journalism Studies* 12, no. 4 (2011): 418.

71 Lewis, "The tension between professional control and open participation: Journalism and its boundaries," 851.

72 Neil Thurman and Anna Walters, "Live blogging – digital journalism's pivotal platform? A case study of the production, consumption, and form of Live Blogs at Guardian.co.uk," 82–101.

Chapter 2

Nothing but the truth

Redrafting the journalistic boundary of verification

Alfred Hermida

As 10 gunmen fanned out across Mumbai at the start of a coordinated terror attack, social media was buzzing with eyewitness accounts and photos. For four days in November 2008, India's financial center was shaken by explosions and shootings. It started with gunmen firing indiscriminately at crowds at a railway station, a hospital and a café, before storming two luxury hotels. As the Indian army fought running battles with the attackers, Twitter was inundated with reports, reactions and rumors about what was going on. A handful came from people on the ground, but many were second-hand, passing on media reports, correcting earlier messages or relaying useful links.[1]

In the midst of the mayhem, BBC News reported on its live event page that the Indian government had asked for live Twitter updates from Mumbai to cease immediately. It quoted an unattributed tweet as saying: "ALL LIVE UPDATES–PLEASE STOP TWEETING (sic) about #Mumbai police and military operations."[2] The information was unconfirmed yet included in the BBC's blow-by-blow account of the attacks that complemented reports from its own correspondents with details from other news outlets, official sources, blog posts, email, and tweets.

But the tweet turned out to be a false rumor, leading to criticism of one of the world's most trusted news organizations. While conceding the need to look into unconfirmed information on social media, BBC News website editor Steve Herrmann defended the use of tweets in a breaking news scenario:

> As for the Twitter messages we were monitoring, most did not add a great amount of detail to what we knew of events, but among other things they did give a strong sense of what people connected in some way with the story were thinking and seeing.[3]

The Mumbai attacks highlighted the new ecology of news, where the first reports tend to come from those caught up in the event itself, facilitated by real-time networked services like Twitter. But they also brought to the surface tensions over quality and reliability when journalists turn to tweets and cell-phone photos or videos to fill the news vacuum that follows a breaking story.

The tweet cited by the BBC as part of its rolling 24-hour coverage turned out to be false. Reflecting on the error, Herrmann conceded the BBC should have done more to check the information. But he also argued

> there is a case also for simply monitoring, selecting and passing on the information we are getting as quickly as we can, on the basis that many people will want to know what we know and what we are still finding out.[4]

The publication of a piece of information without first checking it flies in the face of what has been one of the key tenets in journalism – verification before publication. The discipline of verification is a core normative practice in journalism. It is one of the ways that journalists claim a special kind of authority to define reality and tell audiences what really happened. Verification defines acceptable professional behavior. It serves as a fundamental boundary to differentiate the occupational turf of journalism from other forms of public communication.

Those boundaries are being strained as journalists, who once could claim a monopoly on the supply of everyday public information, contend with citizens who are sharing eyewitness accounts, curating reports or evaluating information on social media. The tensions are most visible at times of breaking news, when information flows tend to be chaotic, contradictory, and changeable. These are the times when verification is most valuable, given the surfeit of speculation, rumour, and opinion on social media. But the strain on established verification practices means that this is when transgressions tend to occur.

The importance of verification

Verification is one of the cornerstones of the professional ideology of journalism in Western liberal democracies, together with related concepts such as objectivity, impartiality and autonomy. A commitment to accuracy and truthfulness is simultaneously a prevailing norm and discursive strategy that exemplifies how journalists define their expertise and claim authority. In their seminal 2001 work, *The Elements of Journalism*, Kovach and Rosenstiel declared the discipline of verification as "the essence of journalism," arguing this is what separates it from "entertainment, propaganda, fiction or art."[5] For them, a commitment to finding out the truth is the first criterion that should be used to evaluate any work described as journalism. Similarly, the Pew Research Journalism Project prioritizes an obligation to the truth, listing it as the first of its nine Principles of Journalism. The practice of journalism is "the professional discipline of assembling and verifying facts," as "accuracy is the foundation upon which everything else is built."[6]

Professional codes of conduct reinforce the primacy of accuracy, for example, by stating that journalists should "test the accuracy of information from all sources and exercise care to avoid inadvertent error."[7] The commitment to the truth is closely linked to journalism's purpose "to provide citizens with the information they need to be free and self-governing."[8] The democratic purpose ascribed to journalism goes back to Walter Lippmann,[9] who appealed for journalism to aspire to "a common intellectual method and a common area of valid fact."[10]

Verification is articulated as a boundary that is vital in deciding whether a form of public communication is or isn't journalism. Zelizer[11] suggests that "journalism's presumed legitimacy depends on its declared ability to provide an indexical and referential presentation of the world at hand."[12] The practice of verification not only confers journalistic communication with a unique status, it also validates journalism as a profession that claims a special kind of authority and establishes professional jurisdiction over the news.[13]

While there is agreement on verification as an occupational norm, it is much harder to agree on what it looks like in practice. Verification is a fluid and contested practice, inconsistent in its application.[14] Studies show a lack of consensus on prescribed procedures for checking information consistently. Machill and Beiler[15] found that German journalists spent only 5.5 percent of their time cross-checking information. A study of British newspaper and broadcast news showed that most reports relied on a single primary source.[16] Moreover, many journalism education books lack explicit references to verification or focus on the necessity to double-check names, ages, and locations.[17] Yet practice is vital to journalistic identity. For journalists, authority is discursively constructed through practice, rather than through knowledge. As Zelizer puts it, "journalistic professionalism is established as much by the representation of knowledge as by the actual possession of knowledge."[18]

The challenge between being fast and being right at a time when the audience itself has access to the same information has become a pressing concern within the industry. The volume of coverage and discussion in trade publications indicates the degree of unease over a potential breach in a key boundary of journalism. Verification, for instance, is a common topic on the site of the Poynter Institute. It was one of the organizations behind a free verification handbook published online in January 2014,[19] and its News University offers a course entitled "Getting It Right: Accuracy and Verification in the Digital Age." Verification is also a frequent issue covered by *Nieman Reports*. The publication devoted its summer 2012 edition to "how the BBC, the AP, CNN, and other news organizations are addressing questions of truth and verification."[20]

Verification under pressure

There is a trade-off between the need for speed with the need for accuracy in journalism. Media mistakes didn't start with the Internet. When Philip Meyer studied U.S. newspapers in the 1980s, he found that three out of five stories contained some sort of error.[21] They ranged from misspelled names to wrong numbers to complaints about quotes being distorted. As Meyer remarked, "the problem is finding the right balance between speed and accuracy, between being comprehensive and being merely interesting."[22]

The rise of social media as a primary source for journalists, above all at times of breaking news, has led to additional strains on the continually contested practice of verification. It presents challenges to the occupational construction and practice of journalism. The role of the journalist as bearing witness to the news is usurped when the public itself takes on the role of documenting events through eyewitness accounts, images and videos. Journalistic presence through being there, at the location of a crisis or disaster, has been key in asserting a claim to authority.[23]

Yet the development of communication technologies such as cellphones, widespread connectivity, and social networking services has reduced the centrality of journalists as eyewitnesses to the news. Being there continues to be highly valued by journalists, even those who have live-blogged events from the newsroom. For example, *Guardian* journalist Paul Lewis stressed that "your vantage point is a computer screen in an office block in London, and as a journalist you always find out more when you're there. Always."[24]

Networked technologies have enabled citizens, officials, and celebrities to bypass the media, undermining the principle that journalists ought to act as gatekeepers on behalf of the greater good.[25] Always-on media systems of immediacy and instantaneity such as Twitter introduce a wide range of actors in the flow of news, reframing or reinterpreting a message, introducing hybridity in news production and news values.[26] Ambient journalism, where networked technologies serve as social awareness streams offering a constantly updated, live representation of the experiences, interests, and opinions of users,[27] means the information previously filtered before publication by journalists may already be in the public domain.

The dynamics of information flows on social media add an extra layer of complexity due to the visibility, velocity, and volume of data. "From the moment 24/7 digital news was introduced the process of verification – the beating heart of credible journalism in the public interest – has been under challenge," noted Kovach,[28] warning about the temptation to publish news just because it was already out there.

Visibility creates an unenviable dilemma for a profession balancing speed and accuracy. If a media outlet ignores information circulating on social media, the public may lose faith in it as a source of up-to-date news. Yet a news outlet risks losing the trust of the public by reporting unverified details that may later turn out to be wrong. Over recent years, there have been numerous cases where prominent news organizations have been caught out, such as in the misidentification of suspects in the Sandy Hook school shootings in December 2012 and the Boston Marathon bombings in April 2013. The cost of getting it wrong is heightened at such times when accuracy is at a premium, yet information is fluid, incomplete, and messy.

Velocity and volume accentuate the strain on verification practices, increasing the likelihood of an error. By 2013, an average of 5,700 messages were posted to Twitter every second,[29] while 100 hours of video were uploaded to YouTube every minute.[30] Twitter, in particular, privileges event-based and event-driven posts, for example through its list of trending topics that "identifies topics that are immediately popular, rather than topics that have been popular for a while or on a daily basis."[31]

Journalists are faced with a medium where topics can take on an instant but transient importance, further increasing the pressure on editorial judgment. The British journalist Nik Gowing has labelled this as the tyranny of real time, questioning how far it is possible to verify information. "You can be *First*, and you can be *Fast*. But in entering the race for the information space[,] how *Flawed* – how mistaken and inaccurate – might you be?"[32]

Gowing was writing at a time when Twitter was emerging as a conduit for breaking news. Van Dijck[33] notes how the company introduced subtle changes in 2009 to stimulate information messages rather than personal exchanges. In her analysis of the evolution of the service, she highlighted how status updating and the sharing of news and information have emerged as dominant uses. The importance of social media, and Twitter specifically, as a network for breaking news was dramatically illustrated during the Mumbai attacks of 2008, the Iranian election protests of June 2009, and the Haiti earthquake of 2010.

All three events served as major tests of the "verify first, then publish" premise of journalism. In all three cases, news organizations bent the rules of verification to address a news vacuum. With Iran, newsrooms turned to social media to make up for the severe reporting restrictions on foreign corres-pondents on the ground in Tehran. Leading news organizations such as the *New York Times* and the *Guardian* used uncorroborated videos and tweets together with reports from their journalists in Tehran.[34] In the immediate aftermath of the Haiti quake, news organizations relied on social media for initial reports of the devastation. Bruno's[35] analysis of the rolling news cover-age by three major news outlets found that only the BBC consistently sought to verify information on social media before publication. It used less content than the *Guardian* and CNN, which chose speed versus verification, at least some of the time.

To suggest that journalism is abandoning one of its key tenets would be an exaggeration. The practice of "verify then publish" has entered the penumbra, an ambiguous grey area at the edges of established norms and conventions. Verification is being adapted to an environment where initial reports are far more likely to come from citizens on the spot than from reporters. The result is that one occupational boundary is loosened – the monopoly on journalistic storytelling. At the same time, another, verification, is being reconfigured through processes of reinforcement, rearticulation, and reinvention, taking place within what Lewis describes as "the professional logic of control."[36]

The resuscitation of verification

The strains on established norms and practices due to the visibility, volume, and velocity of citizen media have paradoxically led to a higher priority to verification at the expense of speed. In his 2009 analysis of the impact of social media on mainstream media, Newman concluded that "news organizations are already abandoning attempts to be first for breaking news, focusing instead on being the best at verifying and curating it."[37] In recent years, news outlets have bolstered the mechanisms of verification through the institutional frameworks set up to elicit and process information sourced on social media.

One of the key ways has been through the creation of teams to appeal for citizen content and then process the material. The most well-known is the User-Generated Hub at the BBC, set up in 2005 after the Asian Tsunami of 2004. By 2009, it was processing 10,000 emails, 1,000 images, and 100 videos in an average week.[38] Its primary role is as gatekeeper, or as one senior BBC executive put it, to sort "through the chaff to find some excellent wheat."[39] Rather than disrupting established practices, the Hub serves to buttress deep-rooted values of accuracy and authenticity.[40] CNN takes a similar approach with its user-generated iReport project. Content checked by its team of full-time producers earns an iReport logo, while most material is labeled as "not vetted."

Other news organizations have outsourced the discovery and verification of social media content to companies such as Storyful. Founded in 2010, Storyful counts among its clients Al Jazeera, the *New York Times*, the *Wall Street Journal* and Reuters. In December 2013, News Corp bought the company for $25 million, with Chief Executive Robert Thomson describing Storyful as "the village square for valuable video, using journalistic sensibility, integrity and creativity to find, authenticate and commercialise user-generated content."[41]

Alongside human-based approaches, there are a number of experimental research projects to develop software tools and systems to identify and verify news on social media. Automated tools address the limitations of established practices given the scale and speed of social media.[42] A prototype developed by Diakopoulos, De Choudhury, and Naaman[43] sought to help journalists find and assess sources in Twitter around breaking news events. Similarly, the Truthy project at Indiana University seeks to map how information spreads to detect patterns that might help discern fact from fiction.[44] The European Union Social Sensor project specifically seeks to measure dimensions of credibility that reflect the concerns of journalists, as verifying social media content was one of the top priorities.[45]

Such initiatives, be they human- or machine-based, are efforts to reassert a professional logic of control within a hybrid media environment. They demonstrate the development of approaches and techniques designed to bolster a norm besieged by the scale and speed of citizen content. They reveal and reinforce long-standing routines of control that frame the audience as sources for raw material that is then subjected to the journalistic mill. Far from being abandoned, verification is being rearticulated.

The rearticulation of verification

Resistance and renewal through guidelines

In March 2011, the professional association representing the top echelons of American journalism staked its position over the use of social media. The American Society of News Editors published its guidelines for best practice, following a review of social media policies at mainstream news outlets. Number six on its list of "key takeaways" was to verify material gathered from social networks before reporting it.[46] It highlighted sample policies from the *Los Angeles Times* and NPR that stressed the need to check the accuracy and authenticity of material gathered online. The language used in the guidelines articulates verification as an occupational boundary, rather than as a service to the public. For example, it chides some reporters for being "too eager to pounce on anything they see online, but being a good gatekeeper means carefully authenticating any information found on Twitter or Facebook."[47]

The ASNE guidelines are emblematic of one aspect of discourse in the industry in recent years over social media and verification. It falls within an interpretative repertoire of resistance in the articulation of professionalism.[48] This repertoire focuses on the assertion of professional expertise. For example, the news agencies Reuters[49] and Associated Press[50] both advise their staff against spreading information that hasn't been verified or confirmed. The guidelines from Reuters frame the tensions raised by social media as boundary violations, stating that "social networks encourage fast, constant, brief communications; journalism calls for communication preceded by fact-finding and thoughtful consideration."[51] Such approaches seek to reinforce the role of the journalist as authenticator, differentiating the profession from the work of others spreading similar information.

However, the guidelines adopted by other news organizations point to an interpretative repertoire of renewal.[52] They indicate an expansion of verification practices to accommodate the fact that accounts, rumors, and speculation are already circulating on social media. Such an approach considers the use of unverified material within the context of the public interest of publishing, rather than withholding, information. While the NPR ethics handbook stresses that "accuracy is at the core of what we do," it also recognizes that "reporting about what's being posted on social media can give our listeners and readers valuable insights into the day's news."[53] Similarly the Canadian Broadcasting Corporation acknowledges that while all citizen content should be verified, "there may be times where because of timeliness or if it is in the public interest, we decide to publish without full verification."[54] Such approaches give greater weight to a commitment to public service than to accuracy, without abandoning verification as a desired ideal.

Implicit is a realization that journalism is operating in an open, networked environment where established practices are stretched to breaking point. The currency of trust shifts from being solely based on the provision of accurate information. Instead, trust is gained and maintained through being transparent about the nature of the information being published. Several leading news organizations, including NPR and CBC, stress the need to be open with the audience when unconfirmed details are shared. "One key is to be transparent about what we're doing. We tell readers what has and hasn't been confirmed," say the NPR guidelines. The boundary of verification gives way to what Lewis describes as a willingness "to find normative purpose in transparency and participation."[55]

The semiotics of boundary work

Transparency emerges as a professional boundary to make up for the loosening of verification practices. In August 2013, reports started circulating about the use of chemical weapons in the Syrian conflict. Initial accounts of the attack came from opposition activists, together with videos showing graphic footage of visibly sick men, women and children. UN chemical weapons inspectors later confirmed that the nerve agent, sarin, had indeed been used in an attack on rebel-held suburbs of Damascus. At the time, news organizations could not confirm what had happened, but there was no way they could ignore it either. In order to report on the attacks but maintain a degree of professional distance, news outlets were transparent about their inability to authenticate the reports. Accounts of the attack were attributed to opposition activists and the distressing footage was published but with the added caveat that it was "unverified." BBC News even published an assessment of the reliability of the unverified material to gauge the credibility of the reports.[56]

The use of attribution is a standard practice in journalism. It is a vital ingredient that adds to the credibility of a story. It is a way of indicating how a journalist obtained the information or quotes in a story. Attribution answers the question "How do you know that?" Attribution has gained in importance with the use of material from the public for two reasons. Often the material comes from a source that is anonymous or difficult to identify, violating the basic tenet of not using unnamed sources. Attributing information to opposition activists or eyewitnesses at the scene of breaking news provides a license to use secondhand information.

The language of attribution also serves to separate professionally produced reports from citizen content. BBC guidelines state that "we should ensure that user generated content is clearly identified as such."[57] Likewise, the *Guardian*'s editorial code emphasizes the need for attribution in the fast-moving digital news environment. "Do not state as fact information about or from someone who we cannot authenticate," says the section on verification introduced in the 2011 code.[58]

Labels such as "unverified" serve as semiotic disclaimers. The language reflects the repertoire of resignation identified by Andén-Papadopoulos and Pantti,[59] where news organizations are resigned to the fact that they have to modify traditional standards of accuracy. The use of labels such as "unverified" or attaching a modifier such as "allegedly" presents a way to work around issues of credibility. The framing signals to the audience that such material is outside the usual boundaries of journalism.

Language emerges as a mechanism to proclaim the boundary between the work produced by professionals from that by the public. It is a way to underscore the authority of the journalist and signal to the audience that some published material has not been held up to the rigorous standards of professionally produced work. Citizen contributors are not acknowledged as peers, but placed outside the club of journalism. It echoes the way news organizations sought to integrate user-generated content such as comments by creating clearly defined spaces on news websites.[60] News editors cannot ignore the reports circulating on social media for fear of appearing to be ignorant of the chatter about a news event. Disclaimers such as "we have been unable to independently confirm" enable journalists to expand the scope of what they publish while simultaneously establishing a professional line of defense.

The reinterpretation of verification

Live blogging was a format pioneered in sports coverage but quickly became an intrinsic part of how news organizations from the BBC to the *New York Times* report breaking news. By 2011, the *Guardian* alone was publishing an average of 146 of these every month.[61] Live blogs have become the default vehicle for breaking news, sports reporting and entertainment events that blend journalistic practices and digital technologies. They are an example of how journalistic practices are being adapted and reframed for a real-time ambient news environment.

Live blogs reflect a shift toward verification as a collaborative, fluid and iterative online process. They mark a shift away from journalism as a framework to provide reports and analyses of events through narratives composed after an event. The conventional newspaper story strives to convey a definitive, authoritative and authenticated account of an event. On a live blog, facts are fluid rather than fixed. They are more open and liquid, and less author-centric, than other forms of journalism. The format presents an iterative and incremental account that synthesizes reports from professional journalists and accounts, images, and video on social media together with commentary and analysis in near real-time. The result presents news as a multidimensional, temporal and mutating product.

The format is journalism in progress. BBC News website editor Steve Herrmann sees live blogs as a way to reflect "the unfolding truth in all its guises."[62] *Guardian* reporter Matthew Weaver suggests the format offers "a more fluid sense of what's happening."[63] Live blogs set a different audience expectation about accuracy. For *Guardian* journalist Matt Wells, it means "you can be very open about whether you have verified this or not."[64]

It would be an over-simplification to say that journalists are abandoning verification. Rather, live blogging is reminiscent of the informal verification process in established practice where journalists make pragmatic compromises on what material to check.[65] The key difference is that these practices tend to play out in public on the live blog. Thurman and Walters[66] found that journalists were adapting verification strategies to minimize the tensions between speed and accuracy, such as relying on sources used in the past. Additionally, journalists compensated for looser verification practices by drawing from a wide range of sources, presenting supporting evidence, including contradictory reports and attributing contributions.

In a live blog, journalistic presence is reimagined. The authority of the journalist is no longer derived from being at the scene and witnessing the news. Given the collapse of "being there" as an occupational boundary, the journalist instead reasserts control as a master of ceremonies. The privileged position of the journalist is reasserted as a trusted professional uniquely qualified to coordinate, authentic and interpret multiple streams of information. To date, the most well-known example of a media professional operating in such an ambient news network is Andy Carvin.[67] The former social media strategist at NPR made his name during the Arab Spring of 2011 when he turned to Twitter to identify and contact credible sources, carry out real-time fact-checking, and aggregate news as it happened.

Carvin reinterpreted the notion of journalistic authority. Twitter became his newsroom and his followers became his researchers, reporters, and fact-checkers. With live blogs, journalists retain gatekeeping control over what gets published. With Carvin, the process of sourcing, filtering, contesting and confirming information took place in public through exchanges on Twitter. He was immersed in a media environment that privileges relationships over broadcast, conversing with others to co-construct the news. Verification was crowdsourced, with Carvin appealing to his network to help him confirm or deny reports or images. Trust and credibility came through openness and collaboration rather than solely verification.

Conclusion

Central to the identity of journalists are what Zelizer[68] describes as the "god-terms" of the profession – facts, truth, and reality. They are the building blocks of an ideological claim to present events as they really are. At a time when members of the public are taking on some of the institutional tasks commonly associated with the journalist, verification has become a line of defense, articulated as one of the key distinguishing features of journalism.[69]

But as Shapiro et al. suggest, verification is "a norm of compromise."[70] In practice, the search for the truth is not a consistent process but a malleable and ambiguous quest. Verification operates on a continuum where some facts, such as names and places, are subjected to far more rigorous checks than assertions and explanations.

In a hybrid media environment, the long-standing tensions over accuracy have risen to the fore in a profession caught between continuity and change. The pressures on traditional norms and practices – given the visibility, volume, and velocity of information at times of major events – have led to reactions of resistance, renewal, and reinterpretation. Verification serves as one mirror that reflects these tensions, from approaches that seek to shore up existing traditions to practices that aim to refashion norms.

The mission to accurately and truthfully reflect society to itself remains a constant in journalistic ideology. However, how that mission is implemented and expressed is changing as the profession negotiates the tension between a claim to objectively parse reality and public participation in the news process. Far from being discarded, verification is being rearticulated and reinterpreted to be in line with a hybrid, open media environment.

Emerging practices indicate a shift toward verification as a collaborative, fluid and iterative online public process that reconfigure the boundaries of journalism. Essentially, journalism is turned inside-out. The practices that would traditionally remain within the confines of the newsroom take place in public on networked and distributed media. Such approaches acknowledge that journalism is no longer just about the production of an artifact delivered to the audience as a definitive rendering of events, while simultaneously expanding the boundaries of professional identity. The journalist moves beyond being the arbiter of "the truth" and instead becomes a trusted professional who is transparent about how a news story comes together, with accounts and rumors contested, denied or verified in collaboration with the public.

Notes

1 Stuart Allan, *Citizen Witnessing: Revisioning Journalism in Times of Crisis* (Cambridge: Polity, 2013).
2 "As It Happened: Mumbai Attacks 27 Nov," *BBC News*, 27 November 2008, http://news.bbc.co.uk/2/hi/south_asia/7752003.stm
3 Steve Herrmann, "Mumbai, Twitter and Live Updates," *BBC News*, 4 December 2008, www.bbc.co.uk/blogs/theeditors/2008/12/theres_been_discussion_see_eg.html
4 Herrmann, "Mumbai, Twitter and Live Updates."
5 Bill Kovach and Tom Rosenstiel, *The Elements of Journalism: What Newspeople Should Know and the Public Should Expect* (New York: Three Rivers Press, 2007), 79.
6 Pew Research Journalism Project, *Principles of Journalism*, www.journalism.org/resources/principles-of-journalism/
7 Society of Professional Journalists, *SPJ Code of Ethics*, www.spj.org/ethicscode.asp
8 Kovach and Rosenstiel, *The Elements of Journalism: What Newspeople Should Know and the Public Should Expect*, 5.

 9 Walter Lippmann, *Liberty and the News* (New York: Harcourt, Brace and How, 1920).
10 Lippmann, *Liberty and the News*, 67.
11 Barbie Zelizer, "When Facts, Truth, and Reality Are God-Terms: On Journalism's Uneasy Place in Cultural Studies," *Communication and Critical/Cultural Studies* 1, no. 1 (2004): 100–119.
12 Zelizer, "When Facts, Truth, and Reality Are God-Terms: On Journalism's Uneasy Place in Cultural Studies," 103.
13 Michael Schudson and Chris Anderson, "News Production and Organizations: Professionalism, Objectivity and Truth-Seeking," in *The Handbook of Journalism Studies*, eds Karin Wahl-Jorgensen and Thomas Hanitzch (New York: Routledge, 2009), 88–101.
14 Ivor Shapiro, Colette Brin, Isabelle Bedard-Brule, and Kasia Mychajlowycz, "Verification as a Strategic Ritual," *Journalism Practice* 7, no. 6 (2013): 657–73.
15 Marcel Machill and Markus Beiler, "The Importance of the Internet for Journalistic Research: A Multi-method Study of the Research Performed by Journalists Working for Daily Newspapers, Radio, Television and Online," *Journalism Studies* 10, no. 2 (2009): 178–203.
16 Justin Lewis, Andrew Williams, Bob Franklin, James Thomas and Nick Mosdell, *The Quality and Independence of British Journalism: Tracking the Changes over 20 Years* (Cardiff University, 2008), www.cardiff.ac.uk/jomec/resources/QualityIndependence ofBritishJournalism.pdf
17 Tony Harcup, *Journalism: Principles and Practice* (Thousand Oaks, CA: Sage, 2004); Geoffrey Harris and David Spark, *Practical Newspaper Reporting*, 3rd edn. (Oxford: Focal Press, 1997); Gerald Lanson and Mitchell Stephens, *Writing and Reporting the News*, 3rd edn (New York: Oxford University Press, 2008).
18 Barbie Zelizer, *Covering the Body: The Kennedy Assassination, the Media, and the Shaping of Collective Memory* (Chicago: University of Chicago Press, 1992), 97.
19 Craig Silverman, ed., *Verification Handbook* (European Journalism Centre, 2014), www.verificationhandbook.com/
20 Nieman Reports, *Truth in the Age of Social Media*, 2012, www.nieman.harvard.edu/reports/issue/100072/Summer-2012.aspx
21 Phillip Meyer, ed., *The Vanishing Newspaper: Saving Journalism in the Information Age* (Columbia, MO: University of Missouri, 2009).
22 Meyer, ed., *The Vanishing Newspaper: Saving Journalism in the Information Age*, 87–88.
23 Barbie Zelizer, "On 'Having Been There': 'Eyewitnessing' as a Journalistic Key Word," *Critical Studies in Media Communication* 24, no. 5 (2007): 408–28.
24 Neil Thurman and Anna Walters, "Live Blogging – Digital Journalism's Pivotal Platform?" *Digital Journalism* 1, no. 1 (2013): 93.
25 Seth Lewis, "The Tension Between Professional Control and Open Participation: Journalism and its Boundaries," *Information, Communication & Society* 15, no. 6 (2012): 836–66.
26 Andrew Chadwick, "The Political Information Cycle in a Hybrid News System: The British Prime Minister and the 'Bullygate' Affair," *International Journal of Press/Politics* 16, no. 1 (2011): 3–29; Zizi Papacharissi and Maria de Fatima Oliveira, "Affective News and Networked Publics: The Rhythms of News Storytelling on #Egypt," *Journal of Communication* 62, no. 2 (2012): 266–82.
27 Alfred Hermida, "Twittering the News: The Emergence of Ambient Journalism," *Journalism Practice* 4, no. 3 (2010): 297–308.
28 Bill Kovach, *Toward a New Journalism with Verification*, 2006, www.nieman.harvard.edu/reports/article/100292/Toward-a-New-Journalism-With-Verification.aspx

29 Raffi Krikorian, "New Tweets per Second Record, and How!," *Twitter Blogs*, 2013, https://blog.twitter.com/2013/new-tweets-per-second-record-and-how

30 YouTube, "YouTube figures from YouTube statistics," *YouTube*, no date, www.youtube.com/yt/press/en-GB/statistics.html

31 Twitter, "FAQ About Trends on Twitter," *Twitter*, no date, http://support.twitter.com/articles/101125-faq-about-trends-on-twitter

32 Nick Gowing, *Skyful of Lies and Black Swans: The New Tyranny of Shifting Information Power in Crisis* (Reuters Institute for the Study of Journalism, University of Oxford, 2009), 30, http://reutersinstitute.politics.ox.ac.uk/publication/skyful-lies-black-swans

33 José van Dijck, "Tracing Twitter: The Rise of a Microblogging Platform," *International Journal of Media and Cultural Politics* 7, no. 3 (2012): 333–48.

34 Brian Stelter, "Journalism Rules Are Bent in News Coverage From Iran," *New York Times*, 28 June 2009, www.nytimes.com/2009/06/29/business/media/29coverage.html

35 Nicola Bruno, *Tweet First, Verify Later? How Real-time Information is Changing the Coverage of Worldwide Crisis Events* (Reuters Institute for the Study of Journalism, 2011), http://reutersinstitute.politics.ox.ac.uk/publication/tweet-first-verify-later

36 Seth C. Lewis, "The Tension Between Professional Control and Open Participation: Journalism and its Boundaries," *Information, Communication & Society* 15 no. 6 (2012): 836–66.

37 Nic Newman, *The Rise of Social Media and its Impact on Mainstream Journalism* (Reuters Institute for the Study of Journalism, 2009), 2, http://reutersinstitute.politics.ox.ac.uk/publication/rise-social-media-and-its-impact-mainstream-journalism

38 Newman, *The Rise of Social Media and its Impact on Mainstream Journalism*.

39 Peter Horrocks quoted in Andy Williams, Claire Wardle and Karin Wahl-Jorgensen, "Have They Got News for Us? Audience Revolution or Business as Usual at the BBC?" *Journalism Practice* 5, no. 1 (2011): 85–99.

40 Andy Williams, Claire Wardle and Karin Wahl-Jorgensen, "Have They Got News for Us? Audience Revolution or Business as Usual at the BBC?" *Journalism Practice* 5, no. 1 (2011): 85–99.

41 Jim Kennedy and Ashley Huston, "News Corp Acquires Social News Agency Storyful," *News Corp*, 2013, http://newscorp.com/2013/12/20/news-corp-acquires-social-news-agency-storyful/

42 Hermida, "Twittering the News: The Emergence of Ambient Journalism."

43 Nick Diakopoulos, Munmun De Choudhury and Mor Naaman, "Finding and Assessing Social Media Information Sources in the Context of Journalism," *ACM SIGCHI Conference on Human Factors in Computing Systems*, 2012.

44 Karissa McKelvey and Fil Menczer, "Truthy: Enabling the Study of Online Social Networks." in *ACM Conference on Computer Supported Cooperative Work and Social Computing Companion (CSCW)*, 19 December 2012, http://arxiv.org/abs/1212.4565

45 Steve Schifferes, Nic Newman, Neil Thurman, David Corney, Ayse Göker and Carlos Martin, "Identifying and Verifying News through Social Media," *Digital Journalism*, ahead-of-print (2014): 1–13.

46 James Hohmann, "10 Best Practices for Social Media," *American Society of News Editors*, 2011, http://asne.org/portals/0/publications/public/10_Best_Practices_for_Social_Media.pdf

47 Hohmann, *10 Best Practices for Social Media*, 11.

48 Cf. Kari Andén-Papadopoulos and Mervi Pantti, "Re-imagining Crisis Reporting: Professional Ideology of Journalists and Citizen Eyewitness Images," *Journalism* 14, no. 7 (2013): 960–77.

49 Reuters, "Reporting From the Internet and Using Social Media," *Handbook of Journalism* (2013), http://handbook.reuters.com/?title=Reporting_From_the_Internet_And_Using_Social_Media

50 Associated Press, "Social Media Guidelines for AP Employees," *Associated Press*, 2013, www.ap.org/Images/Social-Media-Guidelines_tcm28–9832.pdf

51 Reuters, "Reporting From the Internet and Using Social Media."

52 Cf. Andén-Papadopoulos and Pantti, "Re-imagining Crisis Reporting."

53 NPR, *Accuracy, NPR Ethics Handbook*, no date, http://ethics.npr.org/category/a1-accuracy/

54 CBC, "Verification of User Generated Content in News Stories, Use of Social Media," *CBC*, no date, www.cbc.radio-canada.ca/en/reporting-to-canadians/acts-and-policies/programming/journalism/social-media/

55 Lewis, "The Tension Between Professional Control and Open Participation," 851.

56 Bridget Kendall, "Syria 'Chemical Attack:' Distressing Footage Under Analysis," *BBC*, 23 August 2013, www.bbc.com/news/world-middle-east-23806491

57 BBC, "Gathering Material," *BBC Editorial Guidelines*, no date, www.bbc.co.uk/guidelines/editorialguidelines/page/guidelines-accuracy-gathering-material/

58 The Guardian, *Editorial Guidelines: Guardian News & Media Editorial Code*, 2011, www.theguardian.com/info/guardian-editorial-code

59 Andén-Papadopoulos and Pantti, "Re-imagining Crisis Reporting."

60 Alfred Hermida and Neil Thurman, "A Clash of Cultures: The Integration of User-Generated Content Within Professional Journalistic Frameworks at British Newspaper Websites," *Journalism Practice* 2, no. 3 (2008): 343–56; Jane Singer, David Domingo, Ari Heinonen, Alfred Harmida, Steve Paulussen, Thorsten Quandt, Zvi Reich, and Marina Vujnovic, *Participatory Journalism: Guarding Open Gates at Online Newspapers* (New York: Wiley-Blackwell, 2011).

61 Thurman and Walters, "Live Blogging – Digital Journalism's Pivotal Platform?"

62 Quoted in Newman, *The Rise of Social Media and its Impact on Mainstream Journalism*, 9.

63 Quotes in Bruno, *Tweet First, Verify Later? How Real-time Information is Changing the Coverage of Worldwide Crisis Events*, 44.

64 Quoted in Thurman and Walters, "Live Blogging – Digital Journalism's Pivotal Platform?"

65 Shapiro et al., "Verification as a Strategic Ritual."

66 Thurman and Walters, "Live Blogging – Digital Journalism's Pivotal Platform?"

67 Alfred Hermida, Seth Lewis and Rodrigo Zamith, "Sourcing the Arab Spring: A Case Study of Andy Carvin's Sources on Twitter During the Tunisian and Egyptian Revolutions," *Journal of Computer-Mediated Communication* 19, no. 3 (2014): 479–99.

68 Zelizer, "When Facts, Truth, and Reality Are God-Terms: On Journalism's Uneasy Place in Cultural Studies."

69 Patrick Brethour et al., *"What is Journalism?"* – *CAJ Ethics Committee Report* (The Canadian Association of Journalists, 2012), www.caj.ca/what-is-journalism-caj-ethics-committee-report

70 Shapiro et al., "Verification as a Strategic Ritual," 12.

Chapter 3

Divided we stand

Blurred boundaries in Argentine journalism

Adriana Amado and Silvio Waisbord

Introduction

The debate about boundaries in journalism has gained renewed attention amid recent changes that have transformed the news industry and the conditions for journalistic practice. Simultaneous developments have shaken up the old order that once sustained traditional notions of journalistic boundaries: the rise of citizen journalism, the crisis of business models in the news industry, the proliferation of news offerings, growing pressures to produce news content that continuously attracts digital readers, and widespread use of social media in information gathering and dissemination. At a time when boundaries between journalism and external actors have become fluid, it is important to reexamine whether and how journalists are able to draw and firm up boundaries.

The literature has approached the issue of boundaries in/of journalism generally in Western newsrooms, where journalists have generally subscribed to a common "journalistic paradigm" for a considerable period during the twentieth century. The constitutive elements of this paradigm are well-known: journalism should be above the political fray, follow the principles of objectivity and public ethics, report "the truth," and observe specific narrative and stylistic norms. Consensus values underpin the presence of journalism as a single "interpretive community"[1] that outlines specific ways to define boundaries.

The affirmation of an occupational paradigm presumes that a critical mass of practitioners, or at least a good number located in powerful positions in the mainstream media, embrace canonical "best practices" and ethics. There cannot be boundaries without consensus among practitioners about how and where boundaries should be drawn. Without a single unifying "paradigm," there is no solid basis to affirm lines of separation between "professionals" and "non-professionals." This issue deserves closer attention, not only given recent changes in journalistic practice. The scarcity of studies about boundary-making in contexts where journalism lacks established paradigms that serve as the foundation for setting and monitoring boundaries also makes this issue important. The bulk of the literature has been produced in the United States and, to a lesser degree, in some Western European countries where the model of evenhanded, public interest journalism has enjoyed canonical status during the past century. Given this condition, scholars have been interested in understanding how journalists demarcate symbolic boundaries vis-à-vis citizens with journalistic ambitions, politicians appointed to news jobs, celebrities-cum-interviewers, and corporate raiders. Journalism, then, has been seen as another example of how social boundaries are demarcated through symbolic operations.[2] Symbolic operations seem the main strategy chosen by journalism in Western countries to reinforce boundaries, given the absence of legal strategies that classic professions use to ensure borders are tightly controlled. Without legal options, journalism resorts to discursive strategies to separate legitimate professionals from non-professional interests, to excommunicate the "bad apples" in their midst,[3] and to fend off *arrivistes* such as citizen reporters and celebrities-cum-reporters.

Journalists' reactions to assorted assaults on professionalism are only intelligible in contexts where they subscribe to common principles embedded in a master paradigm. Only when a single paradigm dominates professional imaginations, can occupational groups effectively claim to be different from others and patrol boundaries. If physicians believed that each colleague is free to practice medicine as she pleases, or if lawyers endlessly argue over what legal system should rule their practice, neither medicine nor law would be the paragon of classical professions. Adherence to "the paradigm" is indispensable for professions to exercise control over their particular "jurisdiction".[4] Professional boundary-making is possible only as long as members of a profession share basic premises about what they do and how they should do it.

Given the particularities of the contexts traditionally considered by studies about journalism and boundaries, it is worth asking what happens in settings when those conditions are absent. How are boundaries drawn when there is no single paradigm that commands unanimous allegiance from journalists and influential publications? What if journalists are not interested in setting themselves apart from external actors but, instead, are primarily motivated to draw internal boundaries? In contexts where boundaries between journalism and external actors (from markets to the state) remain weak, how does boundary-making work?

These conditions are not atypical in so-called new democracies, where political and economic circumstances have weakened the ability of journalism to keep strong boundaries vis-à-vis non-journalistic interests.[5] As journalism has been historically embedded in party–press relationships and commercial pressures from owners, advertisers, and governments constantly hovered on newsrooms, the notion that journalism could be able to delineate and maintain firm boundaries seem hopelessly utopian. Such conditions, however, do not imply that journalists were not interested in establishing boundaries, that is, in supporting a "professionalizing project"[6] to establish social differences and hierarchies. The difference is the absence of a basic condition that existed in selected Western democracies such as the United States for a considerable period during the twentieth century; namely, the presence of critical numbers of journalists interested in firming up boundaries vis-à-vis other occupations and actors.

To discuss these issues, this chapter examines the situation of "blurred boundaries" in contemporary Argentinian journalism. Argentina is an interesting case to probe arguments about "boundary-making" in journalism, given that the historical development of journalism is markedly different from the better-studied U.S. and other Western democracies. Journalism was subjected to official censorship and persecution during military dictatorships in the past century. Its boundaries vis-à-vis external actors have remained endlessly blurred and contested. In the contexts of chronically divided loyalties inside journalism and weak political and social consensus, Argentine journalism has long been immersed in existential battles. There has never been a strong consensus over the fundamental matters that define journalism and its boundaries – the purpose of journalism as well as desirable ethics and relations with external actors. Journalism has remained divided over questions about whether it is a craft or a profession, or what relations it should cultivate vis-à-vis owners, organized politics, governments, advertisers, audiences and other actors. Put differently, Argentine journalism has been historically a weak profession, unable and unwilling to define and maintain clear boundaries.

The analysis shows that these conditions still remain despite the consolidation of democratic governance in the past three decades. Journalists have engaged in continuous and heated debates over occupational identity and the model of the "good journalist." This has taken place against recent developments during the Kirchner governments,[7] particularly efforts by the state to shake up the media landscape and the persistent precariousness of journalists' labor conditions. These conditions have heightened the historical fuzziness of journalistic boundaries.

We argue that as long as journalism's "professional project" is weak, it remains vulnerable to attempts by commercial and political actors interested in blurring or erasing boundaries. The state of journalistic boundaries is symptomatic of the conditions of professionalism. Here professionalism is understood as the ability of journalism to control its jurisdiction in society – namely, the provision of news according to specific criteria decided and agreed upon by its members.[8] "Professional journalism" refers to a situation in which journalism determines its practices and norms without strong interference from external actors. Journalists, rather than non-journalists (e.g., citizens, politicians, or businesspeople), make key decisions about news content. The demarcation of boundaries, then, reflects journalists' common interests, namely, participating in the constant project of "professionalization."

Both structural conditions as well as human agency are necessary for professional boundaries to be clearly demarcated in journalism. Professionalism demands that members share a sense of belonging and a motivation to differentiate themselves from others. Professionalism means that journalists come together to protect their jurisdiction from external actors who are interested in influencing their operations by injecting different logics.

The forces of unprofessionalism

The absence of a canon dutifully observed by reporters across newsrooms sets Argentine journalism apart from journalistic cultures in many Western democracies. There are no "God-terms"[9] because there is no common professional religion. Neither norms (e.g., objectivity, facticity) nor news-writing practices (e.g., "inverted pyramid") are uniformly followed across newsrooms. Behavioral options are open, always falling in a grey area, as long as journalists do not subscribe to similar principles. Instead, journalists profess allegiance to various credos and remain divided over whether journalism should follow common principles. Without canonical beliefs that bring journalists together around common principles and goals, professional boundaries are imprecise and constantly bended.

Understanding the perennial fuzziness of boundaries in Argentine journalism requires addressing several causes.

Political elites have retained significant power over media economics. There has not been a gradual process of decoupling the economy of news organizations from government. A "market" turn that could have steered press finances away from the state never took full form. Media finances remained firmly embedded in the state, particularly in provinces with low levels of economic development and advertising expenditures. Public officials have controlled significant resources affecting media economics – from advertising, to government contracts, to influence over economic issues of interest, to media owners. Chronic discretionalism in the control of public finances, typically controlled by the executive at national, state and municipal levels, greased the wheels of media patrimonialism.[10] Furthermore, particularly outside large metropolitan areas, powerful political families own leading news organizations. Under these circumstances, political elites exercise constant pressure to gain positive coverage and avoid uncomfortable news. This state of affairs did not eliminate efforts to delineate professional boundaries. Some journalists tried to carve out spaces and fend off intrusions but the alliance between news economics and political-economic interests made the existence of strong boundaries difficult, if not impossible.

Nor have media owners been keen in supporting the professionalization of journalism by keeping newsrooms relatively separated from commercial concerns or editorial agendas or promoting specialized education. Until recently, the Argentine news business did not sponsor or fund journalism programs, as discussed below, to support education in specific, "professional" principles. Paper-thin walls have traditionally separated newsrooms from editorial pages and business offices. Owners essentially viewed journalism as an integral part of business projects rather than as a profession that needed to be guided by its own, public interest principles to serve democracy.

Journalism's divisions were also symptomatic of a society with deep political rifts. It would have been surprising if journalism had stayed immune to the recurrent divisions that fractured Argentine society for much of its recent history. Vicious confrontations that culminated in military dictatorships have dotted national politics during the past century. The endless spiral of violence has engulfed every institution, including journalism. Military coups removed Radical presidents in the 1930s and 1940s. After ten years in power, Peronism was pushed out of power in 1955 by the military and proscribed until 1972 amidst growing political violence. Peronism came back to power in 1973 to be overthrown again by a military junta in 1976. By the time it left power in 1983, the last dictatorship was responsible for the murder and disappearance of more than 10,000 citizens.

Needless to say, this volatile political history reflected the lack of political and social consensus. Divided polities hardly provide fertile conditions for journalists to share a similar vision. Journalism stood on the same fault lines that continuously shook up Argentine politics and society. Media owners dragged newsrooms into their own battles and political calculations. Individual journalists openly identified with warring factions and political parties. Governments maintained a system based on punishments and rewards to discipline media and journalists. Journalism could not escape divided politics nor did it seem interested in staying above the fray.

Nor did reporters follow a common educational path that could have inculcated shared understandings about journalistic norms and practices or outlined a common vision about journalism. Journalists are either trained in newsrooms or, as has happened in past decades, received college degrees in an array of fields. Journalism programs were divided into two types: "applied knowledge" focused on specific journalistic competencies and the "academic" model emphasized theoretical skills and the social science. The "applied" model was illustrated by pioneer programs offered by the Instituto Grafotécnico de Buenos Aires and the Escuela Argentina de Periodismo del Círculo de Periodistas of La Plata established in 1934, the Instituto Superior de Enseñanza Radiofónica founded in 1952, and the Escuela de Periodismo del Círculo de la Prensa set up in 1969. These were tertiary level programs intended to disseminate practical knowledge. In contrast, "academic" programs established in the 1970s had a different orientation, as they understood journalists as "social communicators" trained in critical social science approaches to media industries. In most cases, journalism programs are housed in humanities, social sciences, and communication schools.

The number of journalism programs has multiplied in the past decades amidst the proliferation of media companies, particularly radio stations and cable television channels. Out of 125 communication programs in the country, 19 offer degrees in journalism and eight in radio and television. Out of 47 national universities, 30 offer communication courses and four have a specialization in journalism.[11] Master's programs in journalism were established in Buenos Aires during the 1990s, as a result of partnerships between private universities and leading newspapers such as Universidad San Andrés and

Clarín, Universidad Di Tella and *La Nación* (with Italy's *Corriere de la Sera* and Spain's *El País*) and Universidad del Salvador and *Perfil*. Two public universities, the Universidad Nacional de La Plata and Universidad de Buenos Aires, also offer M.A. degrees.

Journalists are not credentialized. The 1946 "Statute of the Journalist" regulates labor issues and states that no degree is necessary for practicing journalism. Article 2 defines professional journalists as "people who perform regularly assignments in daily and periodical publications and news agencies and receive material compensation." The 1960 law 15.532 includes the figure of the "permanent contributor" to refer to those who carry out more than 24 assignments per year, which entitles them to receive social and retirement benefits.

A new Argentina?

Despite three decades of uninterrupted civilian governments since 1983, a major achievement given the spasmodic evolution of Argentine democracy, professional boundaries remain blurred. This is the result of the combination of persistent structural obstacles coupled with the inability (and unwillingness) of journalists to mobilize behind common objectives. Because political elites wield significant influence over press economics, the media business cozies up to political powers. Media owners are hardly supportive of "professional journalism" as a strategy to produce quality, predictable news content. Journalists remain largely divided over basic principles and the mission of journalism.

Political elites still control public resources that are central to news businesses. Media scholars Guillermo Mastrini and Martin Becerra[12] characterize it as a paradoxical situation of a media market with strong state interventionism but without state policies in support of the public interest. The formation and expansion of large media corporations during the past two decades illustrates this condition. Alliances between media companies and prominent public officials explain the rapid rise of companies (e.g., Vila-Manzano, Pierri, Hadad, Szpolski, and Electroingeniería) that were virtually absent in the news landscape two decades ago. These companies control several print publications and broadcasting stations. Their remarkable growth resulted from their proximity to the government. They benefited from tax exemptions and the selective application of existing regulations, received temporary permits that allowed them to expand while avoiding legal restrictions, and obtained broadcasting licenses without public competition and generous sums of public advertising.

The growth of the national government's discretionary management of public advertising during the Kirchner administrations illustrates the considerable power of public officials to influence news media and journalism. From the time Néstor Kirchner took power in 2003 until 2013, during the second presidential term of Cristina Fernandez de Kirchner, the amount of advertising spent by the national government grew more than 40 times. It is 10 percent of total national media advertising, more than twice the amount spent by the largest private advertiser.[13] More than half of government advertising is distributed among dozens of pro-government news companies with low circulation.[14]

Political-economic relations lubricated by the visible hand of the government continue to shape persistent divisions inside journalism. Journalists who work for companies that benefit from the state are constrained by different editorial considerations compared to colleagues working for companies that receive few or no official favors and who have turned their publications into oppositional platforms.

Nor have media owners fundamentally changed their views about journalistic professionalism. Surveys show that the majority of journalists believe that the main negative influence on their work is the interference of marketing/business offices[15] as well as both government and private advertising.[16] Regrettably, "given the weight of the State ... and persistent economic difficulties, some journalists take for granted that colleagues receive gifts, are willing participants in news management operations, and place advertisers in prominent places in the news".[17] Journalists lack legal support to protect their work against business decisions and government arbitrary actions. Without codes of ethics or legal mechanisms to shelter reporters, self-censorship is widespread.

Also, labor conditions undermine the existence of firm occupational boundaries. Between 1998 and 2002, one out of three reporters lost their jobs.[18] A survey commissioned by a journalists' union shows that more than half of the respondents work as free-lancers, and that 70 percent were paid per published article without receiving a monthly salary.[19] Despite the lack of census data about labor conditions, it is an open secret that journalists regularly moonlight in corporate communication and press relations for public officials.[20] This is certainly not unique to Argentine journalism as it is also common in other countries in Latin America.[21] These practices are particularly common in the provinces where, in addition to reporting, a good number of journalists manage press relations for politicians and private companies and seek advertising for their employers as well as for their own radio and television shows.[22] Regrettably, journalists generally accept precarious labor conditions as natural, such as working for no pay or putting in extra hours for no additional compensation, peddling content to find advertising, and reporting without news-gathering resources or solid editorial processes to ensure quality news (fact-checking and editing).[23]

The consolidation of new economic and work modalities in the media further blurs the boundaries of journalism. One example is journalists who function as independent entrepreneurs renting space from media owners. These practices are common among community radio and FM stations, local cable television, and web pages and blogs. Roles are not strictly separated: journalists are also anchors, producers, salespersons, owners, and social media managers, and others among the wide variety of journalistic jobs.[24] In 2010, a website covering journalism estimated that 280 journalists were working in such conditions.[25]

Another example is the acceptance of special sections ("infomercials") in newspapers and television news fully produced by the public relations offices of governments and business.[26] Both commercial businesses and governments promote these practices as they dole out advertising to hundreds of individual journalists-as-entrepreneurs. An investigation by a leading newsweekly, which has frequently criticized the Kirchner administration for its discretionary assignment of official advertising, showed that government officials have secret lists of journalists who regularly receive monies under "advertising" and other rubrics.

Therefore, whereas "multitasking" conventionally refers to journalists with multiple newswork talents in the U.S. and some European countries, its meaning is broader and more imprecise in Argentina. It includes the ability to act as ad jobbers and have close contacts with politicians and business to obtain funding. Although unethical, these practices are all too common. Quid pro quo dynamics underlay these practices. Legislators and other public officials hire working journalists to have contacts in selected newsrooms, and managers hire journalists with extensive contacts in the world of politics and business. In radio and cable television, including public broadcasting, it is common that journalists rent space from owners, run their own production companies, and seek to attract advertising from companies and governments for their news and talk shows. This practice started in the late 1980s and has become dominant among dozens of cable signals and radio stations in the city of Buenos Aires.[27] Journalists find these good opportunities to supplement their salaries. Advertisers also benefit, as they are low-cost practices that give access to journalists who work across various media.[28] Indeed, some journalists find these practices beneficial for they sustain the financial viability for various news platforms.[29] Although these practices existed in legal limbo, the 2009 media law actually supports them under a curious justification. Article 4 establishes the figures of the journalist as "producer" and "non-traditional advertising" to stimulate the participation of civil society and to diversify broadcasting content. The legislation, then, legitimizes long-standing conditions that blur the boundaries between journalism, advertising, public relations and press offices.

In summary, the political economy of journalism fosters practices that blur boundaries between journalism, public relations and propaganda. Journalists lack basic conditions that could shelter them from the intrusion of politics and commerce. They are too weak to resist pressures from business and political sponsors or to break off their dependence for information and economic subsidies. Nor does it seem that significant numbers of journalists are particularly interested in asserting strong boundaries. Too many benefit from the prevalent relations and matter-of-factly consider the current order as the only way journalism is possible. To define clear-cut occupational boundaries between journalism and other professions (press management or public relations) is shooting themselves in their financial feet.

Failed professionalism amidst internal divisions

Amidst these structural conditions and dynamics, efforts to demarcate professional boundaries have confronted significant obstacles. The main obstacle is
that journalists have not shown major interest in reaching a consensus on
fundamental issues that could be the basis for maintaining boundaries.

Consider the issue of codes of ethics. Given that codes are attempts to regulate
journalistic behaviors and draw lines between newsrooms and non-journalistic
interests, they reflect whether journalists are interested in drawing firm
boundaries both internally and externally and what values are selected to make
such distinctions. Since the return of democracy, there have been several
attempts to institutionalize codes of ethics in newsrooms, but they had, at
best, limited success. The Foro Periodístico Argentino (FOPEA), a professional
association established in 2005, elaborated and adopted a code of ethics.[30]
However, only about 300 journalists are members of FOPEA, and the code is,
in principle, observed by individual journalists and not by news organizations.
Some news organizations such as newsweeklies *Negocios* and *Veintiuno* also
developed codes of ethics in the late 1990s, and Radio Mitre, a leading station
in Buenos Aires, produced ethical guidelines for covering kidnappings. These
proposals, however, did not last, and were gradually abandoned. Consequently, news organizations lack codes of ethics that define basic practices and
norms. Nor do the majority of news organizations use style manuals. Some
newspapers, *La Voz del Interior*, *El Ancasti*, *Clarín* and *La Nación* produced
manuals, but they are not consistently observed. Therefore, the fact that neither
codes of ethics not style manuals are consistently observed reflects the difficulties
for journalists to coalesce around common goals and views.

Likewise, the state of the journalists' labor organization also denotes the
absence of collective efforts to draw boundaries. Precarious labor conditions
contributed to the elimination of union representatives in newsrooms which, in
turn, weakened the presence and influence of unions. Two unions represent
Argentine journalists: the *Federación Argentina de Trabajadores de Prensa*
with 34 branches in the country, and the *Unión de Trabajadores de Prensa de
Buenos Aires* (UTPBA) in the city and province of Buenos Aires where the
largest media companies are based. Their representativeness, however, is
questionable. Only one out of ten journalists is affiliated with UTPBA. Its
leadership has been criticized by several internal factions, and the Secretary of
Labor nullified recent election results in response to workers' protests. Representatives from each news organization decided to set up organizations in
parallel to the unions, and demanded that the Secretary of Labor allows the
formation of joint committees to discuss salaries and social benefits. After
several strikes separately organized by journalists working for different news
organizations, some were able to negotiate individual agreements with their
employers. Despite the existence of unions, labor organization remains divided
and contested.

Nor does the state of professional organizations suggest minimal consensus on where and how boundaries should be drawn. In 1995, a group led by high-profile journalists founded *Asociación Periodistas*. The goal of the organization was to confront "growing threats to the press and independent journalism".[31] It became a partner of IFEX, the international network for freedom of expression. Beginning in 1997, it collected and published information on attacks against reporters and gradually acquired visibility. *Periodistas*, however, could not survive deep disagreements among its members over how journalism and the organization should be positioned vis-à-vis the Kirchner government, particularly its media policies and relations with the press and journalism. While some members of *Periodistas* became prominent critics of the Kirchner governments, others maintained close relations with both presidents and were appointed to managerial positions in government-owned and funded media. The organization disbanded in 2004 after some members criticized the leftist, pro-government daily *Página/12* for censoring journalist Julio Nudler.

This conflict illustrated the deepening rift in journalism under *Kirchnerismo*. The "*divide et impera*" intention of the Kirchner administrations to split journalism and consolidate a sycophantic press enormously benefited from an occupation in disarray, without consensus and strong boundaries. The success of the government in building a network of self-called "militant" journalists and news organizations, in contrast to so-called "professional" reporters, was not the only outcome of its firm intention and admirable ability. The fact that it has reshaped the media landscape through legal and economic strategies in less than a decade was facilitated by the presence of a fractured journalism. Split across myriad lines – ideological, partisan, ethical, labor, economic – journalism was too weak a contender to fend off the Kirchners just as it has been too weak to reassert boundaries vis-à-vis the media business. The government astutely sharpened existing differences that expressed deep-seated problems for the consolidation of a professional project.

No issue has rallied journalists with common interests. Unlike in previous decades, persistent violence against the press has not brought journalism together. Anti-press attacks attracted considerable attention and condemnation across journalism in previous decades. A massive outcry and public demonstrations filled with hundreds of journalists followed the assassination of news-photographer Jose Luis Cabezas in 1997, who was covering a powerful, behind-the-scenes businessman with close contacts with the government for newsweekly *Noticias*. The situation has become arguably worse as measured by the frequency of attacks. FOPEA's monitoring system has recorded that some type of violence is committed every other day, including physical and property attacks, verbal threats, blocking broadcasts, denial to access public information, and censorship. The lack of mobilization around the assassination of journalist Adams Ledesma in 2010, who covered drug-trafficking for a community radio station based in a slum in the city of Buenos Aires, was symptomatic of a weaker collective identity. Except for some community media associations, no journalistic organization or news company paid much attention to the murder or urged the government to investigate it.

Although the number of cases of violence against the press has increased in the past decade, the situation has not prompted demands for unity. It has received little attention from journalists working for news media identified with the Kirchner government (who identify FOPEA as a front organization for the anti-Kirchner press). Rarely have pro-government journalists brought up the issue of anti-press violence or condemned national or local authorities for condoning attacks. When anti-Kirchner journalists denounced the situation in local and international forums (e.g., books, presentations, public testimonies to the International Commission of Human Rights of the Organization of American States) and accused the government of persecution and discrimination, reactions were expected. While pro-Kirchner journalists dismissed the accusations, anti-Kirchner journalists showed solidarity. Likewise, reactions were predictable after tax agents were sent to investigate the finances of journalists who criticized the government in books and public forums. Whereas "militant" journalists dismissed the accusations as trumped-up charges by hired hands of the opposition and the "monopolistic" press, "professional/independent" journalists condemned the attacks. Without a shared interpretative framework inside journalism, all interpretations reflect personal convictions and labor commitments. The escalation of anti-press violence alone is not sufficient to strengthen common bonds and reaffirm boundaries vis-à-vis governments and perpetrators.

Labor conflicts, too, have been embedded in the rabid debate between "official" and "anti-government" journalism. Lacking even minimal consensus on workers' rights or collective action to improve labor conditions, journalists have not offered a common front. Journalists and news media close to the government have covered labor disputes in the anti-Kirchner media and accused owners of anti-labor practices, but they have remained silent on the precarious conditions among journalists working for pro-Kirchner media companies.

Another issue that has reflected internal divisions involved presidential press conferences. Press conferences are a ritual of government news management and news routines in contemporary democracies. They reflect the disparate aspirations of officials and journalists: the former aim to influence news coverage and the latter expect to be considered as legitimate, respectable actors in a democracy mediating the relation between government and citizens. If they are highly ritualized events, it is because both officials and journalists expect to benefit. Unsurprisingly, like many other aspects of political communication and journalism, the situation is different in Argentina. Presidential press conferences are not common rituals for both officials and journalists. Nor are they conventionally understood as open to all accredited correspondents in the presidential palace. Presidential communication handlers have significant discretion to decide when they are offered and who is allowed to attend.

Attempts to institutionalize press conferences have failed. For example, in 2007, the German foundation Konrad Adenuaer sponsored an initiative (*"Preguntar al poder"*) to make press conferences by government offices a common practice. Initially, the idea gathered support from journalists and public officials, including Supreme Court justices, but after a few meetings, participants lost interest. Whereas seven meetings were held in 2007, no meetings took place in 2013.

The Fernández de Kirchner government has refused to hold open and regular press conferences, and, instead, opted for presidential mediated appearances either devoid of journalists' questions or including only "softball" questions from pro-government scribes. It has carefully avoided engaging with reporters working for oppositional news media. Even if press conferences are highly choreographed events, with few if any surprises or free-wheeling exchanges between Presidents and the press corps, the government has preferred "media events" that it controls absolutely. Although it is certainly not unique in the history of Argentine political communication, this decision has not encountered firm opposition en masse from journalists. Given the absence of a solid "press corps" with collective identity and demands, reactions were divided. Whereas anti-Kirchner reporters complained and accused the Presidency of being "anti-democratic" for its unwillingness to debate with the press, pro-Kirchner journalists as well as administration officials explained that the President permanently communicates with the people. Some journalists decided to establish the group *Conferencia de prensa* in 2012 to present collective demands, but after a few press releases and twitter entries (#Queremospreguntar), the group disbanded without significant success.

This episode illustrates again the inability and disinterest of significant numbers of journalists to establish and maintain internal and external boundaries. Those with fluid access to the President and ideologically or economically close to the administration dismissed criticisms. They showed no solidarity with colleagues shut off from the event or mobilized to express opposition. Instead, other journalists found the practice contrary to the mission of journalism and the essence of democratic debate and, briefly, raised their demands.

In summary, virtually every issue related to occupational identity and performance, such as labor conditions, anti-press violence, and press conference access, has illustrated a fractured journalism. Rather than giving opportunities to coalesce around common objectives, reassert a collective consciousness, and renew differences vis-à-vis other fields and institutions, these issues have magnified inner divisions.

Conclusion

The Argentine case diverges from conventional studies about journalism and boundary-making. Based on the experience of Western cases,[32] studies typically approach journalism as a cohesive "interpretive community" mobilized to reaffirm differences in order to sustain claims to authority and hierarchy, particularly at a time of "journalism in crisis". Boundary-making actions are strategies to differentiate "legitimate" reporting from citizen journalism, unethical reporting, propaganda, and public relations. Lines of separation are only intelligible as long as journalists are a unified community behind certain principles and norms. Interpretations and boundaries are established on the basis of unifying notions, learned in journalism schools and newsrooms, and reinforced by professional publications, criticisms, and debates. Only when clear agreement exists about what journalists have in common can they draw firm boundaries.

How are boundaries drawn when journalism lacks shared normative principles? The Argentine case shows different dynamics at work. When there is no master paradigm, journalists do not "repair" paradigms, as scholars have observed in the U.S. case.[33] They lack shared values and a common professional imagination to distance themselves from rogue reporters who flagrantly deceive the public and colleagues and threaten the credibility of journalism.[34] Journalists cannot symbolically excommunicate colleagues when there is no "journalistic community"[35] organized around common values. To stretch the religious analogy: when there is no established liturgy, journalism is devoid of rituals or recurrent moments to solidify a common belonging. Instead, journalists are in a constant state of deliberation and disagreement, questioning the essence, practices, and contours of their field. Given a weak collective consciousness, there is no strong, unanimous push to regulate internal behaviors through codes of ethics or defensive actions to fend off assaults by public officials, advertisers, or media owners. Weak boundaries make journalism chronically vulnerable to powerful actors.

Structural conditions may contribute to or discourage the effective drawing of boundaries. Professionalism demands newsrooms with relative autonomy from political and economic actors, durable social consensus, and cohesion among journalists interested in a common boundary-making project. Specific political, economic and social conditions may be conducive to, or discourage, professionalism. A moderate separation between the political sphere and the economic infrastructure of journalism seems necessary. It is difficult to imagine the existence of strong professional boundaries when public officials exert significant influence on the economics of journalism. Collusion between politicians and media owners is hardly conducive to strong boundaries. Likewise, media owners need to be convinced that newsrooms require relative autonomy for professional aspirations to prosper. Owners for whom newsrooms are appendices of their business and political interests hardly contribute to solid boundaries. Professionalism faces difficult conditions when thin walls separate business/marketing and newsrooms. In addition, certain levels of social consensus about fundamental issues are needed. Deeply divided societies hardly provide appropriate conditions for professional journalism. In summary, when political elites wield significant power over news economics, media owners conceive newsrooms as foot soldiers in their commercial battles, and societies are bitterly divided, journalists' professional ambitions confront formidable obstacles.

We remain skeptical about the possibility that this situation can be transformed. The forces that explain the persistently weak boundaries are not on the wane. Prospects for a collective project with minimal agreements are dim. We do not find strong indications that journalists are coalescing around common objectives. Journalists remain divided across many lines, and work conditions push them to juggle multiple jobs (e.g., ad peddlers, press officers, public relations) that are incompatible with the existence of firm boundaries. Furthermore, the proliferation of news caused by the digital revolution has deepened the state of confusion about professional boundaries. When blogging and social media news have thrown into question the conventional notion of news and journalism, it is less likely that journalists will agree on a common core of values to draw boundaries.

Obviously, this is not unique to Argentinian journalism. At a time when news is everywhere,[36] it seems improbable that journalists can effectively function as a cohesive community with clear boundaries. The current state of uncertainty about "the future of news" also reveals the confusion of journalistic boundaries. If it is true that "everyone is a journalist" and "ambient news" dominates, the challenge of blurred boundaries is not limited to specific journalistic cultures bounded by historical and social conditions, as in the Argentine case. Because journalism is currently subjected to unprecedented changes that question conventional definitions, norms, and practices, the scenario of "blurred boundaries" is hardly unique to specific "national" journalistic cultures that historically confronted enormous difficulties to become consolidated as a profession. The contexts are still different across countries, but the emergent "new normal" is the state of uncertainty about the interest and ability of journalism and journalists to come together as a collective institution around common ideas. This does not imply that all boundaries are completely blurred or are set to disappear. Professionalism requires, precisely, the mobilization of efforts to set up and maintain boundaries against internal and external challenges. Yet such efforts face exceptional challenges when the essence of both news and journalism is under question.

Notes

1 Barbie Zelizer, "Journalists as interpretive communities," *Critical Studies in Media Communication* 10, no. 3 (1993): 219–37.
2 Michèle Lamont and Virág Molnár, "The study of boundaries in the social sciences," *Annual Review of Sociology* 28, (2002): 167–95.
3 Mathew Cecil, "Bad apples: Paradigm overhaul and the CNN/*Time* 'Tailwind' story," *Journal of Communication Inquiry* 26, no. 1 (2002): 46–58.
4 Andrew Abbott, *The System of Professions* (Chicago: University of Chicago Press, 1988).
5 Silvio Waisbord, *Reinventing Professionalism: Journalism and News in Global Perspective* (Cambridge: Polity Press, 2013).

6 Magali Sarfatti Larson, *The Rise of Professionalism* (Berkeley, CA: University of California Press, 1977).

7 Néstor Kirchner was president from 2003 to 2007, and was succeeded by his wife, Cristina Fernández de Kirchner, in 2007. She was reelected in 2011. He died in 2010.

8 Silvio Waisbord, *Vox populista. Medios, periodismo, democracia* (Buenos Aires, Argentina: Gedisa, 2013).

9 Barbie Zelizer, "When facts, truth, and reality are God-terms: on journalism's uneasy place in cultural studies," *Communication and Critical/Cultural Studies* 1, no. 1 (2004): 100–119.

10 Waisbord, *Reinventing Professionalism*.

11 Maria Cristina Gobbi & Juliana Betti, "Formação e cognição: ensino da comunicação no Brasil e no Cone Sul," in *Panorama da comunicação e das telecomunicações no Brasil*, ed. José Marques de Melo & João Cláudio Garcia Rodrigues Lima (San Pablo, Brasil: Ipea Instituto de Pesquisa Econômica Aplicada, 2013), 54.

12 Martín Becerra and Guillermo Mastrini, "Estructura, concentración y transformaciones en los medios del Cono Sur latinoamericano," *Comunicar* 18, no. 36 (2011): 51–59.

13 Ex Martín Becerra, *Quid pro quo. La publicidad oficial en la Argentina y sus múltiples facetas*, 2011, http://poderciudadano.org/wp/wp-content/uploads/2011/12/InformeFinalPublicidadOficiaArgentina20111.pdf

14 Adriana Amado, *La palabra empeñada. Investigaciones sobre medios y comunicación pública en Argentina*, (Buenos Aires: Centro de Competencia en Comunicación, Fundación F. Ebert, 2010).

15 Ex Foro de Periodismo Argentino and Giacobbe, *Sobre los periodistas y su profesión*, 2005, www.fopea.org/Etica/Encuesta_sobre_Periodismo

16 Ex Foro de Periodismo Argentino & CIO Argentina, *Encuesta sobre los periodistas y su profesión*, 2011, www.fopea.org/Recursos/Biblioteca_Virtual/Estudios/Clima_de_la_Actividad_Periodistica_de_la_Argentina

17 César Arrueta, *¿Qué realidad construyen los diarios?* (Buenos Aires: La Crujía, 2010).

18 Eduardo De Miguel, *Niñez y adolescencia en la prensa argentina. Informe anual. Monitoreo 2004* (Buenos Aires: Periodismo Social, 2005).

19 Ex Colectivo de Trabajadores de Prensa, *Las cifras de la precarización*, 2012, http://colectivodeprensa.blogspot.com.ar/2012/06/encuesta-del-ctp-radiografia-de-la.html

20 Adriana Amado and Natalia Pizzolo, "Journalism Studies in Argentina: Background and Questions," *Brazilian Journalism Research* 10, no. 1 (2014): 8–23.

21 Claudia Mellado, "Major trends of journalism studies in Latin America," in *The Global Journalist in the 21st Century*, eds David Weaver and Lars Willnat (New York: Routledge, 2012).

22 Arrueta, *¿Qué realidad construyen los diarios?*

23 Telma Luzzani, "Información cierta para un mundo imprevisible," in *Información, ¿se puede saber lo que pasa?*, ed. Adriana Amado (Buenos Aires, Argentina: Norma, 2005); Stella Martini and Lila Luchessi, *Los que hacen la noticia* (Buenos Aires, Argentina: Biblos, 2004).

24 Daniel Castro, José Marques de Melo, Cosette Castro, *Tendências na comunicação. Panorama da comunicação e das telecomunicações no Brasil* (Brasilia, Brasil: Ipea Instituto de Pesquisa Econômica Aplicada, 2010), vol. 3.

25 Ex Diario sobre diarios, *El loteo periodístico se enfrenta al dilema: cambia o sobrevive*, 2010. www.diariosobrediarios.com.ar/eldsd/zonadura/2010/diciembre/zd-2-diciembre-2010.htm

26 Arrueta, *¿Qué realidad construyen los diarios?*; María O'Donnell, *Propaganda K* (Buenos Aires, Argentina: Planeta, 2007).

27 Acción por los Derechos Civiles, *La publicidad oficial del Poder Ejecutivo Nacional durante 2007* (Buenos Aires: ADC, 2008).

28 Eduardo Anguita, *Grandes hermanos* (Buenos Aires, Argentina: Colihue, 2002).

29 Adriana Amado, *La palabra empeñada*.

30 Pablo Mendelevich, *Ética periodística en la Argentina y en el mundo* (Buenos Aires, Argentina: Konrad Adenauer, 2005).

31 Asociación Periodistas, *Ataques a la prensa* (Buenos Aires, Argentina: Planeta, 2000).

32 Chris Peters and Marcel Broersma, *Rethinking journalism: Trust and participation in a transformed news landscape* (London: Routledge, 2013).

33 W. Lance Bennett, Lynne Gressett and Willima Haltom, "Repairing the News: A case Study of the News Paradigm," *Journal of Communication* 35, no. 2 (1985): 50–68; Stephen Reese, "The news paradigm and the ideology of objectivity: A socialist at the *Wall Street Journal*," *Critical Studies in Media Communication* 7, no. 4 (1990): 390–409; Thomas Ruggiero, "Paradigm repair and changing journalistic perceptions of the Internet as an objective news source," *Convergence: The International Journal of Research into New Media Technologies* 10, no. 4 (2004): 92–106.

34 Elizabeth Blanks Hindman, "Jayson Blair, the *New York Times*, and paradigm repair," *Journal of Communication* 55, no. 2 (2005): 225–41.

35 Matt Carlson, "'Where once stood titans': Second-order paradigm repair and the vanishing US newspaper," *Journalism* 13, no. 3 (2012): 267–83.

36 Alfred Hermida, "Twittering the news: The emergence of ambient journalism," *Journalism Practice* 4, no. 3 (2010): 297–308.

Chapter 4

The wall becomes a curtain

Revisiting journalism's news–business boundary

Mark Coddington

Of all the boundaries detailed in this volume and reified within journalistic discourse, only one is so fundamental to the self-understanding of professional journalism, so thoroughly understood as a cultural and occupational assumption, that it is often known simply as "the wall." That wall, between the journalistic and business-oriented functions of a news organization, is one of the foremost professional markers of journalism, a principle that is reinforced most strongly in the central sites of its socialization – journalism schools, textbooks, and reviews, not to mention thousands of newsrooms large and small. Along with the principle of independence from political factions, the news–business wall is the cornerstone upholding American journalism's sense of autonomy, which allows it to function as a profession – to the extent that it does. The wall is arguably the preeminent boundary in American journalism, the one that helps give it the capacity to maintain its many other boundaries.

Yet journalists' considerable rhetoric around this boundary, both in actively enforcing it and in treating it as an unexamined and unquestioned presupposition, has been the subject of far less scholarly examination than other, less foundational, boundaries. Consider it in contrast to its parallel fundamental boundary, the division between journalism and political interest or influence: Hundreds of scholarly works have examined the way journalists publicly perform that boundary, mostly through the practice of objectivity. But the strategies by which journalists perform the news–business boundary and the principles behind them have come under far less scrutiny. Many media scholars have, of course, examined the varied ways the news–business wall is breached, continually and systemically.[1] But the discursive work that journalists put into maintaining it before the public has been relatively untouched. There is a fairly simple explanation for much of this scholarly reticence: Unlike many other boundaries, scholars – at least the more critical ones who might be inclined to study journalistic discourse – tend to agree with journalists that this boundary should indeed exist. They simply disagree on whether it actually does. The journalistic aims that many scholars have called for – a journalism that serves the public good first and foremost, shielded from commercial influence – are precisely the ones toward which so many of the journalists they criticize would eagerly say they are striving. Thus, scholars have not targeted journalists' rhetoric on the issue, which so often overlaps with their own, but instead the journalists' actions.

This chapter is an effort to explicate this rhetoric, exploring the strategies that journalists and media critics have taken to reinforce this boundary. First, I examine the origins and development of the divide. Next, I outline specific discursive strategies that journalists have used to outline the divide, particularly as they emerged in the market-driven journalism heyday of the 1990s. Finally, I highlight two contemporary issues – native advertising and entrepreneurial journalism – that might be perceived as a threat to the news–business boundary. The most striking finding of this examination is not that the news–business wall itself is crumbling; numerous scholars have long ago exposed it as a professionally advantageous fiction. Instead, what is crumbling now is journalists' willingness to continue to uphold that fiction and maintain a boundary that is increasingly seen as a rather anachronistic relic of a time when the news industry's survival wasn't threatened.

Foundations of the boundary

The news–business boundary is based on a distinctive model of the modern news organization, with two sets of goals: financial viability, on the one hand, and public service or public influence on the other. These aims, as Cranberg et al. note, can be traded off to varying degrees, but they cannot fundamentally be made congruent.[2] Overseeing the departments behind both of these goals is the publisher, station manager, or owner. The strange juxtaposition leads to some professional and rhetorical gymnastics on each side to justify such an arrangement. As Cranberg et al. aptly point out, "No self-respecting distributor of a mass-manufactured consumer product would dare to organize itself this way."[3]

With this irrational arrangement in view, journalists have constructed and enshrined a border between themselves and their organizations' business operations primarily as a way to safeguard their professional autonomy, or journalists' ability to exercise judgment and control their work process.[4] Commercial influences, as well as the organizational influences through which they often manifest themselves, are one of the strongest constraints on journalistic autonomy, far stronger than the weak, semi-professional culture of journalism is capable of defending against.[5] That imbalance has two primary consequences: Journalists have worked exceptionally hard to maintain a strong boundary against commercial influence, making it a core element of their professional values. But despite those efforts, the boundary has been extremely susceptible to encroachment by those commercial influences because of their overwhelming advantage in power.

The heavy influence of commercial interests has led many scholars to declare the notion of a separation between news and business "a fiction, more honored as a principle than as something that existed in practice."[6] Yet the resistance of journalists to commercialization is an important part of the story of modern American journalism – at times because of its small successes in holding off commercial influences, but also because of the important role it has played in shaping and maintaining journalists' professional identity. To fully understand the news–business wall, we must be able to simultaneously assert both its extreme permeability and its foundational role in undergirding journalistic professionalism. As Cranberg et al. note, the wall "was never impenetrable but was of symbolic importance and yielded practical consequences."[7]

The news–business divide has its roots in the shift from political patronage to an advertising-based financial model in the early to mid-1800s. Until that point, newspapers had typically operated in the service of political parties, relying on a combination of political funding, printing, and subscriptions.[8] By the 1830s and 1840s, however, industrialization created a need for the mass marketing of new, mass-produced goods, giving the press a new social purpose through its distinct ability to serve this growing economic system by connecting producers with a wide range of buyers.[9] The influx of advertising corresponded with the rise of the penny press, as newspaper publishers subsidized cheap subscription costs with growing advertising revenues stemming from ballooning circulations. As the political parties' power and patronage waned, newspapers moved from primarily political organizations at the outset of the nineteenth century to primarily market-driven organizations by the end, trading dependence on the political system for dependence on the financial one.[10]

Violations and defenses

Almost as soon as advertising began to move to the center of the American newspaper's business model, advertisers began to influence those newspapers' content. Advertisers began to ask for and receive special treatment – they directed ad placement, had stories killed, and dictated blatantly promotional stories, called "puffs," that existed somewhere between news and advertising. Newspapers openly favored advertisers and threatened non-advertisers. Advertising in many cases functioned essentially as a bribe.[11] Puffs, popular in the mid-to-late nineteenth century, morphed into "reading notices," or ads disguised as news items, in the early twentieth century. For many pre-World War I publishers, newspapers were to fundamentally function as a business; any other public-facing purpose was secondary at best.[12]

At the same time, however, journalists decried such devotion to advertiser's desires and business concerns as unethical and polluting. As early as 1848, James Gordon Bennett's *New York Herald* banned puffs from its pages.[13] In 1869, literary critic Richard Grant White called for the formation of what might be called a prototype of the news–advertising wall: "absolute and without exception, that nothing in the interests of an advertiser, no matter what his importance, shall be admitted into the editorial columns for any consideration."[14] Journalists continued to decry the commercialization of news and influence of advertisers in the early 1900s.[15]

What followed were several decades of stability in the news–business boundary, corresponding with what Hallin has termed the "high modernism" of American journalism.[16] During the mid-twentieth century, the news industry's prosperity allowed journalists to believe they had resolved the conflict between their news and business purposes by constructing the boundary between the two as a "wall of separation between church and state."[17] This equilibrium began to be disrupted during the 1980s and 1990s, in part because of the market-driven journalism era's challenge to the boundary.[18] The consternation over the appropriateness and fate of that boundary is evident in the spike in discourse on the subject in both academic publishing and the trade press. In market-driven journalism, journalism's core aspiration shifts from its professional ideal of empowering citizens with information to participate in democratic life to an effort to meet the audience's expressed desires as a set of consumers, in order to match increasing demands for financial returns.[19] As we have seen, these market-oriented principles have been a fundamental part of American journalism for well more than a century, though they began to intensify in the late twentieth century, partly because of the increase in business rationality and market orientation stemming from public and chain news media ownership.[20] The difference in this incarnation of those market principles was that journalists began to feel this pressure more concretely than they had in previous decades, perceiving a significant shift toward business principles and away from their professional values.[21]

The manifestations of this business-based pressure have been well documented. The most basic is the influence of commercial interests on the size of the newsroom, an inherent crossover between news and business. Financial factors have always – and in a way necessarily – determined newsroom size; otherwise, there would be little preventing newsrooms from reaching ever-increasing scales. Because it is so endogenous to the news organization, this is a commercial influence that often operates without being perceived as a breach of the news–business boundary. That changed during the 1990s and 2000s, when the influence became more obtrusive for journalists as the cutbacks and layoffs began appearing in earnest. Weaver et al. found that a shortage of news-gathering resources was the commercial constraint most frequently cited by journalists – to them, limited newsroom size is often experienced as having too little time to do good work.[22]

A more glaring violation of the boundary is the influence of advertisers on news content and decision-making. Anecdotal examples of such influence piled up in the 1980s and 1990s and survey data confirmed its prevalence: Soley and Craig found that more than 90 percent of newspaper editors reported advertiser attempts to influence their news content, and more than a third of them reported that some of those attempts had been successful.[23] Specifically, the scandal surrounding the *Los Angeles Times*' 1999 Staples Center special section, in which the paper split the section's profits from ad revenue with the arena itself, took on a synecdochical characterization of the breaches of the news–business boundary fostered by the market-driven journalism movement. The backlash it prompted was significant enough to lead to a retrenchment of market-driven journalism; the Staples Center incident was effectively the end of an era.[24]

This chapter's exploratory analysis of boundary work rhetoric centers on that period of market-driven journalism, when discourse around the news–business boundary was at its peak and many of the rhetorical themes that remain in use today were most firmly established. About 140 articles from mainstream news organizations, journalism reviews, trade publications, and journalism blogs between 1989 and 2014 were examined and organized thematically for discursive strategies and themes.

Boundary work strategies

Journalists have developed a variety of tools to defend their jurisdiction from commercial interests. Though boundary work is fundamentally a rhetorical process,[25] one key strategy is more organizational than rhetorical – the distinctly bifurcated structure of news organizations described above, with the news and business departments operating independently from each other and often at odds. This structure also includes buffers between journalists and management, most notably in the form of the editor, who serves a boundary-spanning role as both a journalist and a part of management.[26] The effect of this buffering is that the organization absorbs commercial and advertiser pressure so that it appears to journalists as organizational pressure instead.[27] This organizational separation has historically manifested itself most materially in the physical separation between newsroom and advertising departments, an arrangement that reinforces the boundary both physically and symbolically. Longtime *Chicago Tribune* publisher, Robert McCormick, famously enforced this physical divide with separate elevators for journalists and those in the business operation, the latter of which did not stop on the newsroom floor. When ad executives began appearing on the newsroom floor in the late 1980s, their presence was perceived as a powerful sign of the newspaper's fall from integrity.[28]

Aside from organizational divides, most of the journalists' work in defining and defending the news–business boundary has been accomplished rhetorically. The professional values regarding independence from business are most formally encoded at the organizational level in news organizations' written guidelines and at the professional level in codes of ethics. These tools reify a set of professional norms to which journalists can appeal as their basis to a moral claim when their ethical rectitude is challenged.[29] McManus argues that news organizations' codes of ethics, virtually all of which advocate independence from advertisers and business interests, are based on the fiction of the individual journalist's control, serving to deflect criticism for ethical violations from owners and systemic problems onto employees and individual violators.[30] This function – isolating blame over professional breaches in deviant individual violators in order to hold intact the public image of trustworthiness and authority in the larger profession – is precisely the task of boundary work.

The wall

The central metaphor used to maintain the news–business boundary is that of the wall – perhaps the most direct, forceful, and enduring metaphor in modern American journalism. Its origins have not fully been explored; the idea is often thought to have originated with legendary early twentieth-century publishers such as the *Chicago Tribune*'s McCormick or *TIME*'s Henry Luce, but they didn't actually articulate it.[31] It evokes two distinct ideas: the "Chinese wall" ethical concept of avoiding conflicts of interest that arose in the financial world in the wake of the reforms following the 1929 stock market crash;[32] and the Jeffersonian idea of the "wall of separation between church and state" enshrined in the U.S. Constitution's First Amendment. The latter connotation, as we will see, has been a particularly potent rhetorical weapon for journalists.

The wall is commonly employed in news–business boundary discourse, but it is rarely explained or justified. Instead, it is simply invoked as a pre-existing reality. The primary mention of the wall in many stories on the news–business boundary is simply to refer to its ongoing destruction. In the journalistic imagination, the wall is simultaneously venerable and crumbling, the corner-stone of the profession and something constantly under assault. The wall is being "blasted into history," with editors and publishers "crashing through," or "obliterating" it with a "battering ram."[33] The concrete-ness of the wall metaphor and the language surrounding it allows journalists to emphasize their precariousness and to characterize the encroachment on their occupational territory as not just professional tension, but brutal violence.

Some journalistic discourse has challenged the given-ness of the wall, even within articles voicing concern about breaches of the news–business boundary. One 2002 *American Journalism Review* article on the increasing interaction between editorial and business departments of newspapers began, "Few aspects of journalism are as groundlessly romanticized. The apocryphal 'wall' between newsrooms and advertising departments is often referred to without a hint of self-consciousness as the separation between church and state."[34] Other news executives – most notoriously *Los Angeles Times* CEO Mark Willes, with his pledge to take down the wall with a bazooka – openly advocated the demolition of the wall. Willes preferred the more flexible image of a line, but his paper's media critic, David Shaw, countered with a spirited defense of the wall's strength as a metaphor: "A wall is impregnable and immovable – at least in theory; a line can be breached much more easily, moved so gradually that no one knows it's actually been moved until it's too late, and principles have been irrevocably compromised."[35]

The primary asset for journalists in the wall as a metaphor isn't its strength and apparent impermeability; journalists have actually shown themselves eager to concede the wall's vulnerability to attack. Instead, the greatest rhetorical potency of the wall lies in its tie to the concept of the "separation of church and state." As journalists use this metaphor, they characterize themselves as the church and the business side as the state. That classification is rarely made explicit, but it is evident in the unmistakable strain of religious language that runs through their news–business discourse. The newsroom's territory and the separation itself are often referred to as "sacred" or "hallowed," and violations are considered "heresy" that is "corrupting the body and soul of our profession."[36] In a particularly arresting piece of religious imagery, an *American Journalism Review* article on the Staples Center scandal referred to it as Willes' "assault on the church-state wall – the shot that would reverberate through the sanctum sanctorum of the newspaper world like abortion in the Vatican."[37] Journalists have used the church–state connotations of the wall metaphor to apply the language of sanctity to their own behavior, allowing them to bathe their professional values in moral purity and ascribe moral deficiency and uncleanliness to violators of those values.

Public service and trust

Journalists have widely employed two other rhetorical themes alongside that of the wall: Public service and trust. Journalists often set their public service and commercial goals in opposition to each other – and indeed they often conflict.[38] But journalists often portray them as a zero-sum game, setting them up as mutually exclusive and depicting each gain of commercial ends as a necessarily equal loss of journalists' ability to effectively serve the public. Former *New York Times* executive editor Max Frankel set up this distinction as the fundamental dividing line in the profession: "Serious journalists are not hard to define. Deep down, they think of packaging news not as a business but as a public service."[39] The public-service argument is more than a way to claim social responsibility as a profession; as Squires notes, it is the basis on which journalists defend their First Amendment rights.[40] If that claim is based on journalism's effectiveness as a business rather than its aim to serve democratic ends, journalists' moral case for expansive First Amendment rights – in essence, its formal autonomy from the state – crumbles.

While public service as a theme is meant to set up and defend professional journalism's idealized goals, trust is oriented toward its idealized assets. Like the wall, credibility is characterized both as an immense social asset for journalists – something they possess in enough quantity to drive virtually their entire social value – and as something continually in danger of being emptied out because of violations of the news–business boundary. As Cameron and Ju-Pak note, most editors view advertising as borrowing (or stealing) their credibility.[41] The *Los Angeles Times*' Shaw, in his critique of the Staples

Center fiasco, concluded that "The *Times'* credibility and integrity – *ultimately the only commodities a newspaper has to offer* – have been severely compromised at a time when public confidence in the press is already in deep decline."[42] In this newsroom-centric mindset, the newsroom produces all of the value of the news organization, and it is only borrowed, sapped, or stolen – never enhanced – by the intrusion of commercial values into news.

Violators' defenses

Journalists and news organizations accused of violating the news–business boundary engage in their own rhetorical strategies to reposition themselves within the realm of professional propriety. In some cases they do this by restating their commitment to upholding the boundary, and in others by attempting to shift the boundary to include their own behavior. When questioned about potentially problematic practices, journalists often argue that any potential damage is obviated by the standards to which they continue to adhere – not allowing advertisers to influence news copy in market-oriented special sections, for example, or continuing to keep readers at the forefront in advertiser-suggested product reviews.[43] Sometimes, news organizations attempt to re-establish their professional probity simply by stating their knowledge of the wall, without any further explanation of what that might mean in their case, as with the magazine editor who told the *Wall Street Journal* simply, "I know the difference between church and state."[44] Such statements serve not only to reaffirm one's commitment to journalistic principles, but also to buttress the principles themselves, by portraying them as without need of description or elaboration. Holding to their own knowledge of these professional standards allows journalists to police the news–business boundary on the profession's behalf in public while they simultaneously succumb to the same commercialization within their own organizations.

In some cases, journalists have defended themselves not by reaffirming their commitment to the boundary, but by arguing that the boundary should be reconsidered or shifted to include their own behavior. In the most dominant defensive argument, journalists have made the case that economic hardships in the media industries necessitate increased permeability of the boundary simply to ensure continued survival. The idea that clinging to church–state boundaries will lead to extinction amid the harsh difficulties of competing in modern information and advertising markets picked up steam in the late 1980s and early 1990s, spreading to the point that Underwood called it "gospel" in newspaper conferences.[45] Even those who were defending the boundary felt the need to acknowledge that blurring the boundary could be a crucial element in maintaining news organizations' financial viability.[46] Survival rhetoric often characterizes boundary maintenance concerns as being academic or theoretical, while financial concerns are placed in the more relevant realm of "the real world," as in one article regarding the use of web analytics to guide news decisions: "Any performance metric is going to be anathema to the j-school professor crowd, but these publications say they'd prefer to exist rather than debate these kinds of issues."[47]

Contemporary challenges to the boundary

These general rhetorical strategies of boundary work have held relatively steady since they emerged in the debates over market-driven journalism in the 1980s and 1990s. Those attempting to maintain the boundary continue to invoke the metaphor of the wall and lean on arguments about maintaining their credibility and public-service mission, and those defending their own contested practices continue to foreground the industry's economic hardships and claim they are upholding the boundary. Yet the relative prevalence of each of those arguments points to subtle but significant shifts in the boundary work being performed at the news–business intersection, and perhaps also the location and permeability of the boundary itself. Before briefly examining two particular flashpoints in the struggle over the boundary – native advertising and entrepreneurial journalism – it is worth setting the stage with the role that online journalism has played vis-à-vis this boundary more generally.

As we have seen, challenges to the news–business boundary are not new to the Internet era; rather, they are as old as the boundary itself. Still, journalism scholars have been concerned since the early days of online journalism about the increased potential for blurring between news and commercial content there, due to less institutionalized ethical norms, as well as a general prevalence of advertising content online.[48] Empirical data testing these concerns are limited, but those data have found that online journalists reported more influence from advertisers than did print journalists.[49] Several factors coalesce to produce a more commercialized online journalism space: The lowered barriers to entry create more competition, which, when coupled with a weak online advertising market, creates an environment in which news organizations are more directly responsive to market forces in the form of web traffic and what limited ad revenue is available.[50] In short, as McChesney puts it, "[T]he Internet does not alleviate the tensions between commercialism and journalism; it magnifies them."[51] It is within this environment that we examine the present state of the boundary on two fronts.

Native advertising

The most prominent and controversial realm in which the news–business boundary is being contested is the growing practice of native advertising, or sponsored content, a form of online advertising that is built around its resemblance to editorial content. The practice descends from forms of news–advertising fusion such as the nineteenth century's puffs, early twentieth century's reading notices, and late twentieth century's advertorial, with a few key – and very much contested – differences. In fact, much of the boundary work surrounding this practice is taking place at the very basic level of how to define it.

Native advertising is one of the fastest-growing forms of advertising expenditure within the news industry, with growth of 56.1 percent in news industry revenue from 2010 to 2011 and another 38.9 percent in 2012.[52] The current iteration of this form of advertising was pioneered in the late 2000s by a handful of media companies such as *Forbes*, which allowed advertisers to pay for their own blogging platform modeled after, and thinly distinguished from, the site's own editorial platform.[53] Though it became associated with traffic-driven web publishers such as *BuzzFeed*, native advertising quickly spread to more established traditional news organizations including the *Wall Street Journal*, the *Associated Press*, and the *New York Times*. The practice has come with its own minor fiascos, such as *The Atlantic*'s publication of a particularly tone-deaf native ad extolling the virtues of Scientology,[54] and has drawn the scrutiny of advertising industry groups and the U.S. Federal Trade Commission, which held a conference on the subject in 2013 called "Blurred Lines."[55]

Much of the boundary work regarding native advertising surrounds its contested definitions. Those who are skeptical of the practice tend to define it in terms of its similarity to editorial content, such as the description by *New York Times* media critic David Carr as "advertising wearing the uniform of journalism, mimicking the storytelling aesthetic of the host site."[56] This definition mirrors that of advertorial, the news-lookalike advertising that flourished in the market-driven era of the 1990s but has since fallen out of favor.[57] Native advertising critics likewise emphasize its similarity with advertorial, characterizing it as simply a new manifestation of the same practice.[58] On the other hand, those who defend native advertising define it in terms of its attractiveness to readers; if it is not worthwhile to the reader, then by definition, it is not native advertising. In this vein, journalism scholar and pundit Jay Rosen defines the practice as "advertising that is as worth reading as the editorial into which it is mixed, from which it is distinguished."[59] According to this definition, native advertising is distinguished from advertorial in two respects: It is as valuable to the reader as news content, where advertorial is worthless to the reader, and its primary intent is not to deceive the reader, where advertorial is built solely on deception.[60]

Of course, to those concerned with defending the news–business boundary, the latter assertion is absurd; they describe confusion as the entire goal of the practice.[61] This is the FTC's primary concern, and indeed, even at the commission's behest, advertisers have been reluctant to label their advertisements as such.[62] The advertising and publishing industries are quick to declare transparency and separation of news and advertising content as a core value,[63] but that value is in fact quite ambiguous in practice, as evidenced by one exchange between two ad executives at a conference panel on native advertising: "If it's done well, people don't know it when they see it," said one. Replied the other: "No, if it's done well, they don't care."[64] In that exchange lies the core tension in native advertising: It is an enterprise built on blurring the boundary between news and advertising, but also on simply creating more compelling advertising that's honestly labeled. Both purposes are inherently in conflict, but both are necessary to native advertising's value to advertisers. If either one is absent, it is no longer native advertising.

Just as with previous challenges to the boundary, journalists on both sides of the native advertising debate struggle to define it in terms of either eroding trust or industry survival. Critics express their concern about native advertising's confusion hurting news organizations' credibility, making their brands less valuable for advertisers to associate with.[65] Publishers engaged in the practice go to great lengths to publicly reaffirm their dedication to the news–business boundary, perhaps none as conspicuously as the professional standard-bearer the *New York Times*.[66] But they also employ the rhetoric of survival, describing native advertising as a key to maintaining journalism's viability and depicting those who object as scolds who, in the words of a News Corp. executive, "would rather hide behind ossified church and state walls with absolute positions than find flexible ways to protect both journalism and the business of journalism."[67] Despite the boundary work rhetoric in both directions, those advocating a shift to accommodate native advertising clearly have the upper hand, particularly based on its adoption among journalism's most professionally respected organizations. Those organizations continue to pledge their commitment to maintaining the boundary, but their vision of that boundary is significantly different from that of traditionalists.

Entrepreneurial journalism

A second area that has threatened the news–business boundary in recent years is the spread of an entrepreneurial journalism model that orients journalists toward involvement in nascent and less institutional news organizations rather than the larger and more institutional organizations of modern professional journalism. After several decades in which new news organizations were rare, journalism has seen a boom in startup news organizations. Some of them have been successfully founded with the help of significant outside funding, such as *Politico* and the *Huffington Post*; others have been nonprofit organizations leaning heavily on foundations and donations, such as *ProPublica* and *MinnPost*. Many of these online news startups, such as *BuzzFeed* and *Gawker*, have relied heavily on metrics to influence issue coverage, writing style, and writer incentives. This preoccupation with the use of tools to quantify audience interest is widespread within traditional news organizations as well; in both settings, it can serve to replace news judgment with a thin, incomplete view of the audience driven by commercial considerations rather than professional ones.[68]

Journalism schools have become a significant site for entrepreneurial journalism and the professional tension that surrounds it. Entrepreneurial skills and the business of journalism have become increasingly emphasized in American journalism education, with journalism schools launching entrepreneurship courses and programs and attempting to absorb startup culture by using the language of startups and in some cases even acting as incubators for students launching their own media businesses.[69] These developments are driven by the notion that knowledge of the business of journalism is part of the fundamental set of skills required in young journalists,[70] which is necessarily a function of a vision of a more permeable boundary between news and business. As one Newspaper Association of America staffer and journalism Master's student wrote, "The very fact that the Media Entrepreneurship program in which I'm enrolled even exists demonstrates that we're past a point of editorial-business firewalls."[71] At the same time, however, the instructors who teach these courses complain that journalism schools remain permeated by the traditional notion of "separation of church and state," making it difficult to put business elements at the core of students' journalism education and even breeding resistance on the part of the students themselves.[72]

There is notably little public discourse defending against the advance of entrepreneurial journalism in the name of the news–business boundary. Instead, virtually all of the discourse advocates journalists' increased under-standing of the news business, and most of it foregrounds the rhetoric of survival. According to the common argument, journalists now need to understand the financial aspects of their industry because it is no longer stable enough to afford them the luxury of ignoring it. Journalists have to take responsibility for ensuring their journalistic work continues to reach audiences and remain financially sustainable.[73] A particularly aggressive strain of this argument maintains that journalism's ignorance of business principles is the reason it's in a volatile state in the first place: As entrepreneurial journalism professor Jeff Jarvis writes, "by teaching journalists that business itself is corrupting, we became terrible stewards of journalism and that is one of the key reasons journalism is in the fix it's in."[74] Arguments such as these leave little room for the defense of a strict news–business boundary: The widespread newsroom cuts of the mid-to-late 2000s were a concrete indicator of the power of the profession's business side and the degree to which it must be sated.

Conclusion

Though native advertising and entrepreneurial journalism are contested areas, they are notably less contested than the hot spots that emerged along the news–business boundary throughout the late twentieth century. Journalists still apparently feel some need to defend practices that might be perceived to violate the boundary, but the viewpoint against which they are defending is rarely being publicly vocalized. When the boundary appeared to be under siege as the high-modernist age of journalism gave way to the market-driven journalism era,[75] journalists vigorously contested it through their professional discourse. Now, however, they've largely ceded the metaphor of the wall to the rhetoric of survival and industry crisis. The wall maintains an iconic place in the

American journalistic imagination, but its era as a dominant norm is over. It has been continually contested for at least the last two decades, and now appears to be losing ground to such norms as transparency and integrity – norms that might guard against commercialization, but do not necessarily come with a boundary to protect.

The erosion of this boundary is not necessarily something to be mourned. For decades, it has provided a means for journalists to avoid knowledge of and moral responsibility for the creeping co-optation of their work by commercial interests. It has also left them ill-prepared for an online-oriented media environment in which their work is increasingly vulnerable to the fluctuations of market forces. But the wall has also carried significant practical consequences in giving journalists a symbolic image to remind them of their own role in maintaining a professional practice that fundamentally serves democratic aims rather than commercial ones. As the wall slowly declines in professional importance, it is imperative that journalists develop and defend a less fraught and more robust set of norms that safeguard the profession's integrity and autonomy amid powerful commercial forces and an increasingly skeptical public.

Notes

1 Ben Bagdikian, *The New Media Monopoly* (Boston, MA: Beacon, 2004); Robert McChesney, *Digital Disconnect* (New York: The New Press, 2013); John McManus, "The Commercialization of News," in *The Handbook of Journalism Studies*, ed. Karin Wahl-Jorgensen and Thomas Hanitzsch (London: Routledge, 2009), 218–33.
2 Gilbert Cranberg, Randall Bezanson, and John Soloski, *Taking Stock* (Ames: Iowa State University Press, 2001).
3 Cranberg et al., *Taking Stock*, 98.
4 Claudia Mellado and María Humanes, "Modeling Perceived Professional Autonomy in Chilean Journalism," *Journalism*, 13, no. 8 (2012): 985–1003.
5 Leo Bogart, *Commercial Culture*, 2nd edn. (New Brunswick, NJ: Transaction, 2000); David Weaver et al., *The American Journalist in the 21st Century* (Mahwah, NJ: Lawrence Erlbaum Associates, 2007).
6 Doug Underwood, *When MBAs Rule the Newsroom* (New York: Columbia University Press, 1993), 124; Bagdikian, *The New Media Monopoly*; McChesney, *Digital Disconnect*.
7 Cranberg et al., *Taking Stock*, 100.
8 Kevin Barnhurst and John Nerone, *The Form of News* (New York: The Guilford Press, 2001).
9 Gerald Baldasty, *The Commercialization of News in the Nineteenth Century* (Madison: University of Wisconsin Press, 1992); Theodore Peterson, "Mass Media and Their Environments," in *What's News*, ed. Elie Abel (San Francisco: Institute for Contemporary Studies, 1981), 13–32.
10 Barnhurst and Nerone, *The Form of News*; Denise Delorme and Fred Fedler, "An Historical Analysis of Journalists' Attitudes Toward Advertisers and Advertising's Influence," *American Journalism*, 22, no. 2 (2005): 7–40.
11 Baldasty, *The Commercialization of News*; Delorme and Fedler, "An Historical Analysis."
12 Baldasty, *The Commercialization of News*.

13 Delorme and Fedler, "An Historical Analysis."

14 Cited in Delorme and Fedler, "An Historical Analysis," 15.

15 McManus, "The Commercialization of News."

16 Daniel Hallin, "The Passing of the 'High Modernism' of American Journalism," *Journal of Communication*, 42, no. 3 (1992): 14–25.

17 Bagdikian, *The New Media Monopoly.*

18 Hallin, "The Passing of the 'High Modernism'."

19 Jeremy Iggers, *Good News, Bad News* (Boulder, CO: Westview, 1998); Bill Kovach and Tom Rosenstiel, *The Elements of Journalism*, 2nd edn. (New York: Three Rivers, 2007); Underwood, *When MBAs Rule the Newsroom.*

20 Baldasty, *The Commercialization of News*; Cranberg et al., *Taking Stock.*

21 Underwood, *When MBAs Rule the Newsroom.*

22 Weaver et al., *The American Journalist.*

23 Lawrence Soley and Robert Craig, "Advertising Pressures on Newspapers," *Journal of Advertising*, 21, no. 4 (1992): 1–10; see also Bagdikian, *The New Media Monopoly*; Bogart, *Commercial Culture*; Underwood, *When MBAs Rule the Newsroom.*

24 Michael Schudson, *The Sociology of News*, 2nd edn. (New York: W.W. Norton & Co., 2011).

25 Thomas F. Gieryn, "Boundary-Work and the Demarcation of Science from Non-Science," *American Sociological Review*, 48, no. 6 (1983): 781–95.

26 John Soloski, "News Reporting and Professionalism," *Media, Culture & Society*, 11, no. 2 (1989): 207–28.

27 Mellado and Humanes, "Modeling Perceived Professional Autonomy."

28 Kovach and Rosenstiel, *The Elements of Journalism*; James Squires, *Read All About It! The Corporate Takeover of America's Newspapers* (New York: Times Books, 1993).

29 Iggers, *Good News, Bad News.*

30 John McManus, "Who's Responsible for Journalism?," *Journal of Mass Media Ethics*, 12, no. 1 (1997): 5–17.

31 Kovach and Rosenstiel, *The Elements of Journalism.*

32 James Upshaw, Gennadiy Chernov, and David Koranda, "Telling More Than News," *Electronic News*, 1, no. 2 (2007): 67–87.

33 Greg Mitchell, "And 'the Wall' Came Tumbling Down," *Editor & Publisher*, 132, no. 49 (1999): 20–21; Joanne Lipman, "Hurt By Ad Downturn, More Magazines Use Favorable Articles to Woo Sponsors," *The Wall Street Journal*, 30 July 1991; David Shaw, "An Uneasy Alliance of News and Ads," *Los Angeles Times*, 29 March 1998; Squires, *Read All About It*, 77.

34 Sharyn Vane, "Taking Care of Business," *American Journalism Review* (2002): 60–65.

35 Shaw, "An Uneasy Alliance."

36 Alicia Lasek, "New Ad-Editorial Bridge Goes Up," *Advertising Age*, 61, no. 45 (1990): 28–29; Squires, *Read All About It*, 73; Roy Greenslade, "Journalists as Entrepreneurs? That's Fine, But Not If They Have to Sell Advertising," *The Guardian*, 8 October 2010, www.theguardian.com/media/greenslade/2010/oct/08/entrepreneurs-digital-media; Bill Kirtz, "Is the Fire Wall Burning?" *The Quill*, 86, no. 5 (1998): 6–9.

37 William Prochnau, "Down and Out in L.A.," in *Leaving Readers Behind*, eds Gene Roberts, Thomas Kunkel, and Charles Layton (Fayetteville: University of Arkansas Press, 2001), 189–233.

38 John McManus, "Serving the Public and Serving the Market," *Journal of Mass Media Ethics*, 7, no. 4 (1992): 196–208; Uphaw, Chernov, and Koranda, "Telling More Than News."

39 Cited in Carl Sessions Stepp, "The Thrill Is Gone," *American Journalism Review*, October 1995, http://ajrarchive.org/Article.asp?id=1676

40 Squires, *Read All About It.*

41 Glen Cameron and Kuen-Hee Ju-Pak, "Information Pollution? Labeling and Format of Advertorials," *Newspaper Research Journal*, 21, no. 1 (2000): 65–76.

42 David Shaw, "Crossing the Line," *Los Angeles Times*, 20 December 1999. [Emphasis added.]

43 Lasek, "New Ad-Editorial Bridge"; Prochnau, "Down and Out in L.A."

44 Lipman, "Hurt by Ad Downturn."

45 Underwood, *When MBAs Rule the Newsroom.*

46 Shaw, "An Uneasy Alliance"; Stepp, "The Thrill Is Gone."

47 Josh Sternberg, "Pageview Journalism Gets a Reset," *Digiday*, 16 October 2013, http://digiday.com/publishers/pageview-quota-pay-per-click/

48 Barnhurst and Nerone, *The Form of News*; Jane B. Singer, "Who Are These Guys?" *Journalism*, 4, no. 2 (2003): 139–63.

49 William P. Cassidy, "Outside Influences," *First Monday*, 13, no. 1 (2008), http://firstmonday.org/htbin/cgiwrap/bin/ojs/index.php/fm/article/view/2051/1922;   Tom Rosenstiel and Amy Mitchell, "The Web: Alarming, Appealing, and a Challenge to Journalistic Values," *Pew Research Center for the People & the Press and the Project for Excellence in Journalism* (2008), www.people-press.org/files/legacy-pdf/403.pdf

50 McChesney, *Digital Disconnect*; Singer, "Who Are These Guys?"

51 McChesney, *Digital Disconnect*, 193.

52 Jane Sasseen, Kenny Olmstead, and Amy Mitchell, "Digital: As Mobile Grows Rapidly, the Pressures on News Intensify," *Pew State of the News Media* (2013), http://stateofthemedia.org/2013/digital-as-mobile-grows-rapidly-the-pressures-on-news-intensify/

53 Lewis Dvorkin, "Inside Forbes: Before It Was Called Native Advertising, a Team in a 'Box' Had an Idea," *Forbes*, 4 February 2013, www.forbes.com/sites/lewisdvorkin/2013/02/04/inside-forbes-before-it-was-called-native-advertising-a-team-in-a-box-had-an-idea/

54 Lucia Moses, "After Scientology Debacle, The Atlantic Tightens Native Ad Guidelines," *Adweek*, 30 January 2013, www.adweek.com/news/advertising-branding/after-scientology-debacle-atlantic-tightens-native-ad-guidelines-146890

55 Edward Wyatt, "As Online Ads Look More Like News Articles, F.T.C. Warns Against Deception," *The New York Times*, 4 December 2013, www.nytimes.com/2013/12/05/business/ftc-says-sponsored-online-ads-can-be-misleading.html

56 David Carr, "Storytelling Ads May Be Journalism's New Peril," *The New York Times*, 15 September 2013, www.nytimes.com/2013/09/16/business/media/storytelling-ads-may-be-journalisms-new-peril.html

57 Cameron and Ju-Pak, "Information Pollution."

58 Tracie Powell, "Native Ads Aren't As Clear As Outlets Think," *Columbia Journalism Review*, 5 December 2013, www.cjr.org/behind_the_news/ftc_workshop_on_sponsored_cont.php

59 Jay Rosen, Twitter, 21 December 2013, https://twitter.com/jayrosen_nyu/status/414572505194459136

60 Jeff Sonderman and Millie Tran, "Understanding the Rise of Sponsored Content," *American Press Institute*, 13 November 2013, www.americanpressinstitute.org/publications/reports/white-papers/understanding-rise-sponsored-content/

61 Jeff Jarvis, "In the End Was the Word and the Word Was the Sponsor's," *Medium*, 29 May 2013, https://medium.com/whither-news/72c32793244f

62 Wyatt, "As Online Ads."

63 Sonderman and Tran, "Understanding the Rise of Sponsored Content."

64 Todd Wasserman, "Why Native Advertising Is the Opposite of Porn," *Mashable*, 25 September 2013, http://mashable.com/2013/09/25/native-advertising-porn/

65 Carr, "Storytelling Ads"; Jarvis, "In the End Was the Word."
66 Margaret Sullivan, "Pledging Clarity, The *Times* Plunges Into Native Advertising," *The New York Times*, 19 December 2013, http://publiceditor.blogs.nytimes.com/2013/12/19/pledging-clarity-the-times-plunges-into-native-advertising/
67 Sullivan, "Pledging Clarity."
68 C.W. Anderson, "Between Creative and Quantified Audiences," *Journalism*, 12, no. 5 (2011): 550–66.
69 Michelle Ferrier, "Media Entrepreneurship," *Journalism & Mass Communication Educator*, 68, no. 3 (2013): 222–41; Dena Levitz, "How News Orgs Break Down the Editorial-Business Wall, Ethically," *PBS MediaShift*, 8 November 2012, www.pbs.org/mediashift/2012/11/how-news-orgs-break-down-the-editorial-business-wall-ethically313/
70 Ferrier, "Media Entrepreneurship."
71 Levitz, "How News Orgs Break Down."
72 Ferrier, "Media Entrepreneurship."
73 Jeff Jarvis, "Journalism's Leaky Condom," *BuzzMachine*, 8 October 2010, http://buzzmachine.com/2010/10/08/journalisms-leaky-condom/; Levitz, "How News Orgs Break Down"; Matt Thompson, "Why Journalists Should Explore the Business Side of News," *Poynter*, 4 December 2012, www.poynter.org/how-tos/career-development/196857/why-journalists-should-explore-the-business-side-of-the-newsroom/
74 Jarvis, "Journalism's Leaky Condom."
75 Hallin, "The Passing of the 'High Modernism'."

Chapter 5

Creating proper distance through networked infrastructure

Examining Google Glass for evidence of moral, journalistic witnessing

Mike Ananny

Introduction

In 1937, radio journalist Herbert Morrison interrupted his own recording of the *Hindenburg*'s arrival in Lakehurst, NJ, to report that the ship had exploded into flames. Breaking their long-standing rules against broadcasting recorded material, NBC and CBS aired Morrison's report,[1] marking a turn in the modern history of journalistic witnessing. This history would go on to include the live or near-live reporting of events like the Challenger explosion, the Rodney King beating, O.J. Simpson's slow chase through Los Angeles, U.S. invasions of Iraq, the 9/11 attacks,[2] Kenya's election violence,[3] and the Middle East and North African uprisings.[4] Alongside this history sits a story of innovation as both the tools and techniques of journalistic storytelling reflected broader cultural and technological changes. Reporters now tell stories faster, from farther away, and increasingly alongside audiences who describe feeling immersed in and affected by events that they once had to wait weeks to learn about.

Indeed, journalists are often called upon to be thoughtful avatars: "To be their audience's eyes and ears in situations where individuals less determined to seek out the truth would do well to avoid,"[5] *and* to "convince publics of [a] distant experience or event in a seemingly unmediated style."[6] Especially in the context of contemporary, networked news work – in which journalists' traditions of professional control encounter increasingly active audiences shaping news independently[7] – journalists occupy multiple spaces at once. Sometimes, they must melt into the background as professional observers (proxies in the service of audiences demanding quality information with which to form opinions), but at other times they must foreground their own interpretations (advocating for why issues *should* matter to audiences who still need journalistic guidance). Studying journalistic witnessing thus means studying the boundaries of news work – analyzing how journalists straddle, shift between, and mix their roles as "individual interpreters" creating compelling narratives and their identities as "professional communicators" equipping audiences with information.[8] But these styles of witnessing are not just personal achievements; they exist within a field of cultural, organizational, and technological forces that make them possible and signal their acceptability.

This chapter explores how journalistic witnessing means traversing boundaries between observing or reporting, avoiding or assuming risk, getting close or staying distant, live coverage or post hoc analysis. These are complicated, porous boundaries that have both ideological and material dimensions because they touch on normative underpinnings (assumptions about journalistic witnessing as professional and objective) and media conditions (tools and techniques for representing spaces to audiences). As journalists adopt and respond to the immersive possibilities of media technologies they leave clues about what they think moral, journalistic witnessing means in any given era – what "proper distance"[9] is for journalism. Proper distance requires configuring boundaries, thoughtfully encoding separations and dependencies into the information systems and ethical standards that bring events, journalists, and audiences together to create moral witnessing.

This paper examines how one emerging tool, Google Glass, sits at the intersection of multiple journalistic boundaries of witnessing. I ground the analysis in scholarship on the concept of witnessing, describe the idea of journalistic witnessing, propose the concept of "networked witnessing," and suggest its tracing in Google Glass's user interface, technical documentation, and early adopter discourse.

The idea of witnessing: Three questions

Although the literature on witnessing is vast and diverse, three interrelated questions continue to be asked: Who qualifies as a witness? What does witnessing demand of media? And what is witnessing meant to accomplish? In Peters'[10] oft-cited formulation, witnessing entails a person performing for others: "the witness (speech-act) of the witness (person) was witnessed (by an audience)." Tracing which speech-acts, which people, and which audiences are implicated in witnessing is a perennial concern for any given era of media technology.

Who qualifies as a witness?

Fundamentally, witnessing requires a *person*: someone acting as an "observer or source possessing privileged (raw, authentic) proximity to facts."[11] Someone's proximity to an event is roughly proportional to her legitimacy as a witness since the farther from a scene she is, the more likely she is to depend upon the observations of others. A witness's *physical* presence signals serious commitment and a singular investment. Similarly, witnesses need to be present at the moment an event happens. It is less authentic for a witness to attend after the fact because, like physical distance, temporal distance prevents someone from making the kind of first-hand, real-time observations often seen as the most powerful evidence for influencing future events.[12]

Witnesses also articulate experiences. Often invoked in studies of Holocaust witnessing – to distinguish among people who saw and perished from atrocities, survivors who observed but were rendered mute, and those who saw and recounted their experiences[13] – witnesses are those who are willing and able to translate observations into accounts. They must be *visible*, trusted documentarians who convince others to pay attention – not simply telling compelling stories, but *embodying* the reliability of their testimonies by earning respect in places (e.g., courtrooms, religious institutions, media narratives) that pass moral judgments on events.[14]

Some notions of witnessing go further, expecting witnesses to risk, if not incur, bodily harm.[15] The "*moral* witness," Margalit[16] (emphasis added) writes, "should himself be at personal risk, whether he is a sufferer or just an observer of the suffering that comes from evil-doing."[17] The ideal witness is thus not only physically present, articulate, and institutionally validated, but an embodiment of risk and harm – with religious martyrs as the ultimate trusted witnesses because the "body is authenticity's last refuge in situations of structural doubt."[18]

What does witnessing demand of media?

To *witness* means to experience a personal point of view and then communicate that experience to an absent audience that is relying on your observations to form opinions. In modern eras, this communication entails creating, circulating, and interpreting media – enabling "mediated witnessing"[19] in which witnesses achieve proximity to an event through first-hand mediated representations of it. Indeed, mediated witnessing is often invoked by first-hand witnesses defending themselves against charges of privacy infringement – they see their incursions as *principled* because they contribute to a *system* of mediated witnessing that would be impossible without their recordings. Rejecting the criterion of bodily investment, they claim that such representations can help audience members be witnesses akin to first-hand observers who were present and risked harm.

Indeed, Ashuri and Pinchevski[20] argue that the kind of witnessing required to manage the large-scale social relationships of contemporary, networked life requires: *eye*-witnesses; *mediators* (who create, edit, and circulate media); and *audiences* (spectators who judge accounts and potentially take action because of them). Witnessing, they argue, is a *field* of forces and agents each with different "abilities, interests, and resources" and "operating according to sets of norms and rules."[21] The field of mediated witnessing today is so well populated by observers, media and audiences, it is impossible *not* to witness – people cannot claim to be ignorant of events because they did not see them themselves.[22]

Such a claim, though, needs to be critiqued in light of the structural features of contemporary media environments. Although there is a great deal of media, echo chambers can be filled with homogenous content,[23] filter bubbles can prevent new information from surfacing,[24] platforms can limit conversational styles,[25] and people can purposefully avoid new information[26] or fail to attend to available media.[27] We may not have the chance to be mediated witnesses if search engines, recommendation algorithms, social networks, or personal preferences do not allow media to surface.

For those media that do make it to us, there is the question of whether interpreting media is ethically inferior to first-hand witnessing. Chouliaraki describes a "pessimistic" view of mediated witnessing in which technology is seen to "distort the authenticity of the represented event," bracketing spectators within "the safety of their own living rooms," and "rendering the scene of suffering as small as the television screen itself."[28] The "optimistic" view, though, sees mediated witnessing as a "celebration of communitarianism" in which viewers experience "intimacy at a distance" with far-off sufferers. Such intimacy creates a *potential* "democratization of responsibility" for the conditions that made the suffering possible in the first place.[29] Instead of creating a test for witnessing that depends upon physical proximity and bodily risk, mediated witnessing asks the more pragmatic question of how *seeing* what a witness saw might bring about change: "[C]an we *act* on what we now know?"[30] Mediated witnessing is legitimate if it impacts the events that required witnessing in the first place.

What is witnessing meant to accomplish?

Mediated witnessing must create *meaningful* change. Chouliaraki[31] suggests differentiating between "representations of suffering that may simply bring a tear to a spectator's eye and those that may actually make a difference in the sufferers' lives." In this model, witnessing is storytelling with a purpose: it helps people separate mundane from important events; it helps people create memories that anchor them in time; and it distinguishes among types of suffering.

First, witnesses and mediators must decide which events to record and which media to circulate – to help audiences distinguish "mundane" events[32] from those that are meaningfully unusual, morally outrageous, and deserving focused attention. The contemporary proliferation of media makes it possible for "the monstrous and the mundane [to] occupy the same space" – and for the mundane to dominate.[33] Witnessing makes distinctions – it helps the *field* of moral witnessing pass a pragmatic test[34] by showing how the world would be *meaningfully* different if an event was seen as significant and worthy of attention, not simply mundane and ignored. This is how witnessing exercises "moral and cultural force."[35] But asking for too many events to be witnessed can create "compassion fatigue"[36] – an "apathetic spectator [can become] reconciled with the presence of evil," seeing "the injustice of suffering as an inevitable condition of life."[37] To avoid witnessing that is mundane or fatiguing, it needs to be edited, curated, moderated.

Second, mediated witnessing can create what Tenenboim-Weinblatt[38] calls retrospective and prospective memories. Attending to media events commonly seen as significant can help place people in timelines longer than their own lifespan: they can imagine being part of the historical events that shaped their present circumstances and they can envision how their actions relate to future conditions. Mediated witnessing thus serves a *public* function as people imagine themselves part of constituencies larger than what they are personally able to experience.

Finally, witnessing can distinguish among types of sufferers, construing some as "worthy of our pity and others as unworthy of it,"[39] helping people determine "why *this* suffering is important and what we can do about it."[40] Though harsh, such selectivity can create the kind of conceptual, "proper distance" that Silverstone[41] says ethical uses of media create and sustain. Such distance, he argues, helps people see their own privilege so they might alleviate suffering – a perspective that too much intimacy or perceived similarity makes impossible. Proper distance can also help people see the value of sustaining differences, making them pause before intervening to question whether they truly have the moral standing to change another person's life.

Journalistic witnessing and proper distance

Mediated witnessing is not about reporting events as closely as possible, about immersing audiences as deeply as possible, or about creating change as quickly as possible. It is instead about understanding how boundaries within a field of actors – first-hand witnesses, media technologies, storytellers, audiences, victims – influence how people understand their responsibilities to others and respect their differences from them. Instead of simply using new technologies to immerse observers in distant, real-time events – collapsing spatial and temporal separations between audiences and victims – journalists might actually *create* boundaries that give the *field* of witnessing the time and space it needs to create the proper distance that moral witnessing demands.

But when journalists *create* boundaries they act as advocates. When they enact boundaries they implicitly acknowledge a distinction between witnessing (reporting for a distant audience that would be there if it could) and *moral* witnessing (advocating for an outcome to audiences through their reporting). The moral journalist *justifiably* intrudes upon "the suffering of others with the aim of changing the witnessed reality."[42] Instead of intruding to guarantee a public right to know, the moral journalist intrudes in order to bear responsibility for witnessed events.[43] Her goal is not simply to inform audiences but to *compel* them: testifying "to what it *feels like* to see, and to what seeing means and requires of the witness."[44] This type of journalism requires not just observation – "seeing does not necessarily compel responsibility"[45] – but involvement, justifying infringements upon privacy in order to create and circulate media that impact events.

Journalistic witnessing is frequently defined as *live* reporting. Often seen as the epitome of connecting audiences and events,[46] live reports have an authenticity that comes from reporters' real-time proximity to events; the unpredictability of broadcasting events outside of newsrooms; and the reporter's enforced humility as she is forced to make sense of events alongside audiences.[47] Live reporting is also perceived by audiences as logistically challenging, letting news organizations demonstrate their technological sophistication.[48]

But journalistic witnessing premised on live reporting is widely criticized as unnecessary and contrary to the profession's mission of explaining what events *mean*. Indeed, too much live journalism makes it difficult to distinguish between the mundane and the significant, creating compassion fatigue. Katz describes CNN's abundant use of live, on-site reporting as adding up to "nonstop information without interpretation, and nonstop interpretation without information."[49] Wang, Lee and Wang[50] empirically confirm Katz's complaint: Television journalists required to make live reports after the 2011 Japanese earthquake had far less professional autonomy than their print counterparts who had the freedom to behave more like moral journalists, describing "not only the experiences of the Japanese victims but also their *own* experiences of suffering." And live reporting does not necessarily make "everyday" people more visible: Livingston and Bennett[51] find that even when journalists use mobile video technologies to create live coverage of "unpredicted, nonscripted, spontaneous" events, they still rely heavily on official sources to frame and interpret events.

Recalling Silverstone's[52] concept of "proper distance," we might ask how *journalistic* witnessing not only disseminates information about events, but also distributes responsibility for them among the boundaries of networked journalism.[53] As the contemporary, networked press becomes distributed among various people, locations, and technologies,[54] traditional journalistic actors lose their hold on the norms and dynamics of witnessing. As the press becomes a boundary-spanning phenomenon, so too does journalistic witnessing.[55]

Materiality, infrastructure and the borders of networked witnessing

What exactly do these boundaries of journalism look like? How do they afford and constrain witnessing? And what do we need to know about them in order to make normative interventions into the kind of contemporary, journalistic witnessing so intertwined with digital materiality? These are precisely the kind of questions that scholars of science and technology studies (STS) grapple with as they trace the political meanings of information infrastructures – the materiality of seemingly neutral design decisions that make certain people and ideas more visible than others. Following Leonardi,[56] I mean "material" as both instantiation and significance; some ideas take *form* and some ideas *matter*. By examining the "platforms, technological innovations, and reflective procedures" of witnessing across institutional environments, as Givoni[57] suggests, we can trace how well theorists' *ideals* of witnessing appear in *systems* for witnessing.

These mentions of platforms, innovations, and reflections echo how STS traces phenomena across boundaries and human-object divisions. Latour's actor-network theory boldly positions non-human artifacts as "full-fledged social actors"[58] that, in concert with other actants, make relationships among people and ideas visible, that are usually hidden and assumed.[59] Understanding the contemporary "field of witnessing" that Ashuri and Pinchevski[60] describe means accounting for the networks of socio-materiality that constitute contemporary witnessing. Indeed, such witnessing might be called *networked* witnessing because the normative dynamics of concern to theorists of witnessing live in systems that surface,[61] associate,[62] attend to,[63] and make publicly relevant[64] the events, people, and ideas rendered in media.

How do networks afford witnessing? More specifically: how do different configurations of human/non-human actor-networks create the conditions under which events are instantiated in media *and* judged to be significant – that is, become *material*? And, within the narrower context of journalism: how well does the mix of "institutional platforms, technological innovations, and reflective procedures"[65] meet the normative demands of *moral* witnessing that helps people be both responsible to and respectful of each other?

In the spirit of actor-network methodologies that ascribe agency to non-human actors[66] and infrastructure studies that trace how knowledge work spans cultural, professional and material boundaries,[67] I trace the construction of "proper distance" through a close reading of Google Glass's user interface, technical documentation, and early-adopter discourse. What clues do such materials give about how journalistic witnessing spans the physical, technological, and rhetorical boundaries that Glass creates? And how does Glass's infrastructure complicate and challenge traditional norms of journalistic witnessing? How might the dynamics of "proper distance" in contemporary, journalistic witnessing be different because of the new borders and boundaries that Glass creates?

Analyzing an infrastructure for networked journalistic witnessing: Google Glass

First made available to selected people in the U.S. in April 2012 – "Glass Explorers" who paid approximately $1,500[68] – Google Glass is essentially a computational display mounted on an eyeglass frame and connected through a digital tether to a mobile phone's Internet service. Through a combination of touch, voice, and gestural commands, Glass users can capture images, record video, access websites, compose text messages, and perform a variety of other computational tasks common on smart phones. Although the default duration of video recording is approximately 10 seconds (due to limited battery life, Google claims), Explorers report recording for as long as 45 minutes. To take a picture or record video, Glass users must say a command – "OK Glass, record a video" – or touch the Glass frame, illuminating the Glass display and making "it clear to those around the device what the user is doing."[69] After agreeing to terms of service and obtaining a unique access key, Explorers can create Glass applications – called "glassware" – using Google's Glass Development Kit (GDK) and the Mirror Application Programming Interface (MAPI), with help from the Glass developer community, sample code, design guidelines, and discussion forums.

There is a burgeoning journalistic Glass development community. *The New York Times* developed a Google Glass application linked to its website;[70] Poynter offered a course on journalism and wearable technology in 2013,[71] and the University of Southern California offered a course on Glass journalism in the fall of 2014.[72] There is a Glass journalism Tumblr account,[73] Twitter feed,[74] and a resource website run by journalism professors;[75] and NBC producer Frank Thorp reported a day on Capitol Hill using only Google Glass.[76]

Glass is often described as a tool for journalistic storytelling or news-gathering, but little has been written about Glass and journalistic *witnessing* – examining its infrastructure for evidence of witnessing ideals. An extensive analysis of Glass in light of the entire literature on witnessing is beyond the scope of this chapter; I focus here on reading Glass for evidence of three aspects of witnessing:

- Proximity: recalling that ideal moral, journalistic witnesses are physically located in places, how does Glass infrastructure both require and reflect place-based witnessing?
- Risk: recalling that ideal moral, journalistic witnessing entails risking or suffering harm, how does Glass infrastructure require or entail risk-taking?
- Outcome: recalling that ideal moral, journalistic witnessing results in actions that alleviate suffering, how does Glass infrastructure encourage impact on – not simply recording of – witnessed events?

To trace these ideals across Glass, I conducted close readings of the following: approximately 75 popular press articles and Google promotional media selected for their descriptions of the Glass interface and user experience; Google's[77] technical documentation on the "Glass Development Kit" and "Mirror API" (including guides on how to design user interfaces, how to authorize access to the camera, how to sense location, etc.); online forums populated by early-stage Glass innovators, called "Explorers," as well as software programmers creating applications for Google Glass.[78]

The aim in studying these materials is three-fold. First, to understand Glass as a material object, a technology that enables media capture critical for mediated witnessing. Second, for insight into the kind of functions and uses that the software development environment officially supports: the design principles, best practices and code samples known to play a role in how software engineers design and execute projects.[79] Finally, for insight into the aspirations and

Table 5.1 Google Glass

	Infrastructural element		
	User interface	*Technical documentation*	*Early adopter discourse*
Witnessing ideal: Proximity	Glass is designed to be worn on the face, making it extremely difficult to use *without* being close to it; the form factor tightly couples the user and device. Data overlays can be placed over the users' views, letting them be *virtually* connected to other locations. Voice commands, gestures, and small lights that initiate and indicate audio-visual media capture are perceived close-up, making it difficult for those further away to know they are being recorded.	Glass users can be tracked with GPS signals, cell towers, WiFi routers, and near-field methods using Bluetooth and gravity, acceleration, and gyroscope sensors. Location sensing taxes the battery so documentation advises limited use. Augmented navigation gives turn-by-turn directions to indexed locations or latitude/longitude coordinates; "geo-fencing" lets users receive updates about locations when they enter particular places; and, with authorization, users' last known locations can be retrieved.	Discussion of proximity focuses on: 1) how those unfamiliar with Glass misunderstand location sensing and recording signals; 2) how most people are too boring to record; 3) Glass's similarity to existing, mainstream technologies like mobile phones that track locations and record people; 4) places they were asked to remove Glass, or were ejected from them for wearing Glass.
Witnessing ideal: Risk	Although like traditional glasses, Glass's identifiable form can make wearers targets of those who want to avoid being recorded, or who understand how Glass records, or who know Glass's ability to privately display real-time information about people, locations, and events. The interface makes sensory demands, overlaying data on a wearer's field of vision and transmitting sound through bone-conducting speakers.	Requiring voice commands or gestures to start audio-video recording (and displaying lights while recording) makes recording visible. In contrast to standard data overlays designed to keep wearers aware of their surroundings, specialized Glass experiences called 'immersions' take over Glass's display and demand sustained focus.	Discussion of risk focuses on: 1) negative reactions and threats of violence from non-wearers, who wearers see as naïve; 2) customizing Glass for particular contexts (e.g., a "driving mode" to limit information overload). Except discussion of an incident in which a Glass wearer recorded an arrest and the social risks of being ostracized for wearing Glass publicly, there is little discussion of risks.

Table 5.1 (continued)

	Infrastructural element		
	User interface	*Technical documentation*	*Early adopter discourse*
Witnessing ideal: Outcome	The interface affords three types of outcomes: 1) Glass can provide access to relevant information during a crisis situation; 2) Glass's form factor lets others know who is wearing Glass; 3) Glass recordings are from first-person, eye-level points of view that mimic an audience member's perspective.	Designers are encouraged to create glassware for "increased engagement" in physical settings. A "fire-and-forget" model encourages users to "start actions quickly and continue with what they're doing." Google's sample Glass applications (compass, stopwatch, timer) mention no contexts or outcomes.	The sub-discussion 'Usage Scenarios' describes helpful or enjoyable data overlays. Much discussion focuses on alleviating negative outcomes of wearing Glass, how to avoid being banned or socially ostracized for wearing Glass, and how to reform laws and social norms discouraging Glass.

beliefs of early adopters defining Glass norms: how they propose, critique, and champion features while supporting each other in the face of critics (who often call Explorers "Glassholes" and "Glasstards"). While certainly not describing the entire Glass infrastructure – much would be gained from interviewing Glass designers and Google program managers and analyzing Glassware – these three types of materials offer insights into how the Glass infrastructure affords and constrains ideals of witnessing. The chart below summarizes the analysis of materials (user interface, technical documentation, early adopter discourse) for evidence of the ideals of witnessing (proximity, risk, outcome).

Glass's governance of proximity, risk, outcome

A close reading of Glass's infrastructure elements reveals patterns in how its sociotechnical boundaries structure the proximity, risk, and outcomes that theorists argue are key for moral, journalistic witnessing.

Proximity

Glass governs proximity in three principal ways. First, it *forces closeness* by collapsing boundaries between witnesses and recording devices, tightly coupling them. Remote recording is practically impossible and the gestures and signals that start and indicate Glass recording can only be observed at a relatively close distance. Only those close to Glass and literate with its gestural controls can be fully aware of recording. Second, Glass data overlays create *private, hybrid proximities* that span virtual/physical boundaries; Glass wearers can be simultaneously present in other, virtual locations. Although they share the same physical space as others and have the same information access as observers with mobile phones, the Glass's data-augmented views *situate* Glass wearers in space differently.

Understanding a Glass witness's presence means noting not only their physical proximity to events, but knowing how that proximity is influenced by data-augmented views that only they have. Although live-streaming of Glass video (not technologically feasible with the current version of Glass) makes it possible for *mediated* witnesses to access the Glass wearer's personal, eye-level camera, non-Glass witnesses in the same physical space have little insight into this other, Glass-mediated environment. Finally, Glass *indexes* the space of witnessing. Its GPS directions make it easy to navigate to, observe at, and geocode media within locations indexed by Google Maps – and difficult to do all of these things at locations *not* visible to Google Maps. Although Glass's technical architecture makes it easy to find places, track observations, and geocode recordings, Glass wearers report strong social pressures that prevent them from accessing locations when wearing Glass. Glass's *technological* power to navigate and index space is tempered by *cultural* forces that eject Glass wearers from those very spaces.

Risk

Glass may both ameliorate and exacerbate risk of harm that scholars describe as integral to moral witnessing. First, Glass may *insulate* wearers from risk, erecting a protective boundary between a wearer and her environment. People who recognize Glass's power to record media – or who mistakenly ascribe technical features beyond its capabilities like indefinite, live-streamed video recording – may be less likely to harm Glass wearers and those around them because of the surveillance. Glass wearers are also able to access virtual information and navigate using heads-up, turn-by-turn GPS directions, maintaining a heads-up physical presence with different knowledge than those without Glass. Glass, though, may heighten the risk of harm. Glass users may find themselves unprepared to interpret a scene, represent an audience, record media, or navigate a space if they lose their cellular internet connection and are left without Glass's augmentations. Glass wearers may also be targeted *because* of Glass's ability to record media, with harassers focusing on Glass wearers either because they fear its recording capabilities or imagine features beyond its functionality. If data overlays and immersions demand too much attention or are insensitive to particular contexts, Glass witnesses may lack the situational awareness needed to perceive and avoid harm. Similarly, unlike hidden audio recorders or surreptitiously aimed mobile phone cameras, Google's requirement that wearers gesture to start recording and illuminate the display while recording makes it difficult for Glass mediated witnessing to go unnoticed.

As a boundary object, Glass spans instrumental and symbolic forms of risk. Instrumentally, Glass wearers can capture and disseminate recordings of wrongdoing, acquire web-based knowledge about locations while maintaining heads-up awareness, and navigate quickly to safer locations. But Glass may also represent the very *idea* of surveillance and audience oversight in high-risk situations, setting expectations or inviting judgment because of the oversight and accountability Glass and their wearers may represent.

Outcome

Glass's infrastructure is largely silent on how and why to impact surrounding places and events – when to break the boundaries between observation and intervention, a key feature of moral witnessing. The technical documentation cautions against interfering with a wearer's activities, telling designers to avoid "immersions" that require the wearer's complete attention. It advocates a "fire-and-forget" design principle that aims *not* to affect wearers' behaviors, and offers only generic Glassware examples designed without awareness of the wearer's physical environment. Most of the discourse about outcomes among early adopters focuses on Glass itself – primarily how to minimize the social stigmas associated with wearing it – not what outcomes might be achieved *with* Glass. Curiously, the discussion of Glass's limited battery life, relatively small memory capacity and often unreliable internet connection, is reminiscent of Ellis's[80] requirement that moral witnesses distinguish between "mundane" and important events: many forum comments encourage Explorers to be selective and thoughtful in their recording, recording only things "that count."

Though speculative and requiring further empirical study, Glass may help facilitate interventions of the kind that witnessing theorists call for. A wearer with access to heads-up information about events may be able to more knowledgeably or confidently influence events they observer; bystanders who notice Glass wearers in the area may change *their* behavior as they (rightly or mistakenly) assume that their presence is being monitored and recorded; audiences seeing video of events recorded through Glass's first-person, eye-level camera may empathize with events differently than they do through other media recordings; and Glass wearers themselves may feel a different kind of responsibility to influence events or record for audiences because of the device's unique technological features and the significance others ascribe to it.

Conclusion

In their recent essay "Media Witnessing and the Ripeness of Time," Frosh and Pinchevski[81] argue that we have entered a new era of witnessing in which recorded events are available for immediate and widespread interpretation; ad-hoc communities of attention arise quickly and without formal organization to assess the significance of events; and "cosmopolitan risk publics ... perceive their commonality through representations of shared vulnerability." Contemporary witnessing depends upon how speed, presence, interpretation, community, and vulnerability are encoded by "hybrid assemblages of human and technological agents with shifting boundaries that defy traditional models of mass communication."[82]

Glass journalists may separate themselves from what they see differently than other journalists – seeming to be present and personally invested because they have no overtly visible media tools, but behaving more like embodied avatars as their observations are shaped by and for invisible audiences visible only through Glass. Glass may also become a boundary object for news technology design as app designers and early adopters embed their own assumptions about what journalistic witnessing *should* be as they create Glass apps that govern proximity, risk, and outcomes. As journalists take up, respond to and adapt such boundary objects in practice, they may reveal new types of hybrid techno-journalistic *practice*, reinterpreting the meanings of long-standing journalistic concepts like objectivity, storytelling, and embeddedness as they report with Glass. Indeed, Glass's augmented reality data overlays may blur boundaries between what it means to observe "naturally" occurring scenes. As Glass journalists use the technology to navigate spaces, research events, surveil sources, and link to real-time audiences, it becomes difficult to see them as traditional reporters – they may change the very thing being witnessed, observing from a privileged, data-infused position fundamentally different from others in the space or journalists working without Glass. Glass's novelty may make journalists *less* able to stay in background, observational roles if Glass-literate bystanders lobby them to influence real-time events by linking to and immersing real-time witnessing audiences. Indeed, this may further erode the *temporal* boundaries that have traditionally separated reporters and audiences – letting distant witnesses not only *see* events in real-time, but allowing journalists to *influence* events as the embodied representations of distant, witnessing audiences who wish they had a physical presence.

Finally, if wearable technologies like Glass become more commonplace among journalists, it may spur a public debate about what kind of boundaries journalists *should* preserve. As audiences understand Glass better, will they expect Glass journalists to be more cognizant and thoughtful about how wearable technologies blur traditional distinctions – e.g., affording sources anonymity, eschewing real-time audience feedback, taking Glass off at key moments, labeling reporting as Glass reliant, demanding Google's policies that directly address *journalistic* meanings of confidentiality, avoiding excessive immersion that may lead to audience compassion fatigue? And as a tool that both citizens and reporters alike might use for witnessing, infrastructures like Glass may become not just boundary objects, but boundary *infrastructures*[83] – spaces for normative contestation, to debate what mobile, wearable, real-time journalism *should* look like.

As Glass evolves and eventually becomes obsolete, it is crucial to understand how systems like it act as sociotechnical infrastructures through which audiences and journalists alike negotiate the meaning of "proper distance." Witnessing means traversing boundaries: discovering how you are like or unlike, responsible to or detached from, other people and events. The moral value of such boundary work to witnessing depends not upon simply immersing audiences in far-off places or transmitting news to them as quickly as possible, but upon helping them see the power they have to intervene and the responsibilities they have to doing so thoughtfully. Moral, mediated, contemporary witnessing of the kind that Glass affords might better be described as *networked witnessing*. It emerges from intertwined social, technological, and normative forces that bring audiences close to events, show them why events matter, and help them decide what, if anything, to do about them. It is thus the same type of boundary work that continually makes and remakes journalistic witnessing in any given era.

Notes

1 Edward Bliss, *Now the News* (New York, NY: Columbia University Press, 1991).
2 Barbie Zelizer, "On 'Having Been There': 'Eyewitnessing' as a Journalistic Key Word," *Critical Studies in Media Communication* 24, no. 5 (2007): 408–28.

3 Patrick Meier and Kate Brodock, "Crisis Mapping Kenya's Election Violence: Comparing Mainstream News, Citizen Journalism and Ushahidi," http://irevolution.net/2008/10/23/mapping-kenyas-election-violence/ (accessed April 1, 2014).

4 Andy Carvin, *Distant Witness: Social Media, the Arab Spring and a Journalism Revolution* (New York, NY: CUNY Journalism Press, 2013).

5 Stuart Allan, *Citizen Witnessing* (Cambridge, UK: Polity, 2013), 11.

6 Zelizer, "On 'Having Been There,'" 424.

7 Seth C. Lewis, "The Tension between Professional Control and Open Participation: Journalism and its Boundaries," *Information, Communication & Society* 15, no. 6 (2012): 836–66.

8 James W. Carey, *Communication as Culture: Essays on Media and Society, Media and Popular Culture*, ed. David Thorburn (New York: Routledge, 1989).

9 Roger Silverstone, *Media and Morality: On the Rise of the Mediapolis* (Cambridge, UK: Polity Press, 2007).

10 John Durham Peters, "Witnessing," *Media, Culture & Society* 23, no. 6 (2001): 707–23.

11 Peters, "Witnessing," 709.

12 Keren Tenenboim-Weinblatt, "Bridging Collective Memories and Public Agendas: Toward a Theory of Mediated Prospective Memory," *Communication Theory* 23, no. 2 (2013): 91–111.

13 Paul Frosh and Amit Pinchevski, "Introduction: Why Media Witnessing? Why Now?" in *Media Witnessing: Testimony in the Age of Mass Communication*, eds Paul Frosh and Amit Pinchevski (New York, NY: Palgrave, 2011).

14 Peters, "Witnessing".

15 Matt Carlson, "War Journalism and the 'Kia Journalist': The Cases of David Bloom and Michael Kelly," *Critical Studies in Media Communication* 23, no. 2 (2006): 91–111.

16 Avishai Margalit, *The Ethics of Memory* (Cambridge, UK: Cambridge University Press, 2002), 150.

17 Tamar Ashuri and Amit Pinchevski, "Witnessing as a Field," in *Media Witnessing: Testimony in the Age of Mass Communication*, eds Paul Frosh and Amit Pinchevski (New York, NY: Palgrave, 2011), 135.

18 Peters, "Witnessing".

19 Frosh and Pinchevski, "Introduction: Why Media Witnessing? Why Now?"; John Ellis, *Seeing Things: Television in the Age of Uncertainty* (London, UK: I.B. Tauris, 2000).

20 Ashuri and Pinchevski, "Witnessing as a Field".

21 Ashuri and Pinchevski, "Witnessing as a Field," 136.

22 Luc Boltanski, *Distant Suffering: Morality, Media and Politics* (Cambridge, UK: Cambridge University Press, 1999).

23 Cass Sunstein, *Republic.Com 2.0* (Princeton, NJ: Princeton University Press, 2009).

24 Eli Pariser, *The Filter Bubble* (New York, NY: Penguin Press, 2011).

25 Aaron Shaw and Yochai Benkler, "A Tale of Two Blogospheres: Discursive Practices on the Left and Right," *American Behavioral Scientist* 56, no. 4 (2012): 459–87.

26 R. Kelly Garrett, "Echo Chambers Online?: Politically Motivated Selective Exposure among Internet News Users," *Journal of Computer-Mediated Communication* 14, no. 2 (2009): 265–85.

27 James G. Webster and Thomas B. Ksiazek, "The Dynamics of Audience Fragmentation: Public Attention in an Age of Digital Media," *Journal of Communication* 62 (2012): 39–56.

28 Lilie Chouliaraki, *The Spectatorship of Suffering* (London, UK: Sage Publications, 2006), 24–25.

29 Chouliaraki, *The Spectatorship of Suffering*, 20–28.
30 Chouliaraki, *The Spectatorship of Suffering*, 18.
31 Chouliaraki, *The Spectatorship of Suffering*, 7.
32 John Ellis, "Mundane Witness," in *Media Witnessing: Testimony in the Age of Mass Communication*, eds P. Frosh and A. Pinchevski (New York, NY: Palgrave, 2011).
33 Ellis, "Mundane Witness," 74.
34 William James, *Pragmatism* (Indianapolis, IN: Hackett Publishing Company, 1907).
35 Peters, "Witnessing," 708.
36 Susan D. Moeller, *Compassion Fatigue: How the Media Sell Disease, Famine, War, and Death* (New York, NY: Routledge, 1999).
37 Chouliaraki, *The Spectatorship of Suffering*, 34.
38 Tenenboim-Weinblatt, "Bridging Collective Memories and Public Agendas: Toward a Theory of Mediated Prospective Memory".
39 Chouliaraki, *The Spectatorship of Suffering*, 11.
40 Chouliaraki, *The Spectatorship of Suffering*, 13.
41 Roger Silverstone, *Media and Morality: On the Rise of the Mediapolis*.
42 Carmit Wiesslitz and Tamar Ashuri, "'Moral Journalists': The Emergence of New Intermediaries of News in an Age of Digital Media", *Journalism* 12, no. 8 (2011): 1035–51.
43 Barbie Zelizer, *Remembering to Forget: Holocaust Memory through the Camera's Eye* (Chicago, IL: University of Chicago Press, 1998).
44 Sue Tait, "Bearing Witness, Journalism and Moral Responsibility," *Media, Culture & Society* 33, no. 8 (2011): 1220–35.
45 Tait, "Bearing Witness, Journalism and Moral Responsibility," 1226.
46 Daniel Dayan and Elihu Katz, *Media Events: The Live Broadcasting of History* (Cambridge, MA: Harvard University Press, 1994).
47 John Huxford, "The Proximity Paradox: Live Reporting, Virtual Proximity and the Concept of Place in the News," *Journalism* 8, no. 6 (2007): 657–74.
48 C. A. Tuggle and Suzanne Huffman, "Live News Reporting: Professional Judgment or Technological Pressure? A National Survey of Television News Directors and Senior Reporters," *Journal of Broadcasting & Electronic Media* 43, no. 4 (1999): 492–505.
49 Elihu Katz, "The End of Journalism? Notes on Watching the War," *Journal of Communication* 42, no. 3 (1992): 5–13.
50 Bess Y. Wang, Francis L. F. Lee, and Haiyan Wang, "Technological Practices, News Production Processes and Journalistic Witnessing," *Journalism Studies* 14, no. 4 (2012): 491–506.
51 Steven Livingston and W. Lance Bennett, "Gatekeeping, Indexing, and Live-Event News: Is Technology Altering the Construction of News?" *Political Communication* 20, no. 4 (2003): 363–80.
52 Roger Silverstone, *Media and Morality: On the Rise of the Mediapolis*.
53 Charlie Beckett and Robin Mansell, "Crossing Boundaries: New Media and Networked Journalism," *Communication, Culture & Critique* 1, no. 1 (2008): 92–104.
54 Mike Ananny and Kate Crawford, "A Liminal Press: Situating News App Designers within a Field of Networked News Production," *Digital Journalism* (2014).
55 Allan, *Citizen Witnessing*.
56 Paul M. Leonardi, "Digital Materiality? How Artifacts without Matter, Matter," *First Monday* 15, no. 6–7 (2010), http://firstmonday.org/ojs/index.php/fm/article/view/3036/2567
57 Michal Givoni, "The Ethics of Witnessing and the Politics of the Governed," *Theory, Culture & Society* 31, no. 1 (2013): 123–42.

58 Bruno Latour, "A Collective of Humans and Nonhumans," in *Technology and Values*, ed. Craig Hanks (Malden, MA: Wiley-Blackwell, 2010), 59.

59 Susan Leigh Star and Karen Ruhleder, "Steps toward an Ecology of Infrastructure: Design and Access for Large Information Spaces," *Information Systems Research* 7, no. 1 (1996): 111–34.

60 Ashuri and Pinchevski, "Witnessing as a Field".

61 Langdon Winner, "Upon Opening the Black Box and Finding It Empty: Social Constructivism and the Philosophy of Technology," *Science, Technology, & Human Values* 18, no. 3 (1993): 362–78.

62 Christopher A. LeDantec and Carl DiSalvo, "Infrastructuring and the Formation of Publics in Participatory Design," *Social Studies of Science* 43, no. 2 (2013): 241–64.

63 Taina Bucher, "Want to Be on Top? Algorithmic Power and the Threat of Invisibility on Facebook," *New Media & Society* 14, no. 7 (2012): 1164–80.

64 Noortje Marres, "The Issues Deserve More Credit: Pragmatist Contributions to the Study of Public Involvement in Controversy," *Social Studies of Science* 37, no. 5 (2007): 759–80.

65 Givoni, "The Ethics of Witnessing and the Politics of the Governed".

66 Edwin M. Sayes, "Actor-Network Theory and Methodology: Just What Does It Mean to Say That Nonhumans Have Agency?" *Social Studies of Science* 44, no. 1 (2014): 134–49.

67 Thomas F. Gieryn, "Boundary-Work and the Demarcation of Science from Non-Science: Strains and Interests in Professional Ideologies of Scientists," *American Sociological Review* 48, no. 6 (1983): 781–95; Katherine C. Kellogg, Wanda J. Orlikowski, and JoAnne Yates, "Life in the Trading Zone: Structuring Coordination across Boundaries in Postbureaucratic Organizations," *Organization Science* 17, no. 1 (2006): 22–44; Mike Ananny, "Press-Public Collaboration as Infrastructure: Tracing News Organizations and Programming Publics in Application Programming Interfaces," *American Behavioral Scientist* 57, no. 5 (2013): 623–42.

68 Hayley Tsukayama, "Everything You Need to Know About Google Glass," www. washingtonpost.com/blogs/the-switch/wp/2014/02/27/everything-you-need-to-know-about-google-glass/ (accessed March 11, 2014).

69 Google, "Glass FAQ," https://sites.google.com/site/glasscomms/faqs (accessed March 20, 2014).

70 Sean Hollister, "Google Reveals Glass Apps: New York Times, Evernote, Gmail, and Path," www.theverge.com/2013/3/11/4091426/google-teases-path-skitch-new-york-times-on-project-glass (accessed March 1, 2014).

71 Poynter News University, "Preparing Journalism for the Age of Wearable Devices," www.newsu.org/mobile-wearables (accessed April 1, 2014).

72 Kristen Hare, "Usc Offers Course on 'Glass Journalism'," www.poynter.org/latest-news/mediawire/244697/usc-offers-course-on-glass-journalism/ (accessed March 26, 2014).

73 Robert Hernandez, "Glass Journalism," http://glassjournalism.tumblr.com/ (accessed April 1, 2014).

74 Robert Hernandez, "Glass Journalism," https://twitter.com/GlassJournalism (accessed April 8, 2014).

75 Jeremy Littau, Jennifer Ware, and Chip Stewart, "Glass Journalism," http://glass journalism.com/ (accessed April 1, 2013).

76 Frank Thorp, "NBC Producer Covers Capitol Hill with Google Glass," www. nbcnews.com/video/nbc-news/52820576#52820576 (accessed April 1, 2014).

77 Google, "Google Mirror API Overview," https://developers.google.com/glass/develop/mirror/ (accessed March 2, 2014); Google, "Glass Development Kit," https://develop ers.google.com/glass/develop/gdk/ (accessed April 2, 2014).

78 Google, "Glass Developers," https://plus.google.com/communities/105104639432156 353586 (accessed April 3, 2014); Google, "Glass Explorers," https://plus.google.com/ communities/107405100380970813362 (accessed April 3, 2014); Stack Overflow, "Google Mirror API," http://stackoverflow.com/questions/tagged/google-mirror-api (accessed April 8, 2014).

79 Matthew Fuller, ed., *Software Studies: A Lexicon* (Cambridge, MA: MIT Press, 2008).

80 Ellis, "Mundane Witness".

81 Paul Frosh and Amit Pinchevski, "Media Witnessing and the Ripeness of Time," *Cultural Studies* 28, no. 4 (2014): 594–610.

82 Frosh and Pinchevski, "Media Witnessing and the Ripeness of Time," 594.

83 Geoffrey C. Bowker and Susan Leigh Star, *Sorting Things Out: Classification and its Consequences* (Cambridge, MA: The MIT Press, 1999), 287.

Chapter 6

Hard news/soft news

The hierarchy of genres and the boundaries of the profession

Helle Sjøvaag

Introduction

The boundary between hard and soft news is the dividing line that separates one of the strongest dichotomies of news production. Within the sociological approach to news, journalism is often described as a broad practice ranging beyond political reporting and in-depth investigation to also include lifestyle, celebrity culture, health journalism, traffic reports, and even sports. Here, news is defined as the daily reporting of the large and small events that either challenge or affirm our concepts of normalcy. News is often thought of as disruptions, but typically, news is rather about confirmation.[1] Disruptions are primarily communicated as hard news – such as war reporting, political exposure or investigative journalism. Affirmations primarily come in the form of soft news – entertainment, features and human-interest stories, family life, consumer journalism, and sports. The hard-and-soft dichotomy therefore reflects the hierarchy that separates the higher and lower forms of journalistic genres, professional practices, ethical issues, and journalism's potential socio-democratic impact.

Hard and soft news in the Norwegian context

While this dichotomy in many markets can be found to separate newspapers as either elite or tabloid (such as in the U.K., Germany or the U.S.), in the Norwegian context this distinction is found within newspapers rather than between them.[2] A small national market of five million geographically dispersed inhabitants of a centralized state has created an omnibus press enabled by economic growth and welfare state development.[3] The expanding journalistic professionalism that emerged as newspapers began to break free of party affiliations in the 1970s caused journalists to discover everyday life, and owners to discover new advertising revenue. As a consequence, the omnibus paper in Nordic markets is usually a mixture of soft and hard news. The particular brand of Norwegian newspaper journalism has therefore been described as "schizophrenic" – a type of journalism where everything is equally important.[4]

The consumer orientation emerged in the Norwegian newspaper market at the end of the 1970s. A conservative political turn relaxed regulation in the credit and housing markets, creating growth in the advertising industry that led journalism to focus more on private economy. Growth in the magazine market also created increased segmentation of the press towards a consumer orientation focusing on personal development, consumption, and the good life.[5] As personal leisure time increased, so did demand for information about how to best spend that time. This expanded the newspapers' potential markets for audiences and advertisers.[6] A shift in address towards clientalism meant that readers were more frequently addressed not as citizens but as rights holders. Moreover, the clientalism that characterizes consumer and lifestyle journalism spills over into political journalism and assumes an individualistic orientation where political parties are framed as consumer products, focusing on what the parties can offer you, the political consumer.[7] The growth in lifestyle journalism has therefore not only caused worry because of its proximity to the economic field,[8] it also has been credited with inducing a consumer orientation in the harder news genres.

The Norwegian newspaper market thus provides a fruitful context for studying the contested boundaries between hard and soft forms of journalism. In this chapter, the hierarchy of journalistic genres is investigated through a content analysis of the print and online editions of four regional newspapers owned by the Norwegian media company Schibsted.[9] In the analysis of Schibsted's newspaper chain, questions emerge as to how to delineate, measure and separate lifestyle content and other "soft" journalistic genres from the harder and more politically oriented news. These methodological issues reflect the question of genre boundaries relevant to the professionalization of journalism as a larger vocational project. According to Thomas Gieryn,[10] the rhetoric mobilized in boundary work includes attributing selected characteristics to the discipline that helps to separate it from its closest rivaling fields, providing a rationale for the superiority of the discipline. This repertoire is "guided by its effectiveness in constructing a boundary [that rationalize the discipline's] request for enlarged authority and public support."[11] For journalism, hard news is part of that rhetoric because it serves an effective purpose in maintaining the authority of the field. Soft news is excluded from the repertoire because it may be potentially damaging to the professional ideal. Newspapers that contain a mixture of hard and soft news – as the Schibsted papers do – must contribute in this effort to uphold the rhetorical boundaries of the field, primarily by maintaining the hierarchy of genres. This effort necessarily comes into conflict with the economic aims of the news operation, to which hard and soft content constitute essentially interdependent formats.

There are, however, measures that can soften the impact that the conflict between economic aims and journalistic ideals may have on professional legitimacy. As John H. McManus explains,[12] the news model determines newsworthiness based on an event's expected consequence for a proportionately large audience. In a market theory of news production, however, newsworthiness is determined based on its potential harm to investors, the cost of coverage, and its expected audience reach. The market logic therefore results in news production routines designed to "hide the pervasiveness of the economic logic that forms them."[13] Because lifestyle and consumer journalism imply an uncomfortable closeness to the economic field, these softer journalistic genres are placed lower in the professional hierarchy. And whereas lifestyle journalism may be undergoing a professionalization through specialization, such internal inconsistencies in what the profession is supposed to be, says Gieryn, also "provide diverse ideological resources for use in boundary work."[14] The interests of the field inevitably guide the selection of such repertoires for public presentation. Ideologists manage to endow the discipline with "just those characteristics needed to achieve professional and institutional goals."[15] Communicating the hierarchy of journalistic genres is therefore useful in the profession's boundary work. The financially strained Schibsted newsrooms do this by outsourcing lower forms of journalism to centralized production hubs, while taking care of the more serious journalism themselves.

Data and findings

The content analysis of Schibsted's regional newspapers investigates one continuous week of print and online coverage, from 25–31 January 2013 (Sundays excluded), of Schibsted's four regional newspapers[16]: *Aftenposten*, *Bergens Tidende*, *Stavanger Aftenblad*, and *Fædrelandsvennen*. The newspapers are former broadsheets, liberal or conservative in editorial orientation, published in cities, and carry an omnibus identity while aiming for the top end of the markets where local competition is present. The unit of analysis is the article as printed in the newspaper (n = 2,123), and the front-page story published in the online edition (n = 1,694). Units were analyzed based on a coding scheme of more than 60 variables designed to register stories according to topical content,[17] and along the hard and soft content spectrum.[18] The data facilitates a comparison of content profiles across publications and between platforms within and between the individual titles.[19] The analysis establishes content profiles for the print and online ventures of the newspapers, reveals the uneasiness in mobilizing dichotomous news categorizations, and uncovers the boundary struggle that exists within the professional hierarchy.

The analysis shows that there is a tendency towards content divergence between the print and online platforms, indicating that the publications are moving in different directions, serving slightly different purposes. Online, the newspapers are more local than national or international in orientation, carry more news-you-can-use than politics and economy, and display higher levels of content syndication than print versions. Printed editions have more stories with social impact, including politics, social issues, and economy; they have a more nationally oriented profile and low levels of syndication.[20] This suggests a division of labor along the hard and soft journalism spectrums, where "softer" popular content is subject to syndication whereas more resource-demanding investigations directed at political institutions and social services are produced locally and reserved for printed editions. This divergence tendency is most noticeable along the traditional division between hard and soft news, in the central function of sports and lifestyle journalism, and in the importance of local affiliation. Syndication of content is higher online than in the printed editions (13 percent online versus 3 percent in print) and concentrated in the areas of sports, entertainment and lifestyle journalism. Hence, the consolidation strategies of the parent company are focused on the digital platform, where centralized production hubs increasingly cater to all four publications in supplying sport and lifestyle content.

The division of news into hard and soft, and consequently of soft news into popular and lifestyle journalism, renders a curious picture when looking at the Schibsted papers. While hard news is seen as more societally and politically valuable, very little news can actually be defined as hard. Hard news is universally described as consisting of merely three topical areas: politics, economy, and international affairs. Moreover, the form and address of hard news is limited to the factual, detached, and analytical. According to this definition, hard news[21] makes up only 25 percent of printed news[22] in the four newspapers combined, and 23 percent of the online content[23] – while soft news[24] constitutes 59 percent in print and 66 percent online. A third category, "general news,"[25] makes up 16 percent of the print content and 11 percent of the online content. Overall, this measurement characterizes the Schibsted online news venture as softer than its traditional print medium. But the question remains as to the usefulness of these divisions. Van Aelst and de Swert[26] have characterized traffic stories and accidents as sensational news. However, in an online environment, which is saturated with updates about local traffic conditions and accidents, these stories serve an informative purpose rather than as sensations. Because these online news sites strive to stay relevant to local audiences (especially as paywalls are about to go up), they tend to provide news with high information value that is useful to people's everyday lives. This includes information people need to make it home from work, information about local cultural events that people can engage with in their spare time, and suggestions for tonight's dinner. News items relevant to people's everyday lives may be considered "soft," but they also serve an information purpose, albeit one attuned to the private lives of citizens as consumers.

Outsourcing these softer journalistic genres not only reduces the scope of the type of journalism that is practiced within omnibus newsrooms, it also displays the boundary disputes taking place within the professionalization project. As these newsrooms are induced to reduce staff and cut spending, content production is reserved for the most worthy forms of journalism. The hierarchy that exists within the profession ensures that these newsrooms continue to produce news of high social and political relevance while also maintaining the local focus necessary to retain audiences in regional markets. Meanwhile, general sports stories and lifestyle journalism without a local angle can be produced centrally. Because these newspapers carry more sports and lifestyle journalism than they do other content categories – both in print and online – the amount of outsourcing within this area is also growing. However, while generalist sports coverage and lifestyle journalism may be slowly vanishing from these traditional newsrooms, centralization also ensures that these softer forms of journalism undergo professionalization in the form of specialization. The analysis of the Schibsted newspapers therefore demonstrates how these boundaries between hard and soft represent a professional struggle to protect the field.

Methodological boundaries

The boundary maintaining journalistic hierarchy is also supported by the attention that research gives to the various genres of the profession. Because lifestyle or soft journalism enjoys lower regard within the field, it also captures less interest among scholars. The negation of lifestyle journalism as a legitimate form of reporting within journalism research protects the legitimacy of boundaries established by the profession. Peter Dahlgren[27] has noted how this

> natural tendency to discursive containment ... is now increasingly disputed, churning up the waters of traditional perceptions and practices. In these processes, what is at stake, at least in the long run, is definitional and ideological control over what journalism is, can and should be.

The analysis of the boundary disputes between hard and soft news within the regional news market in Norway thus also reveals how boundaries are defined. This is an issue of some contention.

In surveying the literature on lifestyle journalism, what emerges is an acknowledged uncertainty regarding how to distinguish between various versions of soft news. The only thing that seems to gather consensus is the distinction between what is hard and what is soft. This dichotomy seems to be fundamental to evaluations of quality in journalism, and is often operationalized in content analyses. Based on prior literature, Carsten Reinemann and colleagues[28] identify the key dimensions of hard and soft news used in research and note that scholars seem to have an intuitive understanding of the concepts but that they are poorly defined, thereby making comparisons difficult. They claim that tabloidization and infotainment as concepts have contributed to the widespread use of the hard–soft dichotomy, used to signify both form and content of media, primarily in conjunction with judgments about quality and normative democratic assumptions about the role of news in society.[29]

Discussions do exist as to the veracity of the dichotomous separation between hard and soft news. Nevertheless, hard news is more or less consensually defined in the literature as comprising politics, economy, and international affairs.[30] These broad categorizations often include policy, public administration, and national security. In addition, hard news is sometimes expanded from these core thematic areas to also include social matters[31] and important crime stories.[32] The form of hard news is described in terms of qualifiers such as newsworthiness and neutrality, balance, and accuracy. Hard news is important factual news with influence and ramifications, demanding analysis and commentary,[33] primarily directed at an older male audience.[34] Hard news is often breaking news of high significance that focuses on who, what, where, how and why – presented as longer texts directed at elite audiences, opinion leaders, and the highly educated.[35] According to Reinemann et al.,[36] "The more a news item is politically relevant, the more it reports in a thematic way, focuses on the societal consequences of events, is impersonal and unemotional in its style, the more it can be regarded as hard news."

The umbrella term for the opposite of hard news is soft news. Soft news is either treated on its own, or it encompasses popular journalism, consumer journalism, lifestyle journalism, service journalism, sensational news, and tabloidization. Soft news content includes lifestyle, entertainment, crime, disasters, accidents, sport,[37] culture, arts, celebrities, religion, health, family, education, history, science, technology, royalty, human-interest, advice columns, and "other" stories. These are items of light news of immediate public interest with a low level of information value that can be reported at any time. Soft news is focused on individuals and their personal and emotional experiences, is formulaic and clichéd in presentation, is intimate, spectacular, subjective, off-beat, colorful, and confrontational. Soft news is utilitarian and concerns sensational and dramatic or specific events, often in the form of scoops and scandals, and has a feminized mode of address communicating either human weakness or the heroic achievement and perseverance of ordinary people in the face of adversity, framed within the dramaturgy of heroes and villains. The popular appeal of soft news stories is designed to maximize traffic, is often described as infotainment, and characterized by terms such as popularization, tabloidization, trivialization, sensationalism, and marginalization.[38] Tabloidization is perhaps the most widely used of these characterizations. It generally refers to simplification, exploitation, and vulgarity toward the bizarre, particularly in covering show business, royalty, celebrity, scandals, sex, and murders. "Dumbing down" is a term often accompanying discussions of tabloid journalism.[39]

While clearly some of the topics included in soft news can be reported with high societal relevance without a tabloid or sensational angle, soft news is more about form than content. Soft news is therefore dichotomized between two opposite ends of a scale, where popular journalism entails the most extreme form of soft news, and lifestyle journalism entails a more personalized news-you-can-use. Popular journalism is generally described in derogatory terms as vulgar, exotic otherness directed at a mass culture-consuming, working-class segment.[40] It includes gossip, humor, sex, celebrities, curiosities, heroism, shock, and trauma, and is described as intimate, emotional, melodramatic, vulgar, sensational, bizarre, heated, chaotic, and irrational. Popular journalism is typically characterized by big headlines and large visuals, written in an informal language, with little social responsibility, and oriented toward the private sphere.[41]

At the other end of the soft-news scale we find lifestyle journalism, sometimes also referred to as consumer journalism and service journalism. Martin Eide and Graham Knight[42] argue that there is a distinction between lifestyle and consumer journalism where consumer journalism is about choice and popular cynicism while lifestyle journalism is about identification and immersion. However, in the literature, the three terms are largely overlapping. They all refer to different aspects of consumption, with the aim of guiding readers as clients, patients, rights holders and private individuals geared toward personal development, relaxation, and leisure.[43] The topics covered are travel, food and drink, health and fitness, fashion and trends, property and home improvement, auto and gadgets, computers and gaming, gardening and living, career development, child-rearing and family life, and women's issues. Lifestyle journalism is market-oriented, and audiences are addressed as consumers rather than citizens. Concerned with the private economy of individuals, lifestyle journalism assumes a guidance orientation, intent on helping readers choose the right product, career, holiday destination, car, fitness scheme or television program. It therefore often takes the form of product-testing, advice or review, with a vernacular mode of address. Lifestyle journalism addresses the life-world and everyday concerns of readers. As it assumes a guidance position, it also stands firmly with the reader against the market, or any form of service provider. As such, lifestyle journalism can also assume a conflict orientation, focusing on the grievances of individuals and risks associated with consumer society.[44]

To soften the dichotomy of hard versus soft, some researchers have proposed a more nuanced segmentation of content characterizations. Both Brekken and colleagues[45] and Lehman-Wilzig and Seletsky[46] propose including "general news" as a separate category in content analyses of news. Lehman-Wilzig and Seletsky define general news as recent economic, social or cultural news that should be published but not necessarily immediately. This includes important demographic data, academic reports, scientific discoveries and technological innovations; news that is of importance or relevance for specific groups; important news not on the present agenda, and information that is personally useful for the reader.[47] Van Aelst and de Swert, in a study of political news, break up the dichotomous categorization at the soft end of the scale by introducing sensational news, defined as traffic accidents, disasters, and crime. Their hard-news category includes the standard politics, economy, finances and international relations, while soft news includes culture, sports, celebrity and royalty.[48] Hence, while there is debate as to how to categorize different aspects of soft news – and the reasons for doing so – consensus largely prevails regarding the definition of hard news.

Contested divisions

The argument has been made repeatedly that the hard–soft dichotomy fails to recognize the political dimensions of the private sphere, that it takes a narrow view of relations of power in society, and that it fails to include the female perspective in the public sphere.[49] Expanding markets in the intersection between masses and elites have entailed a shift to popular culture that has ensured commercial success for many newspapers. However, the popular turn also entailed a democratization of information to an expanded audience across classes and social sectors.[50] An Nguyen set out to test this claim – that soft news can help serve an attention-scarce audience with news in an age of media richness and audience fragmentation. He has found that the taste for soft news does not have a statistically significant effect on a person's attachment to the news, and, if so, it is mostly negative. Nguyen therefore concludes that soft news cannot be justified with serving democracy. He attributes this turn towards softer news to the connection between young female audiences and increased advertising revenue.[51]

Commercial motives were indeed responsible for introducing women's pages (and female writers) to newspapers in the late nineteenth and early twentieth centuries.[52] Particularly "female" topics are typically defined in the literature as having a consumerist, entertainment or human-interest angle.[53] The manner in which the hard–soft distinction is linked to male–female readership has been amply criticized in feminist scholarship. Irene Costera Meijer notes how definitions of quality journalism are typically rooted in the education, cultural capital, and social *habitus* of the white male professional managerial class. The risk, says Meijer,[54] arises when immigrant or female citizenship is interpreted as contradictory to this. By neglecting the private sphere, such quality boundaries also exclude everyday life from democratic scrutiny and relevance. Meijer therefore argues that, "Current journalism fails to acknowledge fully the significance of people's immediate world: their family, friendships, neighborhood, town, or country."[55] While this may be true for the traditional "quality" media that Meijer refers to, Shibsted's regional newspapers seem to have embraced this insight in their online journalism.

Gendered, ethicized or class-oriented descriptions and demarcations of the target audiences of various journalistic genres remain generally unchallenged in the research. Analyses are operationalized by commonsense categorizations where hard news and current affairs are assumed as directed at white males, while soft news, sensationalism, and lifestyle journalism are assumed to cater to younger females. Likewise, tabloids speak to the masses, financial newspapers to the elites. These bluntly stated categorizations are treated as factual, while they seldom exist as part of any coding scheme. Instead, the hard–soft/male–female link seems to emerge ex post in the analysis, and is hardly ever challenged. In fact, the act of coding sender intentions, embedded gender codes in the message, and implied reading in the receiver is highly difficult, if not to say impossible.

Because these dichotomies exist as reference frames in our heads, research into the form and content of journalism tends to support the journalistic boundary work that maintains the genre hierarchy within the profession. As the Schibsted analysis reveals, the content of the printed and online editions of these four regional newspapers can most accurately be described as soft news-dominated. The largest content categories both in print and online are sports and lifestyle journalism. While these content areas may constitute the primary activity of these newsrooms, this is not the primary activity communicated by the profession. In the professional ideology, journalism is about politics, disruptions, and exposure. In its daily practice, however, journalism is about local sports teams, traffic updates, and trendy holiday destinations.

Boundaries under dispute

Journalism's lack of formal professional status means its borders are in need of constant patrolling. Journalism does not have a monopoly on professional expertise, but the manner in which its practice is mythologized somewhat compensates for this deficiency. Moreover, the professional canon determines the legitimate subject areas to report on.[56] This hierarchy reflects the route to occupational autonomy – the highest levels reserved for senior writers, war correspondents, and investigative reporters.[57] At the bottom, we find the "smiling professions" that interface with the public, says John Hartley "in the name of pleasure, entertainment, attractiveness, appeal"[58] – or, in more concrete terms, as lifestyle journalism, routine crime coverage, advice columns, and celebrity gossip.[59] The hierarchy of genres exists to promote the ambitions of upward mobility that help to reproduce the norms and ideologies of the field that protects journalism from outside threats.[60] This hierarchy, says Dahlgren,[61] is arranged according to proximity to journalism's classic hard-news text. This creates an in-group/out-group dimension within the profession,[62] producing large vocational groups not really associating their works with the professional canon. However, because journalism is a fluid profession, "Positions on the continuum [between the serious and the tabloid] are negotiable."[63]

Jeremy Tunstall has noted how this "occupational pecking order is inversely related to the revenue goal emphasis in particular fields."[64] Part of maintaining professional boundaries is to keep the discipline autonomous and free from control or intervention. Because journalism is close to the political and economic fields – being both a business and a public service – processes of demarcation are necessary to distinguish the work of members from the practices and products of non-members.[65] According to Folker Hanusch, proximity to the market means that "lifestyle journalism is seen as a frivolous pursuit or a guilty pleasure, barely worth the term journalism."[66] The history of journalism therefore tends to overlook this link between journalism and advertising. The genre boundaries within newspapers result from centuries as bundled products.[67] Because consumers have a higher willingness to pay for a combination of goods than they do for individual goods, newspapers contain a mix of softer lifestyle content that is attractive to advertisers with more serious content that is less attractive. The boundary between genres within the finished product is a result of these factors. Moreover, says Dahlgren,[68]

> The growing gap between the realities of journalism and its official presentation of self means that the status of these multiple and large "remainder" categories is left somewhat indeterminant, while they in fact continue to grow and shape popular expectations of what the press and broadcast journalism are and should be.

A development in this direction is noticeable in the specialization of specific practices – a custom move towards professionalization that involves standardization. According to Dominique Marchetti,[69] the journalistic field is organized around an opposition between generalist and specialist journalism, and lately there has been an increase in specialization. Looking at French media, Marchetti found a higher concentration of specialist journalists in the prestigious national newspapers than in subsequent publications, with growth in the areas of business, science, health, and other topics. Specialization establishes journalistic credibility, says Marchetti, but this trend is also inspired by advertising-driven growth in sections on personal economy, health, science and news-you-can-use. The creation of new specialized areas can upset old hierarchies, and "do not occur without exacerbating recurring identity debates over the definitions of journalistic excellence."[70]

These negotiations are a constant within the field, but they become particularly visible in times of crisis, or when news organizations find themselves faced with permanent transitions of a technological or financial nature. Digitalization processes, and the economic and structural factors that challenge the traditional business model of legacy media, entail permanent transitions that exacerbate the boundary struggles going on within the field. The analysis of Schibsted's newspaper chain reveals one such struggle, namely the negotiations taking place within the hierarchy of journalistic genres. During an effort to cut costs and consolidate production, Schibsted in 2012 moved to establish centralized production hubs in the lifestyle and sport sections, supplying news stories and feature articles in the areas of national-level sports, health and fitness, travel, home decoration and consumer issues. In Schibsted's business model, soft-news content is also increasingly outsourced to affiliated specialist publications whose reports on food and wine, home and auto, technology and child care are syndicated among the printed and online editions of the company's regional newspapers. This type of economic rationalization causes staff reductions and forces newsrooms to prioritize what areas to cover. Politics, social issues and local sports news are therefore prioritized in the newsroom at the expense of lifestyle journalism. Based on market orientation and audience affiliation this seems a rational choice, but it also signals the low regard for lifestyle journalism among omnibus newsrooms. Because lifestyle issues do not need a local angle, scaling down original reporting in this area is preferable to reducing coverage of politics or social issues, where local knowledge is important. So while soft news genres may be undergoing specialization to increase advertising revenue, the regard for these genres remains low, as is reflected in the reorganization of the traditional newsroom operation.

The bundled identity and advertising reliance of traditional news operations nevertheless suggest that lifestyle journalism has become an integral part of the news cycle.[71] Softer forms of journalism may be undergoing a process of professionalization that can also help to defend the boundaries of the media from moving too close to the economic field. Specialization standardizes sports and lifestyle journalism and shifts them closer to the more legitimate forms of professional practices. As a genre, say Eide and Knight, service journalism's legacy lies partly in early forms of campaigning journalism, assuming the political-ideological vantage point of social justice and moral reform. Helping the vulnerable is part of the watchdog function of the press, and important in constructing the legitimacy of the professional status and autonomy of journalism in representing the life-world's encounter with the political and economic system. Lifestyle and service journalism therefore represents a hybrid social subject comprising aspects of the citizen, consumer and client. "If modernity brings everyday life into being, it does so by making the practice of living problematic and resolvable through the application of diverse and changing forms of knowledge, information and advice."[72] Service journalism addresses the relationship between the system and the life-world from the side of the life-world, problematizing this as grievance and risk, connecting journalism to the "more collective, political forms of addressing social problems that characterize the public sphere."[73]

Moreover, the prevalence of this particular mix between hard and soft news within the bundled product could explain why the Norwegian public continues to have one of the highest levels of newspaper-reading in the world. The high presence of lifestyle and everyday life issues in both printed and online versions of the Schibsted regional newspapers suggests that these titles are positioning themselves to stay relevant to people's everyday lives. However, most lifestyle content is not locally anchored and does not contribute to strengthening the local identity of the papers, but rather features as syndication between the newspapers – evidence of the financial strain put on the papers by the parent company.

Conclusions

This chapter addresses the hierarchy of journalistic genres, the boundary struggles that exist between legitimate forms of news, and how these contestations contribute to protect the boundaries of the journalistic profession in the encounter with the economic field. A case study looking at the print and online content profiles of Schibsted's regional newspapers finds slightly diverging identities that suggest the printed newspaper remains the primary operation of the newsroom in terms of resource allocation and legitimate journalistic production. Because newspapers are also commercial products, they need content that will attract advertising, not least to fund its more serious forms of journalism. This bundled business model is reflected in the publication strategies of the Schibsted regional papers. The online platform, not yet fully accepted as equally legitimate to print production, carries added value in this model. While still climbing the occupational hierarchy, the online venture can be used more strategically to attract readers that in turn attract advertising, as reflected in the soft news focus of the online sites. Hence the online platform is an extension of the bundled product that adds to the specialization of journalistic production that enables news organizations to cater to a greater variety of niche markets. Because an increased focus on web production also facilitates content syndication, the online version reduces the cost of production while offering content that is attractive to readers and advertisers alike.

The outcome of economic rationalization that forces newsrooms to make staff and production priorities seems to entail exclusion of the softer forms of journalism from the daily news operation. The centralization of sports and lifestyle journalism and the outsourcing of specialist areas related to leisure, consumption, and everyday life is not only evidence of the low regard for these genres within the profession, it also signals a narrowing of the scope of the omnibus news operation. Because softer forms of journalism do not require local affiliation, newspapers can cut costs by moving production out of the local newsroom. But whereas the local omnibus newsroom may be shrinking, these lower journalistic genres are also undergoing specialization that can ultimately contribute to legitimizing journalistic practices that are largely criticized for operating uncomfortably close to the economic field. The financial strain that compels newsrooms to outsource its lowest forms of content, while still having great need for them to attract readers and advertisers, suggests these hierarchies are still in operation.

The central place that soft journalism genres have in news operations is often overlooked in journalism research. When given attention, its prevalence, form, and function are largely criticized. The research questions asked often negate private life and the sphere of consumption as politically relevant, and tend to ignore the potential that issues close to the private sphere serve in people's roles as citizens. The methods and measurements used to separate hard from soft are usually taken for granted, and built on normative assumptions that exclude the life-world from the realm of the democratically relevant. Methodological operationalizations that separate hard and soft news ultimately serve to support existing journalistic hierarchies, helping to protect the field through the continued exclusion of soft news as legitimate forms of journalism. By being more open and reflective about the assumptions that fuel operationalizations of news in the hard–soft dichotomy, we gain more insight into the boundary work that helps sustain the journalistic field and its professionalization project. This analysis reveals how the hard–soft dichotomy – and, in particular, the projected low regard for lifestyle journalism – contributes to uphold the boundary between journalism and the economic field. Soft journalism sells newspapers and drives online traffic. As such, sports journalism, lifestyle content, and consumer issues protect the boundaries of the field on two fronts. First, it finances hard journalism, and second, by occupying the hierarchical bottom, the hard–soft dichotomy creates a separation between the two forms of journalism that enables hard news to maintain its distance from the economic field, thus protecting the boundaries of the profession.

Notes

1 Michael Schudson, *The Sociology of News* (New York: W.W. Norton & Company, 2003), 8.
2 Martin Eide, *Hodet på blokken: Essays om journalistikk* [*Essays on journalism*] (Oslo: Gyldendal, 2004), 269.
3 Terje Rasmussen, "Veiledningsjournalistikk: Om å lede vei og å gå seg vill" ["Consumer journalism: Guiding the way and losing your path"], in *Nytt på nett og brett: Journalistikk i forandring* [*News online and Tablet: Journalistic Changes*], eds Martin Eide; Leif Larsen and Helle Sjøvaag (Oslo: Universitetsforlaget, 2012), 215–30.
4 Eide, *Hodet på blokken: Essays om journalistikk* [*Essays on journalism*], 235.
5 Folker Hanusch, "Broadening the Focus: The Case for Lifestyle Journalism as a Field of Scholarly Enquiry," *Journalism Practice* 6, no. 1 (2012): 2; Rasmussen, "Veiledningsjournalistikk: Om å lede vei og å gå seg vill" ["Consumer journalism: Guiding the way and losing your path"].
6 Hanusch, "Broadening the Focus: The Case for Lifestyle Journalism as a Field of Scholarly Enquiry," 7.
7 Rasmussen, "Veiledningsjournalistikk: Om å lede vei og å gå seg vill" ["Consumer journalism: Guiding the way and losing your path"], 228.
8 Hanusch, "Broadening the Focus: The Case for Lifestyle Journalism as a Field of Scholarly Enquiry," 4.
9 Schibsted is Norway's largest media company, established in 1839. Its newspaper subsidiary Schibsted Norge was established in June 2009 as Media Norge.
10 Thomas F. Gieryn, "Boundary-Work and the Demarcation of Science from Non-Science: Strains and Interests in Professional Ideologies of Scientists," *American Sociological Review* 48, no. 6 (1983): 774.
11 Gieryn, "Boundary-Work and the Demarcation of Science from Non-Science: Strains and Interests in Professional Ideologies of Scientists," 787.
12 John H. McManus, *Market-Driven Journalism: Let the Citizen Beware?* (Thousand Oaks, CA: Sage, 1994).
13 McManus, *Market-Driven Journalism: Let the Citizen Beware?* 85.
14 Gieryn, "Boundary-Work and the Demarcation of Science from Non-Science: Strains and Interests in Professional Ideologies of Scientists," 792.
15 Gieryn, "Boundary-Work and the Demarcation of Science from Non-Science: Strains and Interests in Professional Ideologies of Scientists," 792.
16 Circulation figures for 2013: *Aftenposten* 653,000; *Bergens Tidende* 216,000; *Stavanger Aftenblad* 165,000 and *Fædrelandsvennen* 94,000 (TNS-Gallup 2013).

17 The categories were designed to be mutually exclusive and registered variations within the following broad topical categories: Politics, Crime, Economy, Social System, Culture, Everyday Life, Sport, and Accidents (and Other).

18 The content categories were subsequently divided into hard news, soft news, and general news. See Notes 21–25 for details.

19 Inter-coder reliability was established using 2 independent coders measuring Cohen's Kappa (k) on content: 84%/.80 (n = 238). As Cohen's Kappa is a conservative measure (in cases of high distribution and low variance), measures above .70 are considered acceptable. Kimberly A. Neuendorf, *The Content Analysis Guidebook* (Thousand Oaks, CA: Sage, 2002): 143–51.

20 Helle Sjøvaag, "Homogenisation or Differentiation? The Effects of Consolidation in the Regional Newspaper Market," *Journalism Studies*, forthcoming (2014).

21 Defined as politics (including politics, international politics, war, terrorism and political violence, state administration, and demonstrations); serious crime (financial crime and police matters); and economy (business and industry, finance and banking, markets, energy sector, and the agricultural sector).

22 n = 2,123.

23 n = 1,694.

24 Defined as soft crime (including murder and suspicious deaths, violence, vice, smuggling, trafficking and possession, crime of gain, and petty crime); everyday life issues (family, leisure, religion, traffic, consumer issues, weather, and construction); culture (arts, popular culture, media and advertising, royalty, curiosities, anniversaries and time-specific events); accidents; sports, and other stories.

25 Defined as socially relevant crime stories (restricted to trials); economy (science and technology, the tourism trade, and personal economy); and social issues (including work, health, global social issues, environment, education, minority issues and immigration).

26 Peter van Aelst and Knut de Swert, "Politics in the News: Do Campaigns Matter? A Comparison of Political News during Election Periods and Routine Periods in Flanders (Belgium)," *Communications* 34, no. 2 (2009): 149–68.

27 Peter Dahlgren, "Introduction," in *Journalism and Popular Culture*, eds Peter Dahlgren and Colin Sparks (London: Sage, 1992): 1–23.

28 Carsten Reinemann, James Stanyer, Sebastian Scherr and Guido Legnante, "Hard and Soft News: A Review of Concepts, Operationalizations and Key Findings," *Journalism* 13, no. 2 (2012): 221–39.

29 Reinemann et al., "Hard and Soft News: A Review of Concepts, Operationalizations and Key Findings," 222–23.

30 Tove Brekken, Kjersti Thorbjørnsrud and Toril Aalberg, "News Substance: The Relative Importance of Soft and De-Contextualized News," in *How Media Inform Democracy: A Comparative Approach*, eds Toril Aalberg and James Curran (New York: Routledge, 2012), 64–80; Sam N. Lehman-Wilzig and Michal Seletzky, "Hard News, Soft News, 'General' News: The Necessity and Utility of an Intermediate Classification," *Journalism* 11, no. 1 (2010): 37–56; Reinemann et al., "Hard and Soft News: A Review of Concepts, Operationalizations and Key Findings"; van Aelst and de Swert, "Politics in the News: Do Campaigns Matter? A Comparison of Political News during Election Periods and Routine Periods in Flanders (Belgium)."

31 Brekken et al., "News Substance: The Relative Importance of Soft and De-Contextualized News."

32 Lehman-Wilzig and Seletzky, "Hard News, Soft News, 'General' News: The Necessity and Utility of an Intermediate Classification."

33 Gaye Tuchman, "Objectivity as Strategic Ritual: An Examination of Newsmen's Notions of Objectivity," *American Journal of Sociology* 77, no. 4 (1972): 660–79.

34 An Nguyen, "The Effect of Soft News on Public Attachment to the News: Is 'Infotainment' Good for Democracy?" *Journalism Studies* 13, no. 5–6 (2012): 706–17.
35 Brekken et al., "News Substance: The Relative Importance of Soft and De-Contextualized News"; Lehman-Wilzig and Seletzky, "Hard News, Soft News, 'General' News: The Necessity and Utility of an Intermediate Classification"; Reinemann et al., "Hard and Soft News: A Review of Concepts, Operationalizations and Key Findings"; David Rowe, "Modes of Sports Writing," in *Journalism and Popular Culture*, eds Peter Dahlgren and Colin Sparks (London: Sage, 1992), 96–112.
36 Reinemann et al., "Hard and Soft News: A Review of Concepts, Operationalizations and Key Findings," 233.
37 Also referred to as the "toy department" of the newspaper. Row, "Modes of Sports Writing."
38 Brekken et al., "News Substance: The Relative Importance of Soft and De-Contextualized News." Dahlgren, "Introduction"; Hanusch, "Broadening the Focus: The Case for Lifestyle Journalism as a Field of Scholarly Enquiry"; Lehman-Wilzig and Seletzky, "Hard News, Soft News, 'General' News: The Necessity and Utility of an Intermediate Classification"; Libby Lester and Brett Hutchins, "Soft Journalism, Politics and Environmental Risk: An Australian Story," *Journalism* 13, no. 5 (2012): 654–67; Nguyen, "The Effect of Soft News on Public Attachment to the News: Is 'Infotainment' Good for Democracy?"; Reinemann et al., "Hard and Soft News: A Review of Concepts, Operationalizations and Key Findings"; Rowe, "Modes of Sports Writing"; Tuchman, "Objectivity as Strategic Ritual: An Examination of Newsmen's Notions of Objectivity"; Van Aelst and de Swert, "Politics in the News: Do Campaigns Matter? A Comparison of Political News during Election Periods and Routine Periods in Flanders (Belgium)."
39 Steven Barnett, "Dumbing Down or Reaching Out: Is it Tabloidisation wot don it?," *The Political Quarterly* 69, no. B (1998): 75–90; Lester and Hutchins, "Soft Journalism, Politics and Environmental Risk: An Australian Story."
40 Dahlgren, "Introduction."
41 Martin Eide and Graham Knight, "Public/Private Service: Service Journalism and the Problems of Everyday Life," *European Journal of Communication* 14, no. 4 (1999): 525–47; Lehman-Wilzig and Seletzky, "Hard News, Soft News, 'General' News: The Necessity and Utility of an Intermediate Classification"; Irene Costera Meijer, "The Public Quality of Popular Journalism: Developing a Normative Framework," *Journalism Studies* 2, no. 2 (2001): 189–205; Michael Serazio, "Rethinking a Villain, Redeeming a Format: The Crisis and Cure in Tabloidization," in *The Changing Faces of Journalism: Tabloidization, Technology and Truthiness*, ed. Barbie Zelizer (London: Routledge, 2009), 13–16.
42 Eide and Knight, "Public/Private Service: Service Journalism and the Problems of Everyday Life."
43 Martin Eide, *Den fjerde servicemakt: Noter til forståelse av norsk veilednings-og kampanjejournalistikk* [*The Fourth Service Estate: Notes Towards Understanding Norwegian Guidance and Campaign Journalism*] (Bergen: Institutt for massekommunikasjon, 1992).
44 Eide and Knight, "Public/Private Service: Service Journalism and the Problems of Everyday Life"; Hanusch, "Broadening the Focus: The Case for Lifestyle Journalism as a Field of Scholarly Enquiry"; Rasmussen, "Veiledningsjournalistikk: Om å lede vei og å gå seg vill" ["Consumer journalism: Guiding the way and losing your path"], 228.

45 Brekken et al., "News Substance: The Relative Importance of Soft and De-Contextualized News"; Dahlgren, "Introduction."

46 Lehman-Wilzig and Seletzky, "Hard News, Soft News, 'General' News: The Necessity and Utility of an Intermediate Classification."

47 Lehman-Wilzig and Seletzky, "Hard News, Soft News, 'General' News: The Necessity and Utility of an Intermediate Classification," 47–48.

48 Van Aelst and de Swert, "Politics in the News: Do Campaigns Matter? A Comparison of Political News during Election Periods and Routine Periods in Flanders (Belgium)," 159.

49 Dahlgren, "Introduction"; Meijer, "The Public Quality of Popular Journalism: Developing a Normative Framework."

50 Eide, *Hodet på blokken: Essays om journalistikk* [*Essays on journalism*], 256; John Hartley, "Communicative Democracy in a Redactionary Society: The Future of Journalism Studies," *Journalism* 1, no. 1 (2000): 40.

51 Nguyen, "The Effect of Soft News on Public Attachment to the News: Is 'Infotainment' Good for Democracy?," 715–16.

52 Hanusch, "Broadening the Focus: The Case for Lifestyle Journalism as a Field of Scholarly Enquiry," 6.

53 Lehman-Wilzig and Seletzky, "Hard News, Soft News, 'General' News: The Necessity and Utility of an Intermediate Classification"; Nguyen, "The Effect of Soft News on Public Attachment to the News: Is 'Infotainment' Good for Democracy?"

54 Meijer, "The Public Quality of Popular Journalism: Developing a Normative Framework," 190–94.

55 Meijer, "The Public Quality of Popular Journalism: Developing a Normative Framework," 198.

56 John Soloski, "News Reporting and Professionalism: Some Constraints on the Reporting of the News," *Media, Culture & Society* 11, no. 2 (1989): 210.

57 Herbert Gans, *Deciding what's News: A Study of CBS Evening News, NBC Nightly News, Newsweek, and Time*, (New York: Vintage Books, 1980).

58 Hartley, "Communicative Democracy in a Redactionary Society: The Future of Journalism Studies," 40.

59 Dahlgren, "Introduction," 8.

60 Gans, *Deciding what's News: A Study of CBS Evening News, NBC Nightly News, Newsweek, and Time.*

61 Dahlgren, "Introduction."

62 See also Teun A. van Dijk, *Ideology: A Multidisciplinary Approach* (London: Sage, 1998), 6.

63 Dahlgren, "Introduction," 14.

64 Jeremy Tunstall, *Journalists at Work. Specialist Correspondents: Their News Organizations, News Sources, and Competitor-Colleagues* (London: Constable, 1971), 108.

65 Gieryn, "Boundary-Work and the Demarcation of Science from Non-Science: Strains and Interests in Professional Ideologies of Scientists," 782.

66 Hanusch, "Broadening the Focus: The Case for Lifestyle Journalism as a Field of Scholarly Enquiry," 5.

67 James T. Hamilton, *All the News That's Fit to Sell: How the market transforms information into news* (Princeton: Princeton University Press, 2004).

68 Dahlgren, "Introduction," 7.

69 Dominique Marchetti, "Subfields of Specialized Journalism," in *Bourdieu and the Journalistic Field*, eds Rodney Benson and Erik Neveu (Cambridge: Polity, 2005), 64–84.

70 Dominique Marchetti, "Subfields of Specialized Journalism," 67.

71 Folker Hanusch, "A Profile of Australian Travel Journalists' Professional Views and Ethical Standards," *Journalism* 13, no. 5 (2011): 669.
72 Eide and Knight, "Public/Private Service: Service Journalism and the Problems of Everyday Life," 526
73 Eide and Knight, "Public/Private Service: Service Journalism and the Problems of Everyday Life," 529.

Chapter 7

Internal boundaries

The stratification of the journalistic collective

Jenny Wiik

The long-time professionalization process of journalism is a fact and a global phenomenon, but lately there has been a growing range of counter-moving developments. The freedom of journalism is currently threatened by external as well as internal forces, causing professional boundaries to shake. The crisis is, among other things, ascribed to "plummeting circulation, declining revenues, new technology, conglomerate ownership, and layoffs,"[1] mainly in the newspaper industry, and has contributed to an increasingly tough working environment for journalists. Media organizations have not yet succeeded in the reformation of business models but are desperately seeking to adapt to the new, fierce competition. Journalists are finding their terms of employment being redefined, and work opportunities are substantially reduced.[2] What consequences will this development have for the collective identity of journalists, their internal hierarchies and professional loyalty? This chapter will mainly focus on the internal mechanisms of journalists struggling to maintain their common professional identity, as the journalistic field as a whole is becoming increasingly insecure and fragmented. Following Gieryn,[3] what consequences might a possible stratification of the work force have on how journalistic boundaries are understood? Can we rightly regard journalism as one cohesive profession anymore, or is it, in fact, falling apart into smaller fractions and sub-identities?

Possible sub-identities may form in line with a variety of uniting factors, such as social background, organizational belonging, and gender. I will therefore limit my scope by taking the aspect of working conditions as a starting point. From this perspective, the ongoing restructuring of news production frames the negotiation of professional boundaries. What we see is journalism balancing a fine line between the acceptance of new competencies and the defence of long-established practices. The question becomes how are conditions changing and how can these changes be traced in the professional identity of journalists? While the issue is relevant in the majority of Western countries, I will here concentrate on the case of Sweden by using a mixed-methods approach. Empirical support will be drawn partly from the Swedish Journalist Survey, conducted five times during 1989–2011, and partly from an open-answer questionnaire to trainee students on the journalism M.A. at the University of

Gothenburg. While the survey offers a general view of the profession, the students, being trainees in a wide range of newsrooms, bring a cross-media insight to the developments currently marking the Swedish news business.

A collective splitting up?

The knowledge-intensive labor of journalism is all about performing similar work tasks with some amount of freedom for the individual to judge how, and with what measures, the task that should be performed. For those workers, intellectual capital is their most valuable resource. The mobilization of occupational members in erecting and protecting professional boundaries serves to secure the consistency, quality and accumulation of that capital. From a Swedish perspective, this process has been incredibly successful since it took off in the 1960s and 70s, and the democratic importance of journalism has even been stated in a series of official reports.[4] The professional identity of Swedish journalists is built on the notions of guarding democracy, explaining complicated events to the audience and letting different opinions be heard. Previous research shows this identity to be increasingly homogeneous over time and that the ideals of scrutiny and explanation are being accentuated in that process: as many as 99 percent of the journalists today consider these functions to be the most important elements of their professional role.[5]

The homogenization processing of journalistic ideals does, however, face clear counter-tendencies at all levels of news production. One such tendency is the global trend of individualization. Individualization means the increasing importance of the individual at the cost of the influence of collective actors. A popular assumption in line with this trend suggests that late-modern identities are no longer being ascribed but chosen to a greater extent than before. They are supposedly not as dependent on group ties anymore, instead allowing more freedom for the individual.[6] Nevertheless, such development has not removed the existence of collective movements in any way; according to Castells,[7] they are merely organized in a different manner. He hypothesizes that subjects may no longer be constructed in line with the civil societies that are dissolving, but rather as extensions of collective resistance to power in transition. Identities thus become created defensively in relation to new forms of power that are mainly being formed at the globalized level. This development is, on a macro-level, paralleled by evidence of increasing fragmentation and differentiation.[8] To a late-modern labor force, this means resisting strong forces in the direction of flexibility and adaptiveness.[9] Well-established professions now suffer from reorganization and boundary-breaking processes. In addition to this, increased commercial demands imply the bureaucratization and standardization of previously free occupations.[10]

Behind these forces is the process of globalization, which sometimes, but not always, is working in favour of professional journalism. In terms of labor, globalization is said to create an intellectual and cultural elite of mobile knowledge workers, whereas the majority remain immobile and dependent service workers.[11] This is also visible in journalism. Expanding applications of different journalistic skills and personnel, accompanied by far-reaching reorganizations of journalistic labor, contribute to the creation of new hierarchies. Ursell[12] suggests a division of the journalistic field into three strata: top-layer journalists who may indeed be regarded as being involved in the rule-setting of the field and enjoying some mobility and autonomy, while the bottom layer comprises replaceable production news workers. The majority of journalists land somewhere in between: holding reasonably secure terms of employment, but finding their autonomy drastically curtailed by their existence as corporate employees.

The practical consequences of this development still have to be disentangled. There is a rich collection of myths surrounding the business, and studies on actual working conditions are scarce. However, the working environment of journalists is transforming very fast, and although the linkage between ideal and practice is subtle and difficult to grasp, I will try here to make that connection. Previous research shows that changing conditions influence the way journalists perceive their role in society and how they build their professional identity.[13] By focusing on the case of Swedish journalists, I investigate the ideals and standpoints shaping their common identity on an aggregate level. This allows an analysis of whether this identity is stable in all groups of journalists or if the ongoing stratification of the workforce is having a fragmenting impact on the common grounds of journalism.

Understanding the field

In order to understand the relationship between the guiding ideals of journalists and their practical conditions, I will here apply the field perspective of Pierre Bourdieu.[14] Among other things, he pointed out the importance of demographic and structural factors to identity formation, focused by the terms *habitus* and *capital*. Actors in a field compete with each other to attain legitimate power – or, in the words of Abbott,[15] to gain jurisdiction. They do this by the accumulation of *symbolic capital*, which is most easily explained as the attributes that are acknowledged by other actors in relation to certain field rules. Bourdieu theorized mainly on economic and cultural capital, embracing resources such as money, property, education, and titles. Symbolic capital includes these and all other forms of capital regarded as legitimate in the field. These may accordingly be exchanged for preferential rights of interpretation.[16] Gender could, as an example, be interpreted as a form of capital as being a man generates a favorable position in the constant struggle for power in most fields.[17] Gender differences in the professional identity of journalists could thus be explained by the diverse starting points of men and women when entering the profession.[18] The concept of *habitus* is in many respects similar to the identity concept inasmuch as it represents the accumulation of experience, capital, and struggles shaping a person. However, here I prefer the identity concept as I find it less static and more fruitful in explaining changes of collective mind-sets and values. I furthermore consider the professional ideals of journalists as building blocks of their common professional identity.

Bourdieu's concepts are *relational*, which means that journalistic production must be understood as derived from specific competitions among actors in the field.[19] The relational character of the concepts complies well with the comprehension of professionalism. Considering journalism as a professional field allows an analysis of what is considered high and low in that field – the status of different media types, different news areas, and various positions. For instance, the credibility of various news outlets may be arranged hierarchically, as may the status of individual journalists within the newsroom. These positions are determined by a complex evaluation frame for capital forms, set and maintained by the dominant actors of the field. Several researchers have drawn attention to the struggle of journalism for legitimacy, status, and exclusivity,[20] and Bourdieu's terminology makes it possible to ascertain the actual means of this struggle and how definitions of symbolic capital change over time. This includes mapping historical transformations based on demographical and morphological factors – such as the number of agents entering the field, social characteristics, gender and education – that are central to understanding the reproduction and manifestation of values, as well as change.[21]

Changing working conditions, changing ideals?

A common explanation for the fragmentation and decreasing autonomy of the journalistic field is the ubiquitous influence of the market.[22] The influence of market logic affects professional fields in several ways: it challenges the boundaries between practitioners and laymen (i.e., journalists and audience), as the passivity of the "laymen" can no longer be taken for granted. The audience have transformed into customers whose taste and demands become imperative, blurring the line between journalistic ideals and market ideals. Moreover, deregulation and broken monopolies as well as technological change require professionals to prime multi-functionality instead of speciality.[23] Journalistic marketization has had immense implications ideologically: while the field has always mirrored the dominating class and its inherent tension between an intellectual pole and an economic pole, it is now increasingly sliding towards the economic side. Embodied in the hybrid figure of the "media intellectual" is the economically successful journalistic enterprise where the original tension has been washed off, suggesting synonymy between proper and profitable journalism.[24]

In a Swedish context, these developments have transformed the news business in many ways, rapidly changing the working conditions of journalists. For many years there have been repeated redundancies in national newspapers as well as in smaller local dailies. An investigation of the regional market of the province of Skåne, for instance, revealed the cutbacks in staff over the years 2010–2013 have reduced the total workforce of journalists by a quarter.[25] For young, recently graduated journalists entering the business, the situation is tough, and many give witness to an insecure existence, switching between different kinds of loose contracts and temporary positions. An additional trend is the growing reliance of media houses on staffing companies. In a 2011 report, the industrial organization *Medieföretagen* [The Media Companies] claims, however, that the Swedish news business is dominated by tenured posts and that only 4 percent are being hired via staffing companies. Ten percent of the media company employees are said to hold some kind of short-time position.[26] On the other hand, a survey from 2012 conducted by the Swedish Journalist Union showed that a majority of the reporters employed through staffing companies were unhappy with their conditions. The low status and limited autonomy of their work influenced, in a negative way, their salaries, opportunities for planning their lives, and the freedom to perform their work. One of those journalists said, "I see no future ... the risk of being used and burnt out is way too obvious."[27]

The practical conditions are changing but the ideological consequences of this transition are yet to come. The professional identity of Swedish journalists has proven to be increasingly homogeneous over time,[28] so the basic starting point is that any sign of fragmentation represents a trend break. Besides the forceful reorganizations characterizing the business, there is also a current alternation of generations. Swedish journalists make up an aging community with fewer members under 30 than over 60 (see Table 7.1).

Journalists born in the 1940s and 50s are retiring, taking their certain constellation of ideals with them. Replacing them, the online generation is now entering the profession, and the journalistic field they face is, in many respects, completely different to the situation of their predecessors. These changes of age structure and working conditions may have brought new mind-sets into the professional community. In this chapter I will empirically focus on a few attributes – or forms of capital – that are closely tied to those structural changes of the field, and around which new subgroups of journalists may align: namely, *age* and *employment status*.

Table 7.1 Age distribution among Swedish journalists 1989–2011 (percent)

Age	Year		
	1989	*1999*	*2011*
<29	11	15	10
30–39	33	30	26
40–49	37	27	23
50–59	14	24	24
60>	5	4	17
Total	100	100	100
n	850	1097	1409

Source: *SJS*

Study design

To explore the impact of those individual attributes on professional ideals, I use questions from the *Swedish Journalist Survey 1989–2011*. This survey has been conducted five times since 1989, by the Department of Journalism, Media and Communication at the University of Gothenburg (JMG), in cooperation with the Swedish Journalist Union (SJU). The union membership register was used as a sampling frame, and some 1,000–2,500 journalists were included in the survey each time. In Sweden, the majority of journalists are affiliated with the union (there were around 17,500 in 2011), which means the selection is highly representative.

The *Swedish Journalist Survey* is an ambitious questionnaire, with a wide range of questions concerning different aspects of journalism as a profession and as a democratic institution. It also includes background data such as age, class, education, and working conditions. In my analysis, I treat a question focusing on the professional role of Swedish journalists – or, more specifically, how they think journalists should regard themselves as professionals – by offering a number of different statements. The positions of the respondents are then measured on a five-degree scale. The exact wording of the statements and the given response set are presented in connection to the tables below. Measurements used to analyse the empirical data are based on percentages and Kendall's tau-C. The age and employment variables have been controlled against other factors such as gender, education, and organizational belonging, something that is commented on in relation to the results in case they have made any relevant difference.

The statistics have been complemented with an open-answer survey given to 30 students studying on the Masters program in Journalism at JMG, University of Gothenburg. The program begins with a full-term internship in a wide range of Swedish newsrooms. This may be in magazines, commercial broadcasting, public service companies or regular newspapers. During this internship, students work full-time for half the ordinary salary, thereby gaining experience beyond standard university schooling. Their views on their own entrance to the labor market and the state of the newsrooms were collected in the autumn of 2013. This material is used here to illustrate and explain the statistical data. Although it cannot be seen as representative of the opinions of all Swedish journalists, it can be said to give some insight into the current development of the news business, as experienced by new journalists.

The online generation differs

How should journalists regard their role as professionals? Considering the agreement of Swedish journalists on the different standpoints offered in response to that question, it is fair to say that their opinions are still very uniform. This is especially true regarding the professional ideals of scrutinizing people in power and explaining complicated events to the audience. The majority of the journalists consider these missions to be important elements of the journalistic role, and the agreement on this has increased between 1989 and 2011. Those ideals can be seen as the ideological umbrella keeping the journalistic collective together. Below this we find a range of standpoints where the journalists position themselves more freely and in relation to individual as well as organizational attributes.

While journalists in general seem to agree on many ideals, the younger generation diverges in most aspects (Table 7.2). They do agree with their older colleagues regarding the all-embracing opinions of scrutiny and explanation. Those two ideals are so fundamental that very few journalists nowadays say anything else – that would be unprofessional! Putting these standpoints aside, the online generation reveals a quite different professional identity than the rest of the group. It is no surprise that new and fresh journalists show a higher intensity in their opinions. Young people tend to be more radical and less willing to compromise, coming directly from university with high hopes and standards. The difference in attitude compared to more mature generations may thus partly be explained by the fact that the latter have had time to mold their views against the reality of practical work life.

But not altogether, though: considering the way young journalists diverge, they appear to be deeply marked by the liberal interpretation of what journalistic professionalism is. Objectivity is the most obvious example of this:

Table 7.2 Swedish journalists' perceptions of professional ideals, organized by age, 2011 (percent that *fully* agree with the statements)

		Age groups					
	All	<29	30–39	40–49	50–59	60>	Tau-c
Scrutinize power holders	82	86	87	82	80	77	−.05**
Explain complicated events to the audience	75	75	77	76	78	66	−.04*
Let different opinions be heard	62	72	65	62	59	54	−.08**
Objectively mediate news and information	58	75	59	55	56	52	−.07**
Criticize social injustice	48	56	48	49	46	49	−.02
Neutrally report social events	38	55	41	32	36	35	−.07**
Influence public opinion	19	16	18	20	21	20	.08**
Mirror public opinion	19	31	19	20	19	13	−.07**
Provide recreation and amusement	17	22	16	17	15	15	−.01
Average number of responses	1,365	131	360	321	323	238	

Note: The question was worded 'A journalist should consider him/herself as...a scrutinizer of those in power/...someone who explains complicated events to the audience/...someone who lets different opinions be heard' and so forth.
* Significant at the 95 percent level. ** Significant at the 99 percent level.
Source: *SJS 2011*

while only one out of two of the oldest journalists fully agree that this is important, 75 percent of the youngest do so. Thereby, they clearly lean towards the Anglo-American model, resting heavily upon ideals such as objectivity and neutrality.[29] The strong support for the ideal to criticize social injustice further verifies this approach. The objectivity norm has spread continuously over the world in recent decades,[30] but what it means is culturally dependent. An international survey in the beginning of the 1990s showed that Swedish journalists favored the meaning "going beyond the statements of the contending sides to the hard facts of a political dispute," while American journalists preferred to see objectivity as "expressing fairly the position of each side in a political dispute."[31] The tenor of the objectivity concept is likely to have changed both in Sweden and the U.S. since then, but from a Swedish point of view it signifies a continued de-politicization of journalism – and a movement toward the commercial pole of the business.

Furthermore, the strengthened objectivity norm among young journalists could be a consequence of the academification of the occupation. A majority of Swedish journalists today hold some kind of university degree, often in journalism. From a journalistic perspective, academic/professional objectivity has come to conquer the more advocacy-oriented approach of the 1970s and 80s. This development also signals a movement from the participatory stand of that time, something that can be seen in the support for the mirroring ideal. The view that journalists should mirror public opinion has been outdated for a long time. In a cultural context where social constructivism is being commonly acknowledged, the mere thought of "mirroring" becomes ridiculous. However, among younger journalists, again, there appears to be a growing support for the mirroring ideal. One third of journalists under the age of 29 think this is a very important task for journalists, compared to the average 19 percent in the collective as a whole.

Another aspect of the growth of liberal ideals in this generation is that it appears to be driven by female journalists. Regarding the ideals of mirroring, neutrality, and objectivity, there is a clear predominance among women. For instance, 79 percent of female journalists under 29 fully agree with the objectivity ideal, while the share of men in the same group is 69 percent. Women often express more distinct ideals than their male colleagues. Their motives for applying for journalism in the first place are primarily based on an interest in social issues and the democratic perspective, while men tend to be attracted by the expressive features of the occupation and the excitement of being where the action is.[32] The proportion of women among Swedish journalists has grown steadily, and the gender division is now fifty-fifty, something that could be a sign of a feminization of the occupation. What the embracing of liberal ideals by young women more specifically signifies does, however, need further investigation.

Finally, we can also see that the ideal to provide recreation and amusement is showing a slight upswing in the younger generation of journalists. This is probably a sign of the overall market orientation of the Swedish media, and parallels well the ongoing liberalization of the profession. Nevertheless, taken together, Swedish journalists are still very skeptical about the commercial side of the news business; a total of merely 17 percent agree that entertainment and recreation is an important task for journalists. Somebody once said: "Journalism is printing what someone else does not want printed; everything else is public relations." The quote is of uncertain origin, but could yet illustrate the basic approach of Swedish journalists. They clearly adhere to the professional mind-set of liberal journalism, but with the Scandinavian touch of skepticism toward exaggerated market influence in public arenas.

Employment status

Although the professional identity of Swedish journalists has been growing increasingly homogeneous over time, the younger generation of journalists seems to be breaking this development by taking a new direction toward a more liberal, Anglo-American view of journalism. Aside from the above-mentioned reasons for this development, there are also more general patterns in society that are influencing this trend: the globalization of values in many industries, and the communication industries in particular; the overall liberalization of Swedish society; and the difficult financial situation of many news outlets. The latter situation has fallen hard on new actors trying to work their way into the field. The *Swedish Journalist Survey* shows that, in 2011, a majority of the respondents had tenured positions, but that this situation – unsurprisingly – did not apply to journalists under 29.

One out of two journalists in this group hold tenured positions, while the rest are obliged to take various kinds of temporary employment. This is only natural, as it takes a while to establish oneself in a new occupation. However,

Table 7.3 The employment status of Swedish journalists, 2011 (percent)

	Age groups					
	All	*<29*	*30–39*	*40–49*	*50–59*	*60>*
Tenure position	73	54	69	77	80	76
Supplementary position /stand-ins	7	22	13	3	1	1
Other temporary positions, e.g. project engagements	3	10	5	3	–	–
Freelancer	15	12	10	15	17	20
Unemployed	3	2	3	2	2	3
Total	100	100	100	100	100	100
Number of responses	1,379	132	353	323	332	239

Note: Significant at the 99 percent level. Kendall's Tau-c: -.061.
Source: *SJS*

the situation is only gradually better in the group of journalists aged 30–39, about 30 percent of whom are still outside the safety net of tenured employment.

This means that the variations in perceptions of professional ideals are connected, not only to age, but also to terms of employment: that is to say, the younger generation is also the one holding temporary positions of various kinds, which means the socialization process into the professional identity construction is prolonged and delayed. It is possible, and perhaps even likely, that professional loyalty is weakening among the young journalists who are experiencing difficulties in becoming established in the labor market. In the network society, they face a new type of polarized job-sharing – between a well-educated core staff with special training and great independence, and the other part of the workforce that is flexible and hired when needed. In network organizations, working procedures and professional structures are being redefined; some positions are being up-valued, gaining status and autonomy, while others are being automatized, down-graded and held by low-wage earners.[33] This situation is confirmed by the trainee students at JMG in the open-answer survey. One of the students, working at a tabloid, comments on the development as follows:

> This reasoning clearly captures the way the *Kvällspostens* newsroom works. There are a few specialized and experienced journalists with tenure positions left. But, basically, the paper would not survive without the "dispensable" workers – here in the shapes of interns, stand-ins and freelancers who just have to content themselves with switching between work tasks and news beats as required.

Another problem facing new journalists entering the field today is that, in a time when the business could expect a large-scale shift of generations, this shift is slowing. Older journalists are retiring but are not being replaced by the young to the same extent. This is especially evident in the realm of newspapers, where the workforce is continuously shrinking. During the period of 1990–2005, the total number of newspaper employees dropped from 18,000 to 10,000.[34] The downsizings have accelerated since then, but there are no statistics available to cover those yet. Often it is the senior journalists aged 50 and over who are being included in redundancies, as organizations tend to prioritize the less-specialized and cheaper labor. The well-experienced journalists then continue on the freelance market, offering heavy competition to their younger colleagues. Another JMG student describes the constitution of his internship newsroom:

> Interns also appear to make up a small, but important percentage of workers in the sector. In the *Aftonbladet TV* department there are four interns within a total number of approximately 40 workers. Also, within this total number there are six freelancers and four stand-ins.

These tendencies constitute difficult challenges to the boundary work of journalists, as the community is based on the sense that everybody is fighting the same battle. All professions have built-in hierarchies, and journalism is no exception, but the foundations for these hierarchies are now shaking. The main assumption has always been that you start at the bottom and then work your way up, which gives new recruits something to strive for. Today, an increasing number of doors appear to be closed straight from the start, and the value of each individual is much more insecure. One student describes news production as a factory:

> This is a flexible working place, where almost every person that I ask what their role is answers that they "do a little bit of this and that." One day reporter, another day editor and the third day project leader. I recognize the image of a newsroom where the backbone is the editorial system, and the journalists are changeable bits around this. In sum, those systems function exactly as they should: work is flowing and top-quality products are being made at the same time. But the decline in autonomy does, on the other hand, have an influence over the journalist's daily life. When I, after only a few months, occasionally feel I'm just a part of the production line, then how do those who have been here for ten years feel? I definitely believe that the standardization and modeling could limit journalistic creativity.

The flexibility of news organizations affects various groups of journalists differently, but it creates new strata within the professional community that in the long run could have a fragmentizing effect on the professionalism of journalists. It is obvious that frequent stand-ins and an extensive use of short-term jobs diminish journalistic engagement. However, journalists in Sweden still seem to like their work very much. Few of the questions in the *Swedish Journalists Survey* show any clear evidence of disappointment or dissatisfaction among any group of journalists. There are indications that older, male journalists from the local press are those having the greatest difficulties adapting to the new media environment. They feel somewhat deprived of autonomy on an individual level, but still seem fairly happy with their work. Regarding the younger journalists, the problem with insecure working conditions appears to some extent to be redeemed by the extensive fighting spirit and self-confidence of this generation. A JMG intern at a local TV station says:

> I can't see that someone better educated should be regarded as more competent. In fact, stand-ins and persons with insecure employment can sometimes do that little extra work which is unexpected and well received. The new labor force who is coming in is often the one representing new and revolutionary ideas. This was especially evident in my newsroom since the staff largely included individuals under 40.

It is thus important to remember that the development toward temporary positions and replaceable media workers does not affect all young journalists the same. Those having skills and competences in the area of online/mobile publishing or advanced research methods/data mining are, at the moment, gaining excellent positions in most organizational settings. While online publishing was initially considered as an additional field to the "real" press and broadcasting production, the tables have now turned and the status of online journalists has increased in just a few years. Editors rarely have the skills or insight needed in the digital sphere, which makes such competencies extremely valuable, generating extensive individual autonomy to those having them. This development adds another dimension to the professional expulsion mechanisms, as the competition for jurisdiction increasingly seems to appear in the conflict line between generations. There is a growing complexity in the age–status relationship of the journalistic field, compared to before. Older age and longer work experience have previously been related to higher status in the business, but may today sometimes be an impediment as renewal and innovation are becoming prime requirements. The ongoing shift of generations in the work force is therefore no less than a renegotiation of journalistic boundaries, redefining our understanding of what journalism really is.

The rise of new hierarchies in the field

This chapter has investigated journalistic boundaries with reference to structural changes of external as well as internal character. The field is far from static, and drastically changed working conditions are likely to have some influence on how journalists regard their role. Furthermore, divergent working conditions among different groups might lead to increasing stratification and the rise of internal divisions. The initial question was thus whether journalism can rightly be seen as one cohesive profession any more, or if it is breaking into fractions. By using a methodological combination of survey data and freely formulated observations from newsroom interns, I have attempted to capture the relation between the professional ideals and the field constitution of news production. Post-modern identities are, according to Castells,[35] in a turbulent state, and various sub-identities are developing in response to new pressures. In relation to the labor market, however, Peetz[36] argues that the individualization process should not be mistaken for the *individualization of attitudes*, but instead regarded as an *individualization of the employment relationship*. He means that the discourse of individualism fits the "dominant, market-based view of society, in which all relationships are transactional,"[37] but that this discourse does not always match what data tells us.

Broadly, the journalists' answers showed the ideological foundation of Swedish journalists to be more homogeneous than ever before, and that this foundation is concentrated on the watchdog role and the ideal of explaining complicated events to the public. There are many reasons behind this concentration of ideals: first, the social homogeneity of the journalistic group is increasing. The typical Swedish journalist is a Swedish native with a middle-class, academic background, living in one of the larger cities; very few represent anything else. This social streamlining is a contributing factor to the equally streamlined professional role. In that sense, boundaries are as firm as ever. Second, the professionalization process has far from ceased: journalists are still fiercely struggling to maintain their status and legitimacy as professionals – although the odds are increasingly against them. The intern students speaking out in the open-answer survey state that the development of news firms is characterized by a delimited autonomy for journalists at the benefit of organizational efficiency. The homogenization of ideals among journalists could, in that light, be seen as an intensified act of boundary work by a profession under pressure.

So the professional identity stays firm on an ideological level, but looking at the actual working conditions, Peetz[38] appears to be right: employment relations are increasingly being negotiated on an individual level, a procedure that risks eroding the collective basis in the long run. Repeated editorial budget cuts, low salaries and job insecurity may cause a decline in professional commitment and efficacy – trends eventually leading to cynicism, burnout, and detachment from professional aims. What is clear from the *Swedish Journalist Survey* is that the youngest generation of journalists deviates from the rest regarding both professional ideals and terms of employment. They are more likely to hold temporary positions and are more orientated towards typical liberal ideals such as objectivity and neutrality than their older colleagues. This follows a general tendency predicted by Hallin and Mancini[39] ten years ago, suggesting that the Anglo-Amercian model promoting those ideals would advance internationally. Swedish data prove them right. It is a process visible on many levels, and the attitudinal turn of the new generation of journalists is one of the most evident signs.

The shift in ideals among new journalists may not necessarily indicate an accelerating lack of conformity, but it could be the start of a general change of values led by the online generation – thereby expanding the meaning of professionalism in this context. Their view of the role of journalism is shaped partly by the network society in which they grew up, but also partly by the changing material conditions for journalistic labor. The testimonies of the intern students shows that many of them have internalized the view of the entrepreneurial self, where entrance to the labor market is intimately connected to a constant process of personal branding and identity-building. They are fully aware of their own value, and criticize the old-fashioned attitudes and practices of the industry. At the same time, their positions in the field are insecure and wavering. There is an impending risk that these young journalists are not choosing but are being forced to attune their view to what seems legitimate and feasible in their situation. Temporary employment is perhaps not the best foundation for progressive and radical thinking in this realm; instead it tends to create submissive workers trying to cope. This coping involves, apart from a number of practical maneuvers, a negotiation of values – the professional ideals versus the actual working conditions and career ambitions of each individual.

Furthermore, the pressure on journalists, and young journalists especially, may have the effect of homogenizing the group ideologically, even as this professional identity, on the other hand, may become increasingly flat. The personal enterprise and increasing career focus of journalists may be one reason for the strengthening objectivity ideal. By cultivating a flexible and non-partisan approach, journalists stand available for a wide range of different tasks and positions.[40] They then become the perfect employees for media organizations inasmuch as they can take on various assignments without any bias and always from a professional perspective. So far, so good. What could be problematic, however, is if this development is driven by a negative industrial development and aggressiveness toward individuals, rather than a collective forward-looking within the profession itself. The professional identity may then be transformed from a guiding ideological frame, securing (or at least striving for) the democratic relevance of news production, into a legitimizing window display only.

For the business, there now stands a challenge to pick up and utilize the energy and self-confidence of the young journalists, otherwise they will probably head off for new adventures. For the profession lies the challenge of maintaining the sense of community, but not only ideologically: the community foundation is truly under pressure now, and the rise of internal polarization is in progress. These internal hierarchies are, and always were, tied to the prerequisites offered by organizational settings, something that is becoming increasingly important to acknowledge. For journalism scholars, finally, there is the important task of continuing to investigate the relationship between ideals and practice in news production. Having data from statistical studies is useful, but there is also a great need for more in-depth research. As has been indicated in this chapter, there is an increasing discrepancy between what journalists say and how they go about performing their work. Professional autonomy is a privilege that increasingly seems to be reserved for a few, high-profile journalists with very specialized skills. These journalists bring us great journalism, but they also bear the risk of becoming culprits in the dismantling of the journalistic profession as the gap within the group widens.

Notes

1 Scott Reinardy, "Newspaper Journalism in Crisis: Burnout on the Rise, Eroding Young Journalists' Career Commitment," *Journalism* 12, no. 1(2011): 33–50.
2 Robert McChesney and John Nichols, *The Death and Life of American Journalism: The Media Revolution That Will Begin the World Again* (Philadelphia, PA: Nation Books, 2010).

3 Thomas Gieryn, *Cultural Boundaries of Science: Credibility on the Line* (Chicago: University of Chicago Press, 1999).

4 Pressutredningen [Press commission]. *Vårt dagliga blad: stöd till svensk dagspress [Our Daily News: Support to Swedish Press]* (Stockholm: Fritze, 1995).

5 Jenny Wiik, *Journalism in Transition* (Sweden: University of Gothenburg, 2010).

6 Douglas Kellner, "Popular Culture and the Construction of Postmodern Identities," in *Modernity and Identity*, eds Scott Lash and Jonathan Friedman (Oxford: Blackwell, 1992).

7 Manuel Castells, *The Information Age: Economy, Society and Culture. Vol. 1, The Rise of the Network Society* (Malden, MA: Blackwell, 2000).

8 Anthony Weymout and Bernard Lamizet, *Markets and Myths* (London: Longman, 1996).

9 Frank Webster, "The Information Society Revisited," in *The Handbook of New Media*, eds Leah Lievrouw and Sonia Livingstone (London: Sage, 2002).

10 For example, Kerry Wilson and Eddie Halpin, "Convergence and Professional Identity in the Academic Library," *Journal of Librarianship and Information Science* 38, no. 2 (2006): 79–91; James Faulconbridge and Daniel Muzio, "Organizational Professionalism in Globalizing Law Firms," *Work Employment Society* 22, no. 1 (2008): 7–25.

11 David Angell and Brent Heslop, *The Internet Business Companion: Growing your Business in the Electronic Age* (Reading, MA: Addison-Wesley, 1995).

12 Gillian Ursell, "Changing Times, Changing Identities: A Case Study of British Journalists" in *Identity in the Age of the New Economy*, eds Torben Jensen and Ann Westenholz (Cheltenham, UK: Edward Elgar, 2004).

13 Jenny Wiik, "Identities under Construction: Professional Journalism in a Phase of Destabilization," *International Review of Sociology: Revue Internationale de Sociologie* 19, no. 2 (2009): 351–65; Jenny Wiik, "Towards the Liberal Model," *Journalism Practice* (2014): 1–10.

14 Pierre Bourdieu, *Distinction: A Social Critique of the Judgement of Taste* (London: Routledge, 2010).

15 Andrew Abbott, *The Systems of Professions: An Essay on the Division of Expert Labor* (Chicago: University of Chicago Press, 1988).

16 Beverley Skeggs, *Formations of Class and Gender: Becoming Respectable* (London: Sage, 1997).

17 Toril Moi, *What is a Woman?: And other Essays* (Oxford: Oxford University Press, 1999).

18 Margareta Melin-Higgins, "Female Educators and Male Craftsmen? The Professional Ideals among Swedish Journalists," *Nordicom Review* 1 (1996): 153–69; Monica Löfgren Nilsson and Jenny Wiik, "A Gendered Dimension of Journalism. Professional Ideals in Transition," Paper presented at the conference *Gender, Journalism and the Press*. Rennes, 15–16 May 2008.

19 Christian Vermehren, "Bourdieu and Media Studies" in *Pierre Bourdieu: Language, Culture and Education*, eds Michael Grenfell and Michael Kelly (Bern, Switzerland: Peter Lang, 1999).

20 For example, Jan Hovden, *Profane and Sacred. A Study of the Norwegian Journalistic Field* (Bergen, Norway: University of Bergen, 2008); Tamara Witschge and Gunnar Nygren, "Journalism: A Profession under Pressure?" *Journal of Media Business Studies* 6, no. 1 (2009): 37–59; Silvio Waisbord, *Reinventing Professionalism: Journalism and News in Global Perspective* (Cambridge: Polity Press, 2013).

21 Rodney Benson, "Mapping Field Variation: Journalism in France and the United States" in *Bourdieu and the Journalistic Field*, eds Rodney Benson and Eric Neveu (Cambridge: Polity Press, 2005), 105–12.

22 John Keane, *The Media and Democracy* (Cambridge: Polity Press, 1991); John H. McManus, *Market-driven Journalism: Let the Citizen Beware?* (Thousand Oaks, CA: Sage, 1994); Pierre Bourdieu, *On Television* (New York: New Press, 1999); Robert Picard, "Commercialism and Newspaper Quality," *Newspaper Research Journal* 25, no. 1 (2004): 54–65.

23 Valerie Fournier, "Boundary Work and the (Un)making of the Professions" in *Professionalism, Boundaries and Workplace*, ed. Nigel Malin (Florence, KY: Routledge, 2000), 67–86.

24 Patrick Champagne, "The 'Double Dependency': The Journalistic Field between Politics and Markets" in *Bourdieu and the Journalistic Field*, eds Rodney Benson and Eric Neveu (Cambridge, Polity Press, 2005), 48–63.

25 Newsøresund, "Var fjärde skånsk journalist har fått gå [Every Fourth Journalist had to Go]," *News Øresund* (2013), www.newsoresund.se/

26 Medieföretagen, "Så jobbar vi i media – anställningsformer i mediabranschen [How we work in media – forms of employment in the media business]," Report by the Media Companies/Almega, 2011.

27 Hanna Lundquist, "Enkät visar tuffa villkor för bemanningsanställda [Survey shows tough conditions for staffing company employees]," *Journalisten [The Journalist]*, 29 March 2012.

28 Wiik, *Journalism in Transition*.

29 Michael Schudson, "The Objectivity Norm in American Journalism," *Journalism* 2, no. 2 (2001): 149–70; Daniel Hallin and Paolo Mancini, *Comparing Media Systems: Three Models of Media and Politics* (New York: Cambridge University Press, 2004).

30 Jyotika Ramaprasad and James Kelly, "Reporting the News from the World's Rooftop: A survey of Nepalese journalists," *Gazette* 65, no. 3 (2003): 291–315; Jyotika Ramaprasad, "Nepalese Journalists: Idealists, Optimists, and Realists," *Harvard International Journal of Press/Politics* 10, no. 1 (2005): 90–108; Wiik, "Towards the Liberal Model," 1–10.

31 Thomas Patterson, "Political Roles of the Journalist," in *The Politics of News, the News of Politics*, eds Doris Graber, Pippa Norris and Denis McQuail (Washington, D.C.: CQ Press, 1998), 22.

32 Monica Löfgren Nilsson and Jenny Wiik, "A Gendered Dimension of Journalism. Professional Ideals in Transition"; Jenny Wiik, *Journalism in Transition*.

33 Gunnar Nygren, *Yrke på glid: om journalistrollens de-professionalisering [A Sliding Occupation: on the De-professionalization of Journalism]*, (Stockholm: Sim, 2008).

34 Nygren, *A sliding occupation*.

35 Castells, *The Information Age: Economy, Society and Culture. Vol. 1, The Rise of the Network Society*.

36 David Peetz, "Are Individualistic Attitudes Killing Collectivism?" *Transfer: European Review of Labor and Research* 16, no. 3 (2010): 383–98.

37 Peetz, "Are Individualistic Attitudes Killing Collectivism?" 394

38 Peetz, "Are Individualistic Attitudes Killing Collectivism?"

39 Hallin and Mancini, *Comparing Media Systems: Three Models of Media and Politics*.

40 John Soloski, "News Reporting and Professionalism: Some Constraints on the Reporting of the News" *Media, Culture & Society* 11, no. 2 (1989): 207–28.

Part II

Encountering non-journalistic actors in newsmaking

Chapter 8

Journalism beyond the boundaries

The collective construction of news narratives

David Domingo and Florence Le Cam

Introduction

On May 31, 2012, the police were not surprised when a crowd of dozens of young Muslims gathered in front of the commissary of Molenbeek, a northwest Brussels neighborhood with a majority of Muslim inhabitants, shouting angry slogans. They had been convened through mobile text messages that claimed that a woman wearing a niqab had been forced to take off the traditional clothing in front of policemen at the commissary, after refusing to show her face when confronted in the street by a patrol. Wearing an integral veil has been forbidden by law in Belgium since 2011. The police had been tipped off about the demonstration, and even if the chief of police had no doubts about the correctness of the detention proceedings and considered the rumors in the text messages unfounded, he ordered a security cordon around the commissary. The mayor of the municipality did not hesitate to be there that evening during the protest, not only to try to calm the angry mob of young people that threw rocks at the building, but also to give the journalists present on the scene the first elements of an interpretation of what had happened, in order to make sure they framed the demonstration as a disproportionate reaction to a minor incident. The next day, as protests repeated in the evening under the searchlight of the police helicopter despite a curfew, the mayor decided to use a different channel than mainstream journalism to calm the community: he called the imams to a meeting so that they could explain to their congregations in the mosques that he would not let a minority of radicals ruin the image of a municipality that had been praised for its efforts to foster multicultural respect.

Analyzing the boundary work that professional journalists engage in, as chapters in the previous section do, is crucial to understanding how they are adapting to a scenario full of uncertainty.[1] In this chapter, though, we want to expand the exploration to a wider scenario that includes the daily interactions of a plurality of actors that participates with (and sometimes without) the journalists in a collective construction of news narratives about current events. Research tends to categorize these other actors as sources and audiences, already setting them on the other side of the journalism boundary,[2] even though such boundaries are blurrier than ever.[3] We believe that in order to achieve a better understanding of how news is being produced, circulated and used today, we need to de-emphasize the attention on the contours of professional boundaries. To this aim, instead of exploring the boundaries around journalistic identities, we propose focusing on the diversity of actors playing a role in news narratives, and in doing so we want to highlight the boundaries of news practices. We examine actors who engage in the construction of news narratives, regardless of their position inside or outside journalism as a profession. We prefer to conceptualize journalism as a social practice, defined by the activities that are necessary for the creation of news, rather than by institutionalized structures and professional positions. From this perspective, we may not prejudge a priori what the role is of each actor in making news, or distinguish some practices as legitimate journalism and others as irrelevant just because they are not performed by professional journalists or by professional media. Our hypothesis is that journalism as a practice is "in dispersion,"[4] that the professional boundaries of journalism represent only one of its configurations, historically and symbolically constructed. Other social actors outside institutionalized journalistic organizations are also actively participating in the co-construction of news. In doing so, they extend the meaning of what we should consider as part of the social activity of making the news. The mayor of Molenbeek talking to the imams to reach a public that does not consume mainstream media is a good example of relevant practices we may be missing if we focus solely on the professional boundaries of journalism.

Tracing news practices allows us to pose a different set of questions regarding contemporary journalism. We can ask whether diverse actors reproduce similar strategies in their production and circulation of newsworthy materials, and to what extent professional products are a model to imitate or not. We can explore the emergence of new narrative forms proposed by specific actors and how others adapt to these innovations. Again, to know whether this happens inside or outside of the newsrooms would be an empirical finding: if we did not look at all the actors involved in sharing discourses about issues of collective interest, we would be missing part of the picture of what is journalism. We can still interrogate the relationships between the actors and what roles they assign to themselves and to others implicitly through their interactions and explicitly through the representations they enunciate in research interviews. The boundaries of news practices are likely to be more unstable, and therefore more intriguing, than those of the profession. In this context, professional affiliation is just one factor among others to be traced in order to explain who engages with journalism and how. Moreover, the variety of news practices and the actors performing them may change as every new controversy may motivate new players to enter the public space to contribute to the collective news narrative. By focusing on the preservation of professional boundaries, we would risk erasing the complexity of the construction of news, the strong role that many other actors besides professional journalists may have in the shaping of the narratives about a specific event.

This chapter is the result of a dialogue between two researchers sharing the same fieldwork to test this hypothesis by applying the theoretical background each of them feels more comfortable with. First, we discuss how actor-network theory[5] allows us to approach news practices without defining any boundaries and invites us to trace how the interactions between actors shape their actions. It is through their relationships that we can make sense of how they co-create news narratives, what is the position of professional journalism in the process, and what role professional boundary work plays in configuring the network of relationships. Second, we present the perspective of dialogism,[6] which suggests that every discursive practice has embedded in itself previous discourses and future discourses. The news narrative, then, is the fragile result of a polyphonic and dialogic discursive interaction between the various actors. In their actions and attitudes, actors produce specific, diverse narratives, stemming from the knowledge they have about the strategies, practices, and discourses of other actors, as well as their anticipation of discourses that can affect their own speeches and those of others. Boundaries are symbolically understood and eventually known, but they continuously move according to the discourses produced.

The Djato controversy

The day after the detention of the veiled lady, journalists managed to discover her name and her background: Stéphanie Djato was a Belgian recently converted to Islam and was involved with the Salafist group Sharia4Belgium that wanted to impose Islamic laws in the country. The group was behind the demonstrations and had actually brought many participants from their headquarters in Antwerp. On the evening of June 1, Sharia4Belgium convened a press conference in which its leader and the woman in niqab gave their version of events and called for revenge. Every actor knew that the topic was very touchy, mixing radical extremism, multiculturalism and an electoral context with municipal elections approaching in few months. A controversy was deemed sure to arise.

Controversies[7] are a unique opportunity for researchers, the best moment to make sense of the mechanisms of the collective construction of news.[8] Actors feel the urge to position themselves in the wake of events that resonate with their social principles or political goals, and their ideas crystallize in discourses that most often reveal existing tensions as their relationships are explicitly laid out for the researcher to examine. Selecting a specific controversy, like the Djato case, also makes the discussion of news practices with the diversity of social actors more tangible, and the reconstruction of the process of production and circulation of information about the event allows one to trace the interconnectedness of the actions and discourses involved in the process.

We took as a strategic point of departure the news published by mainstream media (French-speaking national and local newspapers and the public television) in order to identify the sources used by journalists to cover the incident.[9] This sample was not only convenient, but also significant in order to know what narratives had been produced by those formerly known as the chroniclers of history. Our focus being on tracing the participation of all the social actors, not just the journalists, in the construction of the collective news narrative, taking the professionals' production as the starting point may sound paradoxical, but it seemed the most reasonable and feasible option. They were the actors that would surely have been involved in reporting about the controversy, and they could lead us to the rest: politicians, the police and other public institutions, experts, members of the public. During the in-depth interviews with eight journalists, they mentioned other actors not quoted as sources in their news stories about the controversy but with whom they had regular interactions.[10] This allowed us to devise a snowballing strategy to trace the rest of the actors actively involved in the controversy, even if they did not appear in the mainstream media coverage: Muslim community media, NGOs, and activist groups.[11]

An actor-network approach

The epistemological approach of actor-network theory (ANT) is especially well equipped to explore evolving social practices.[12] For journalism studies, it offers the opportunity to address the analysis of the production of news without imposing the traditional categories associated to specific roles.[13] Actors are what they do in their interactions with others, or more precisely, actors are what others make them do, their roles contingent on the network of relationships traced by the researcher. The resulting picture is that of a struggle between actors to impose their ideal configuration of relationships on others and to force them through an "obligatory point of passage"[14] that shapes their actions in ways that fulfill the needs of the hegemonic actor. Within the extensive articulation of an alternative research program for the analysis of the social (Latour 2005), this concept of an obligatory point of passage is the one that this chapter will focus on, as it lets us explore the position of professional journalism in the wider context of the controversy, and rethink the boundaries of journalism as the evolving outcome of daily practices and interactions. From an ANT perspective, keeping a hegemonic position requires mobilizing a lot of resources and the support of other actors adhering to the configuration who are unable to foster alternatives. The case of Stéphanie Djato shows how fragile, actually, journalism is as an obligatory point of passage for the news narrative of the controversy.

Mainstream media as an obligatory point of passage

The news practices of the spokesperson of the police, the mayor, and the radical Salafist group all had something in common: they were consciously adapted to the needs of professional journalists, in order to make sure that their point of view was reported through mainstream media. In the case of the police, they hold a daily morning meeting to select the events they have dealt with that will be most attractive to the media. Systematic press clippings have taught the spokesperson the rules of this obligatory point of passage. If he wants coverage that boosts the image of the police, he gives journalists what they need. He distributes a press release with the selected events, and is available on his cell phone anytime for clarification. Sharia4Belgium was very active at using social media, and especially YouTube, to spread its version of the incident between Djato and the police, but the group also made sure they created the perfect event for journalists: a press conference where the victim would explain first-hand the events of the previous day. Despite the fact that the conference was forbidden in Molenbeek and ended up being held in a small apartment in a village on the outskirts of Brussels, many local journalists attended it. They were reluctant to give voice to the hate speeches of the leader of the Salafist group, but the proposal fitted so well their need for explanations about the initial news narrative created around Djato that they did not want to miss the press conference.

The professional boundaries of journalism were an important symbolic resource in the construction of the obligatory point of passage of mainstream media. Actors outside the newsroom recognized the role of journalists in society as the legitimate narrators of current events, and press releases and press conferences are news practices that exist to effectively reach the professionals from outside of the boundary. This obligatory point of passage became more evident when we reached out to the other actors who were active in the construction of the news narrative but who did not comply with the requisites imposed by the mainstream media. The clearest case were the members of the Muslim community in Brussels, who felt that Sharia4Belgium did not represent the majority of peaceful, moderate citizens professing Islam. They were systematically excluded from the mainstream media coverage, even if some journalists explained to us that they had contacted some of them to understand their interpretation about the demonstrations in Molenbeek. News agency reporters argued that their contacts within the Muslim community could not be quoted as sources in their articles because they were not an institutional source: at that point they were still treating the story as an incident, not as political news, and the police, the prosecutor, and the mayor were the trusted sources. Other journalists just did not know whom to address to get the opinion of the Muslim community once the story became a political controversy about integration. They perceived this community as being too diverse, without clear spokespersons, and, most importantly, lacking the skills to provide reliable regular information. The adjunct director of the Center for Equality, a state-funded non-profit organization, also shared a similar experience: he had tried for months to open up an honest debate about the prohibition of the integral veil, but newspapers had first misinterpreted his words and then later ignored his point of view. He acknowledged that his discourse did not fit the polarized oversimplification of the coverage that quickly fell into dichotomies (us vs. them, democracy vs. radicalism, integration vs. integrism) – all of it fed by politicians, Sharia4Belgium, and what he perceived as the news production dynamics in the media. He decided not to react to the Djato incident and only ended up being quoted in the news when journalists asked him for an opinion regarding the possibility of outlawing the Salafist group, a question that fitted the polarized narrative under construction.

This configuration suggests a very successful boundary-building activity of professional journalists as the legitimate narrators of the controversy, accepted and reinforced by the core actors involved in it, and neglecting those discourses that did not adapt to the obligatory point of passage. Even community media was attracted by the news practices of the mainstream, trying to reproduce them because they shared a lot of the professional ideology (focusing on the facts) and the practices (relying on the official sources) and because they did not have resources to do their own reporting on the ground. However, this hegemony of mainstream media in shaping the news practices of other actors did not grant them control over the collective narrative about the controversy. In fact, the actors that better adapted their practices to the media needs (especially the police, Sharia4Belgium, and, more generally, the politicians) played a crucial role in taking the news narrative in the direction they wanted. During the first evening, the media expertise of the police spokesperson was combined with the fact that over the years he himself had become an obligatory point of passage for crime reporters: he was their trusted source, and the accusations of police abuse towards Djato were always framed by the official discourse that they were unfounded, with the definitive fact that one of the policewomen had her nose broken by Djato in her attempts to resist detention. Later, as Sharia4Belgium managed to transform the incident into a media event and national politicians started calling for a ban on the Salafist group, political reporters took over the relay in constructing the evolving news narrative with this new actor. The police spokesperson felt less at ease in dealing with these reporters because the well-established practices that worked in his relationship with crime reporters were not valid for the new news producers entering the scene. But he quickly understood that it was not the time for facts anymore, but the time for interpretation, the job of politicians.

Circumventing the obligatory point of passage

Despite the prevalence of the professional boundaries of journalism in setting mainstream media as an obligatory point of passage for the narrative of the controversy, it did not deter the other actors from actively engaging in news practices themselves, most often aimed at interacting with the journalists, and at other times consciously circumventing the obligatory point of passage. This is a crucial revelation from an ANT approach focusing on practices rather than positions in the field: the multiplication of news practices and discourses beyond the newsrooms and professional boundaries. The effectiveness of some actors in shaping the news narrative that mainstream media shared with the majority of the population did not stop them from using other communication practices to spread their interpretations of the events. We saw the case of the mayor of Molenbeek at the beginning of the chapter. The Center for Equality had worked with Muslim women on other occasions through workshops, even if they did not develop this kind of initiative as a direct response to the Djato incident. And all the actors shared a fascination for social media as a space where the public participated in the construction of news narratives in a much more visible way than in the traditional public sphere. Journalists admitted that they felt uneasy with social media, as they could not mediate the information and rumors shared on those platforms, and at the same time they were attracted to it as a representation of how public opinion formed in real time. They admitted, though, that they hardly have the time to systematically use social media as a source. The police spokesperson, the mayor, and the director of the Center for Equality wanted to have a more robust presence on those spaces, to reach the communities directly, sharing the intuition that relaying their messages un-mediated by journalists may have advantages worth exploring. Their problem was also lack of time in developing the skills to effectively use online tools. Among the main actors in the story, Sharia4Belgium was the one that was most at ease with social media. Its videos on YouTube had a life of their own, circulating through retweets and Facebook walls. The fact that the videos were embedded in some of the mainstream news websites the day after the incident suggests that professional journalism is interconnected to a broader network of interrelated practices that co-construct the narrative about current events. In this case, Sharia4Belgium started by circumventing mainstream media with the use of YouTube, but interestingly enough the visibility they gained with that strategy granted them the access to the media they were openly pursuing – and persuaded journalists to go to the more traditional setting of a press conference.

The mutual shaping of actors' roles

The roles of each actor in the Djato case were not the result of improvised relationships or configurations that would vanish as soon as the event was forgotten in the cafés of Molenbeek. The "news network"[15] we traced was the result of years of daily interactions between some of the actors, and their adjustments to specific circumstances of this controversy. News networks evolve over time, and controversies are privileged moments to study them because they may shake the existing positions, alter the relationships, or change the obligatory points of passage. In this case, the event easily fitted the established channels, the narrative almost predictably shaped into polarized positions. Actors who exerted their power over others were efficient at keeping business as usual by neutralizing the news practices of an outsider like

Sharia4Belgium, who although receiving the media attention it wanted, was quickly framed through rhetorical condemnation that was soon followed by the jailing of its leader.

In this context, actors mutually shaped the roles of each other through their relationships. The police spokesperson saw himself as the provider of official truth and the facts that journalists needed to construct their stories. Journalists were indeed comfortable with granting that position to the police, even more when it provided conveniently formatted news bites every day. Belga, the national news agency, was the certifier of official information, a crucial tool for other journalists. This role shaped their selection of sources, marginalizing those that did not provide that kind of information. Politicians were not supposed to merely provide facts, but interpretations, which were the natural substance of the narrative once breaking news had settled. Sharia4Belgium is as much the product of its ideological radicalism as of its effective news practices: the media coverage triggered by these practices simply corroborated their extremism and its widespread rejection by the majority of society. The saddest part of this story is how invisible moderate discourses are in the media coverage, simply because they did not find their place in the configuration of the news network.

If we acknowledge that this mutual shaping of roles is performed and reflected by the news practices of the different actors involved in the controversy, we can then see that the professional boundaries of journalism are not only a symbolic asset that journalists mobilize in their interactions but that other social actors understand and recognize them as granting journalists a specific role in society. The boundaries are more tangibly interpreted by the actors as a set of practices they can learn, in order to adapt their own news practices and maximize their appropriateness for the mainstream media newsflow, and therefore the likelihood that their discourses will be adopted by the professional news narratives.

A dialogic perspective on the controversy

A controversy can be seen as a series of interspersed discourses. Social actors produce a variety of interpretations of the event. These discourses could be seen, from a Bourdieusian approach, as if one was trying to dominate the public debate, while the others wanted to strategically find a way to reach it. From the perspective of Bakhtin's work, a controversy is the interweaving of discourses, understood as practices and speeches linked with previous discourses as well as with the anticipation of the effects of these new discourses. In that sense, this dialogic approach cannot directly focus on the boundaries of professional journalists producing the news. It has to take into account the plurality of discourses and their interactions, understand the perspective of each actor, and how each of them, while narrating the news, constructs, in the meantime, a discursive territory. Focusing on the boundaries of journalism as a specific territory is contradictory with a discursive approach and especially with the essential nature of a controversy as a debate: the circulation of discourses, words, and ways of narrating and interpreting events.

Three primary elements can help to understand the controversy from the dialogic approach. First of all, the controversy has to be interpreted as a new discursive element in a broader narrative (not only constructed by the media, but also by politicians, police, the citizens involved, etc.). Social actors do not react to an event spontaneously. They use words already existing that have been used in specific contexts, and the discourses they produce have sometimes already been circulated for another event. What they say, how they socially position themselves, are the result of their own history with the debate. The second element to be taken into account in this approach is that discourses are also dialogic with each other: discourses cannot be analyzed as independent from one another. Speeches involved in the public debate are always constructed with reference to other discourses: they respond to each other, they may contradict, strengthen, or even ignore the others. Together, they form a coherent set of social expressions of differentiated positions. Finally, the third element has to do with the anticipation actors perform in their discourses. A social actor never takes a social position without thinking (even unconsciously) about the consequences of his discourse. Actors (individually or collectively) anticipate how their discourses will interact with others, the way they may change or not the position of others, how they will construct or strengthen their social position. Discourses are often built to perform actions: sometimes they work, sometimes not. But, while thinking on how to express their positions, individuals anticipate how their discourses will integrate with the series of interspersed discourses. Ultimately, what may emerge from this controversy, from an inductive perspective, is the way in which boundaries are conceived by the actors themselves, rather than a validation (or falsification) of boundaries conceptualized by the researcher.

A continuum of interwoven discourses

Each controversy has its own historical origins and a specific continuum of interwoven discourses. In the Djato case, the news narrative carries within it the traces of all previous discourses that focus on the niqab (through the debate around the law in Belgium, and earlier in France), on social and cultural integration (a few days before, a minister made the headlines with harsh opinions on this topic), on the presence of the Muslim community in Brussels – a node of the debate about multiculturality in Belgium – and obviously on the past history of the radical group, Sharia4Belgium, that was already well known in the northern federal region of Flanders. During the coverage of the event the interdiscursivity was quite explicit, clearly expressed by all the actors of the news when answering to each other's interpretations. Actors underlined their own domain of discourse and what made them different from the discourses of others. They were all playing their own part, using arguments to discredit the others. The most obvious dialogic confrontation was between politicians and Sharia4Belgium, but we can also analyze how the mayor of Molenbeek – speaking in the street to citizens, or in a room with the imams – constructed a discourse not only for his community, but also to reinforce his own position in the media and political spheres. He explained in the research interview that other politicians had attacked him because of his conciliatory approach when dealing with multiculturality in his municipality. His discursive practices during the controversy also show an anticipation of the elections scheduled for five months later. The electoral context played a role in the continuum. It also shaped the discourses around a new event that occurred a few weeks after the Djato case. A man arrived from France and tried to stab a policeman in a subway station in Molenbeek. He defended his action by saying that he wanted to defend his Belgian Muslim brothers, and he had a copy of a news story covering the Djato incident in his pocket. This new event revived the media and political interest, and interacted with the ongoing news narrative of the Djato controversy as it evolved into a court case with the menace of a complaint against the police by Djato that never happened in the end, and the prosecution and condemnation of the leader of Sharia4Belgium. By definition, there is never a discursive end to news narratives; they are chained to one another and evolve in new directions. But, for our study, we took the last mention of Stéphanie Djato in mainstream media as the closure of our effort to trace the contributions of the different actors.

The Djato case as a polyphonic interdiscourse

This controversy, as with any other discourse, is in explicit or implicit rela-tionship with other discourses.[16] This interdiscursivity defines the dialogism: each word stays under the influence of the contexts to which it belongs. In that sense, the relationships between discourses are unbounded. The Djato case is a continuum of discourses, and this interdiscursivity has to be taken into account to understand how the narratives about the topic of multiculturality (before, and all along the development of the event) interfered with the dis-courses of the actors (media, politicians, policemen, citizens, members of the community, etc.) about the Djato incident, when they tried to construct their own public position and to interact (or not) with others. As we saw, social actors position themselves according to the positions of the others, adjusting their discursive territories – that is, their boundaries. Some examples can highlight the fact that institutional, journalistic and community discourses are mainly constructed in reference to previous discourses and are aware of the potential effects of the positions expressed. The discourses of the mayor during the controversy were influenced by his historical position in favor of the Muslim community in Brussels, and the fact that he had defended, for many years, the construction of mosques and at the same time fostered the ban of the niqab in his municipality before the Belgian law was passed. He knowingly plays with the media according to his previous political declarations. He has constructed his own public figure, and he anticipates what the media expects of him: direct speech, sometimes very provocative. At the same time, he also imagines the reactions of the citizens, the fact that they are used to seeing him on the ground talking to them while the event occurs. In a different configuration, the same happened with the director of the Center for Equality. He couldn't participate in the debate over the Djato case because of previous positions he had held in an open debate about the niqab. As he was in favor of a rational prohibition of the niqab – to confine religion to the private sphere – he silenced the position of the center to avoid a new controversy about the center itself, trying to protect the institution from a debate about radicalism. They both seemed to anticipate their own territory of actions according to the context – as the context changed, their discourses were adjusted.

The narrative of traditional journalists is then crossed by all these institutional positions. But journalists are at the same time orientated by the past coverage of similar events, by their own editorial policy, and by the knowledge that local reporters have of the field. Journalists act in regard to their collective identity (as members of a professional group historically constructed, mainly performed through the images they think their audiences have of them), but also in regard to the media context, their competition with other media and journalists, and the relations they have built with sources. The example of a particular freelance journalist is especially interesting. A few months before the Djato case, he wanted to report on the emerging personalities of the Muslim community, so he contacted members of Sharia4Belgium, hitherto unknown in Wallonia, and filmed a portrait of them. During the interview, the leader threatened to destroy the iconic Atomium, a gigantic monument that can be seen from many places in Brussels, and the video became very famous. In that case, the reporter used previous discourses about this radical group to make news and to try to build his professional career at the same time. His attitude during the Djato case was strongly influenced by this first contact. He stayed away from the controversy, considering the case to be uninteresting once Sharia4Belgium had become a "media personality." The narrative of traditional journalists acts as the mirror of the discourses of others, but it produces another discourse, by highlighting the positions of some (in particular Sharia4Belgium and the politicians) and discarding others (like the Muslim community).

The neglect of discourses of the Muslim community in mainstream media does not mean that Muslims did not have a specific discourse, but that their speeches were not directed towards the media sphere: they were circulated within the community itself. The actors seemed to distance themselves from the media and the interpretations they anticipated journalists would make. They produced discourses that were the result of their own representation, as well as a direct consequence of the way they had been previously reported in the media. A hypothesis concerning this distance is that it could be the result of a distrust of the media, or the expression of a strong diversity of discourses in the community itself. In doing so, the Muslim community built its own discursive boundaries, trying to control the circulation of their speeches. The practices of orality they used were highly significant for their community, and could be interpreted as a way to bypass traditional media. The mayor was conscious of these news practices and engaged himself in them to reach the Muslim community.

The very few Muslim community media encountered in the field are constrained by a double discourse: they are part of the community and of media discourses. The monthly local Moroccan magazine did not discuss the case, in part because of its editorial policy aimed at promoting a positive self-image of the community, but also because of the abundance of discourses about Muslim radicalism in the mainstream media – extremism they do not want to promote or even to talk about. They reacted to ambient discourses and to traditional media and politicians, who tend to express negative opinions about the community. They did not want to participate in the perpetuation of these discourses and preferred to focus on positive social issues. Their discourses acted as another frame that dialogued (in silence for their public) with other discourses. The interdiscourse is implied, but it becomes the basis of the production of a specific posture and the drawing of their boundaries.

The community radio revealed a different position. The French-speaking journalist working for this local station, with its limited funding, had to use the narrative of traditional media with the websites of mainstream media and the news agency as his main sources. This journalist thought of his work as part of the media system, but he defended a specific framing of the news, anticipating the reactions of his audience. He explained how he had to distinguish his news from traditional media, but at the same time taking them as a reference ensured the objectivity and veracity of the news he produced. His discourse combined the specificity of news expected by his audience with a very professional attitude about the quality of his journalistic practices, consistent with what is expected from traditional media.

This analysis of the dialogic perspective unveils the polyphony of discursive references used by social actors. Some build their discourses according to their previous career, based on previous or current political discourses or electoral situations, or through their wish to spread a specific interpretation of the event in the public debate. At the same time, all the actors try, through their discourses, to distinguish themselves in the public sphere, to imagine and construct their boundaries. This approach allows us to focus on the continuum of discourses in which social actors participate in the construction of the collective news narrative: a continuum of editorial policies and of discourses on multiculturalism, but also a continuum of journalism as a social practice that has to be anticipated by sources, that has to be integrated by some community actors, and that has to be managed by the journalists themselves. Dialogism emphasizes the interdiscourse that creates the news through a continuous process of impregnation between discourses. Boundaries constructed by actors are then fluid and, always, in adaptation to others. The discursive practices reveal this fluidity and the fact that boundaries are both multiple (every actor builds his or her own territory) and contextual: every event, especially a controversy, as an unbounded narrative, can transform the way actors think of their boundaries.

Conclusion

The two theoretical approaches explored in this chapter through a specific controversy unveil the complexity of contemporary newsmaking, and recontextualize the professional boundaries of journalism in a wider context that relativizes their significance for the collective production of news narratives. Actor-network theory and dialogism offer different but complementary perspectives, both underscoring the contingency, historicity, and diversity of news practices. Contingent, because they are (re)defined constantly by the actors in their relationships and their interdiscoursivity; they react to what others are doing and saying. Historically constructed, because practices in the present are shaped by previous experiences and discourses, by the evolution of the relationships between the actors and the adaptations they have made over time in their practices in order to achieve their goals. And diverse, because there is a multiplicity of actors contributing to the news narrative, and journalists may not be the ones determining how the controversy ends up being told: other actors have enough skills and strategy to shape it in the direction they wanted. When we put the professional boundaries of journalism in the context of news practices, the picture is one of an unbounded interdiscourse, a network of relationships where the interactions are more significant than the positions.

Narrating reality is obviously not the exclusive prerogative of journalists. Sources, community media, and citizens produce their own narratives, often mediated by the media or through other channels. But what is of interest here, from a dialogic perspective, has to do with the fluidity of boundaries as they are conceived by the actors themselves. If journalists have historically imagined the boundaries of a professional group, other actors also build their territories based on contextual or specific practices. These actors actually think of the boundaries of journalists by adjusting their own practices, but they also construct the boundaries of their discursive production through dialogism. We may then hypothesize that the narration of news, as a collective process, proceeds through interactions between different discourses. In this sense, a complex set of interdiscursivity is involved in the production of news. News is then the product of the discursive polyphony of all these actors. If we consider that news is the result of the interactions of all these discursive productions, news could be understood as a discourse made by a set of actors (not just journalists) and a set of past and future speeches. The concept of professional boundaries then becomes just an element in the process of understanding who produces the news and how is it produced. News seems, at least in this case, collectively produced by practices and discourses, the result of an unbounded interdiscourse, necessarily fluid and whose affiliations and incarnations may vary depending on the nature of the controversy.

The concept of the obligatory point of passage, on the other hand, provides insights into how the professional boundaries of journalism interact with the rest of the actors. Politicians and activists are aware of the boundaries that legitimate journalists as the narrators of events. But rather than deterring them from proposing their own narratives, they adapt to what they perceive as an obligatory point of passage to successfully convey their messages. Similarly to the controversy in Philadelphia analyzed by C.W. Anderson,[17] social actors seek through journalists the validation of their discourses to reach the widest public possible. Our case also shows how different actors have diverse degrees of success in adapting their news practices to the needs and expectations of journalists, and, more importantly, how sometimes their practices circumvent mainstream media as they try to address specific publics. By doing this, actors are not really challenging the professional boundaries of journalism, which they acknowledge and even encourage as they find that the mediation of mainstream media may fulfill the useful social role of legitimating their discourses. Nonetheless, our case shows that professional boundaries do not stop other social actors from performing practices that imitate, with much sophistication, the ones traditionally associated with journalists, or from exploring other forms of communication that still serve the most basic role of newsmaking: explaining and interpreting what is going on around us.

Notes

1 Seth C. Lewis, "The Tension Between Professional Control and Open Participation: Journalism and its Boundaries," *Information, Communication & Society*, 15, no. 6 (2012): 836–66; Michael Schudson and C.W. Anderson, "Objectivity, Professionalism and Truth Seeking in Journalism," in *The Handbook of Journalism Studies*, eds Karin Wahl-Jorgensen and Thomas Hanitzsch (New York: Routledge, 2008).

2 David Domingo, Pere Masip and Irene Costera-Meijer, "Tracing Digital News Networks: Towards an integrated framework of the dynamics of news production, circulation and use," *Digital Journalism*, 3(1), 53–67.

3 Denis Ruellan, *Le journalisme ou le professionnalisme du flou [Journalism, or the blurred professionalism]*, 2nd edn. (Grenoble, France: Presses Universitaires de Grenoble, 2007), 25–37.

4 Roseline Ringoot and Jean-Michel Utard, *Le Journalisme en Invention: Nouvelles practiques, nouveaux actants [Journalism in invention: New practices, new actants]* (Rennes, France: Presses Universitaires de Rennes, 2005).

5 Bruno Latour, *Reassembling the Social: An Introduction to Actor-Network Theory* (New York: Oxford University Press, 2005).

6 Tzvetan Todorov, *Mikhaïl Bakhtine. Le principe dialogique. Suivi de Ecrits du Cercle de Bakhtine [Mikhaïl Bakhtin. The dialogical principle. Series of articles of*

the Bakhtin Circle] (Paris: Seuil, 1981); Julia Kristeva, "Bakhtine, le mot, le dialogue et le roman," [Bakhtin, the word, the dialog, and the novel] *Critique*, 239 (1967): 438–65.

7 Michel Callon, "Pour une sociologie des controverses technologiques," [For a sociology of technological controversies] *Fundamenta Scientiae*, 2, 3/4 (1981): 381–99; Bruno Jobert, "Représentations sociales, controverses et débats dans la conduite des politiques publiques," *Revue française de science politique*, 42, no. 2 (1992): 219–34.

8 Sophie Moirand, *Les discours de la presse quotidienne. Observer, analyser, comprendre [The discourse of newspapers. Observing, analysing, understanding]* (Paris: Presses Universitaires de France, 2007).

9 David Domingo and Florence Le Cam, "Journalism in Dispersion: Exploring the Blurring Boundaries of Newsmaking Through a Controversy," *Digital Journalism* 2, no. 3 (2014): 310–21.

10 Domingo and Le Cam, "Journalism in Dispersion: Exploring the Blurring Boundaries of Newsmaking Through a Controversy."

11 Florence Le Cam and David Domingo, "Narrating multiculturalism: polyphonic news discourses in Brussels." Paper presented at the conference "Local journalism around the world: professional practices, economic foundations, and political implications." 27–28 February 2014, Oxford, Reuters Institute for the Study of Journalism.

12 John Law, "After ANT: Complexity, naming and topology," in *Actor Network Theory and After*, eds John Law and James Hassard (Oxford: Blackwell, 1999), 1–14.

13 Domingo, Masip and Costera-Meijer, "Tracing Digital News Networks: Towards an integrated framework of the dynamics of news production, circulation and use."

14 Emma Hemmingway, *Into the Newsroom. Exploring the digital production of regional television news* (London: Routledge, 2008), 226.

15 Hemmingway, *Into the Newsroom. Exploring the digital production of regional television news,* 27; Domingo, Masip and Costera Meijer, "Tracing Digital News Networks: Towards an integrated framework of the dynamics of news production, circulation and use."

16 Dominique Maingueneau, *Genèses du discours [Origins of discourse]* (Brussels: Pierre Mardaga, 1984).

17 C.W. Anderson, "Journalistic Networks and the Diffusion of Local News: The Brief, Happy News Life of the Francisville Four," *Political Communication* 27, no. 3 (2010): 289–309.

Chapter 9

Redrawing borders from within

Commenting on news stories as boundary work

Sue Robinson

Introduction

Online commenter "HankandDagney" corrected reporters' articles and other citizens' statements within the commenting sections of his news organizations. "Wbennetti" interviewed city officials to report "facts." "Ivy Lee" posted a story of herself as a New Orleans hero during the 2005 Hurricane Katrina at its anniversary – a stark contrast to the dark remembrance in the attached news articles. And then there was "Guest" who took to the reader forums in 2012 to bear witness to the rallies commemorating the 2011 Wisconsin protests that erupted over the governor's assault on unions, reciting numbers of people and detailing signs. With online interactivity, these citizens writing on news sites become fact custodian, storyteller, and historian – three roles traditionally occupied by journalists. They exchange information, report, and analyze in these spaces. They sympathize, remember, mock, antagonize, criticize and even deliberate here. They check each other's facts with links and eyewitness reports and often engage in back-and-forth exchanges in which each commenter publishes his or her "say" in a public forum. And with every post, these citizens – albeit a small proportion of the news organization's audience – challenge the reporters who authored the original story they are riffing off. And they do so from within the sanctioned borders of the news organizations. With these acts of content production, commenters populate spaces once dedicated only to professionals.

Utilizing Bourdieu's theory of journalism as a "field," this chapter will consider the emergent roles for the citizen in what used to be journalist-only, boundaried spaces. At one time, citizens appeared only as archetypes in journalists' news narratives. Now online commenting spaces for citizens offer a non-threatening, non-onerous pathway to contribute to – and even to author – the daily stories about life in America. Considering press scholars' delineated roles for journalists, which include fact custodians (and watchdogs), storyteller, and historian,[1] this chapter will explore how citizens craft stories and interpret events while often "repairing" newswork alongside these mainstream takes. I will call on a collection of my own data gathered over the course of half a dozen years analyzing commenting spaces such as article forums. I wanted to know how the traditional boundaries for America's press were being negotiated and redrawn by commenters within news website forums. Could these citizens be legitimate actors as Bourdieu might describe them for the field of journalism within the public sphere?

After virtually analyzing the public words of "HankandDagney," "wbennetti," "Ivy Lee," "Guest" and their fellow commenters, I documented an emergent position-shifting happening in the field of journalism. My evidence found that citizen commenters are assuming the traditionally journalistic roles of fact custodian, storyteller, and historian. Citizens adapt journalistic norms of evidence sharing, linking, terminology and other role exercising in these press-controlled spaces. I am arguing that in adopting these positions, they assert value systems through a developing *habitus* (that is, a way of interacting in order to achieve some goal) of community practice that extends across news organizations' forums. This chapter considers how they do this and what the implications are for the boundaries of journalism. In the conclusion, I ponder how effective these actors (typically anonymous and ephemeral) in such spaces (often so hidden from view) and their content (always so fragmented) can be as viable field components. These seemingly inconsequential, individual commenters create a special challenge to the journalism field – but only in aggregate. The commenting places themselves operate as ambiguous boundary objects that can be used by participants to re-conceptualize news events according to alternative perspectives than those represented in the formal article on the page. Ultimately these user-generated sections, existing as they are within the news publications themselves, must be thought of as a grand, collaborative spatial agent of transformation for the overall journalistic field.

Boundary work in scholarship

This chapter takes up the notion of professional boundary work specifically, with journalists the "in" group and the hypothesis that citizens jockey for "in" group status. Many scholars have examined how fields construct an ecological authority over their topical or specialty domains.[2] Boundary work often arises from a need to distinguish a population by creating binaries.[3] Bourdieu[4] related boundaries to fields of space and posited that forces at work in the field could be used to create in and out groups in order to demarcate a community. Fiske[5] suggested that people develop ways of thinking about "others," categorizing individuals according to race, gender, class and other categories. Gieryn[6] typologized boundary work into expulsion, expansion, and protection of autonomy. One way to expel, expand or protect the autonomy of a field is by developing "linguistic ideologies" that result in ways of speaking within groups.[7] Another way is to celebrate in-group perspective and diminish others' points of views.[8] All of this works to preserve resources, restrict access, and present opportunity within the community.[9] Star and Griesemer[10] and others[11] offer the term "boundary object" to describe the ways in which this can be done, such as scientific classifications or press passes. These objects serve as a transitory space between two social worlds as materialities that are "both plastic enough to adapt to local needs and the constraints of the several parties employing them, yet robust enough to maintain a common identity across sites".[12] For Barley et al.,[13] boundary objects represent opportunities for both new and old agents to make claims, create (and re-create) meanings, forge alliances and perform other relational activity that can redefine a community and its borders. Within boundary objects, actors must be able to explore multiple meanings (as opposed to a singular value) for the space – and ultimately, the community. Essentially, I am suggesting that comments can be considered boundary objects.

The field of journalism

One way to think about boundaries in regard to journalism is to call upon Bourdieu's conceptualization of journalism as a field made up of actors who maneuver for position as influential information disseminators.[14] Reporters encompass this field along with other agents such as public relations people, government officials, specialists, and audience members. Everyone in the field operates according to cultural, political, economic, historic and other forces that erect a fluid set of borders. Without an exclusive authority over public information, news organizations' existence – financial, cultural, physical – is threatened. Over the last century, reporters have spent much time policing these boundaries through a variety of mechanisms, including claims of objectivity and paradigm repairwork.[15] Reporters used power-elite "sources," "quotations," and agreed-upon ways of attribution, formulaic writing, and terminology (linguistic ideology) such as "confirm." To be considered members of the profession (and the field), all journalists must follow the rules of objectivity and other professional tenets.[16] These could be considered the field agents' *habitus*; in field theory, an actor's *habitus* incorporates his or her background, norms, values, and belief system that guides what they do according to their position in the field.

For much of the last century, journalists have operated within their field as the nation's official storytellers, watchdogs, historians, psychologists, soothsayers, patriots, and fact custodians.[17] These roles were why the field existed and was perpetuated. As a public mass disseminator of information, reporters learned "truths" and relayed them via frames, value depictions, character archetypes, and other mechanisms;[18] these norms and routines represented the *habitus* of the field agents.[19] Reporters "bear witness" and then use their agreed-upon conventions – such as quotations, third-person writing, inverted pyramid leads – to craft a narrative. In doing so en masse to the public, reporters are able to explain American values (such as responsible capitalism or hard work) and help people learn right from wrong, grieve and move past crises, feel nationalistic, vote and govern, be a good citizen, and generally conceptualize both an individual and a collective identity for themselves. Up until two decades ago, citizens received these "lessons" directly from the authoritative newspaper or television news broadcasts, without much formal interference (though, of course, many personal influencers help people navigate the meaning of these messages).

Interlopers in the field

Calling paradigm repairwork a "professional ritual," Berkowitz[20] argued that when journalists publish criticism of those who deviate from the accepted norms of the field, they protect their authority as information disseminators by undermining those who step outside the community standards. Field outsiders have traditionally been marginalized in some way, via this repairwork and other reflexive communication about the profession.[21] However, Bourdieu makes the important note that when interlopers enter the field and commit challenging acts on a consistent basis, they can shift the boundaries[22]:

> In each field ... there are those who dominate and those who are dominated according to the values internal to that field ... But heteronomy – the loss of autonomy through subjection to external forces – begins when someone who is not a mathematician intervenes to give an opinion about mathematics. ... and is listened to.

The success of an interloper hinges on Bourdieu's statement, "and is listened to." Without influence, a new agent has little chance of changing anything. That said, once an actor attains authority, he or she can force some field movement. As Bourdieu[23] wrote: "The boundary of the field is a stake of struggles."

Bloggers, commenters, Facebook posters, and tweeters engage in "acts of news" that are transforming power dynamics within the field of news production.[24] Anderson[25] argued that emerging networks of blogs and other forums were restructuring the Philadelphia news ecosystem. Lewis[26] studied the impact of the Knight Foundation's funding of many journalistic projects on the ecology of news, finding that "by recasting the rhetorical and actual boundaries of journalism jurisdiction, [the Knight Foundation] has opened space for professional innovation – principally the introduction of participation as an ethical norm." The very institutions infusing dollars into the field to shore up its health are rethinking the field's supposed boundaries. "Boundaries between the world 'out there' and the internal world of the newsroom are no longer sustainable as the tendrils of the network permeate everywhere."[27] In his monograph, Lowrey[28] documented one way in which certain interlopers – health bloggers – position themselves to attain legitimacy (via connections to legacy media, stabilizing content strategies, development of organizational norms, etc.). The population of the health media ecology he examined also radically changed over time, through such developments as increased specialization and hybrid forms of content. The more new agents act in novel ways in a field, the more evolution is observed and we witness more "relaxing of the edges" of journalism boundaries.

Commenting spaces

Citizens can now "comment" within news sites. I am arguing in this chapter that conceiving of commenting spaces as boundary objects could illuminate the shifting power dynamics of the journalistic field. Online comments allow citizens to take over parts of what had been historically journalists' acting roles, and, thus, commenters may be agent interlopers who conduct boundary work. Comments are often attached to news or allowed in user-dedicated forum spaces in most online news organizations today. Much research has examined the nature and effect of comments.[29] So far, this scholarship has determined that what is being written in the comments is influencing how people perceive the topic or issue presented.[30] For example, Walther et al.[31] showed that commenters represent an "influence agent" for people viewing public service announcement video about marijuana use. Similarly, Anderson et al.[32] conducted an experiment using an article with comments about nanotechnology that supported the claim that uncivil comments exacerbate polarization. Analyzing the policy development in one newsroom along with their exchange with commenters about that policy,[33] I argued that user-generated content offered a place where citizens challenged the textual authority that journalists try to maintain on their sites, and that citizens were developing a competing value system for these places.

For this chapter, I am drawing from two sets of data: the first group of comments came from a study on Hurricane Katrina's anniversary in September 2006,[34] when I looked at user-generated comments;[35] the second dataset comprises comments appended to Wisconsin news articles during the 2012 anniversary of the Wisconsin protests.[36] Both involved thousands of comments in online news articles from media organizations throughout the two states involved, Louisiana and Wisconsin. Both incorporated a two-week period of time, around the anniversaries. For this chapter, I approached all of this data thinking about Bourdieu's considerations of agents within a field, particularly interlopers who have the power supposedly to assume positionality within a field and thus transform that field's border. First, I will cull from the data evidence of the new kinds of roles and functions that commenters adopt in these spaces, highlighting three of the most studied roles of journalists – fact custodian, storyteller, and historian.[37] Then I will discuss how field theory can be used to think about the ways in which these actors are shifting traditional boundaries of journalism.

Fact custodian

Jamieson and Waldman, Kovach and Rosenstiel and others[38] argue that a journalist's job includes gathering evidence in a balanced manner to produce some kind of a truth so that we can self-govern. Scholars show how journalism relays "elite" information from "elite" agents who can help journalistic organizations maintain their own elite position within the overall structure.[39] Journalists share a common *habitus*; Schudson described this dynamic as: "journalists all breathe the same air of their occupation and develop habits of judgment of great, sometimes stupefying, uniformity."[40] This uniformity results in agreed-upon "evidence" as "facts" and a self-imposed news judgment that builds social capital and solidifies acting position in the field as "fact custodians." Commenting spaces introduce new players to this practice of uniformity over facts, and I was curious to see whether new *habitus* processes emerged in attempts to build some kind of social capital among the commenters.

In their spaces within the news sanctuary, commenters in my various samples attempted to negotiate "evidence" on their own. They often contradict the reporter's evidence, as in this comment by "Bobpacker"[41] (2012) from the Wisconsin protest anniversary: "The story says 35,000. You say 60,000. The recall leaders say they have 1 million siganture [sic] to recall Walker, others say 750,000–800,000 Whose facts are we to believe? [sic]" These users accept the role of the space – to understand what happened – and they seem to hold what other citizens, that is, nonprofessionals, write on an equal basis with journalists. In one comment about coverage of the Hurricane Katrina anniversary, "Canteen"[42] adopts the journalistic terminology "confirms" and demands a "clear and succinct explanation of what happened,what is the current status, and what will be done to prevent future train wrecks [sic]" from other commenters. Thus, the commenter not only mirrors the journalistic *habitus* in her lexicon adoption, but also the journalists' position in the field as fact-checker and protector of credible information. Some commenters went further, deliberately trying to uncover wrongdoing as in this comment by "keepingitreal"[43] criticizing a conservative-funded fact-checking group: "The MacIver 'news service' will underestimate the crowd by at least 10,000. MacIver is a purveyor of right-wing propaganda masquerading as a news service." It should be noted, however, that the only evidence presented here comes from the "news sources" themselves, and the writer uses quotation marks not to indicate evidence being cited, but rather as a sarcastic questioning. Another asks for "facts" only to cite "evidence" without any attribution[44]: "Any FACTS to back up your statement? Wisconsin has a net loss in jobs since Walker has taken over." Comments on the anniversaries of Hurricane Katrina and the Wisconsin protests offered a constant debate over the nature of "facts," particularly who had them and who was using them correctly. This tension revealed an intense competition in these commenting realms over who had the most authoritative information – a key characteristic of journalists continually vying for position in the field.

Journalists, Bourdieu reminds us, "are in a competitive relationship of continuous struggle."[45] Still other commenters cited outside sources (as in one writer on the Wisconsin data who urged people to "read your Politifacts! and get the facts first"[46]) or "reported" directly from the field, as in this comment from the Katrina data: "Today on Inside Jefferson Parish, I asked Council Chairman Capella specifically about the 17th Street Canal floodwalls. He stated that he was comfortable with the pump stations operational ... "[47] Here we note that citizens adopt the hierarchy that already exists in the field. Commenter "wbennetti" attempts to gain social capital to attain a position of authority by citing an authoritative source. Thus we can see how the commenters use the space to push their way into the world of the journalist, turning the forum into a boundary object that encourages roleplay reflecting the existing field's value system.

Storyteller

Jamieson and Waldman,[48] Gans,[49] and Lule[50] have documented how mainstream journalists tell stories as a way to establish a certain value system. The nation's storytellers "transform the raw stuff of experience into presumed fact and arrange facts into coherent stories" to "create a way of seeing individuals and events as well as a way of making sense."[51] Lule goes so far as to call this storytelling a matter of mythmaking that results in binary good-versus-evil accountings. For Gans, reporters have an ideological value system that plays out in content, "teaching" readers about "responsible capitalism," "individualism," or "small-town pastoralism," for example. We[52] found in both the Wisconsin and Katrina datasets that commenters largely reflected these values. In the following comment, "Ivy Lee" in the NOLA forums (the online product of the New Orleans news organization *Times Picayune*) at the Katrina anniversary adopts Gans' stated values of moderation, responsible capitalism and rugged individualism in addition to themes such as God and family:

> this evacuation came with an eerie reality as we, the lone car for miles, headed in the opposite direction to the city of New Orleans as Katrina approached. If nothing else, I being a nurse, thought that push comes to shove, I'd be of some assistance to someone who might need a little TLC or a Band-Aid while we stayed at the hotel. Once in the hotel, ... Katrina has changed my thinking on the issues of material things and their priority in my life. I won't over spend in the supermarket, especially during the storm season. I promised myself to pay more than the usual attention to my spiritual and family life. Nothing is more important when "things" lose their value.[53]

Through the telling of this narrative, "Ivy Lee" portrays herself as a (would-be) hero undergoing a harrowing journey and triumphing – even completing the tale with her story of redemption and personal growth. Those of us reading – presumably we are the ones who ultimately determine whether someone's position-taking in a field is successful – note her effort to bear witness while also making meaning of her acts. Like a reporter on the front lines, she proved authentic. Like a reporter reinforcing the dominant structure and hierarchy that work as scaffolding for this particular field, the commenter reifies the accepted institutions of cultural life – church, family, supermarkets – and signals a willingness to accept the field's core ideology.

Yet in their assertion of these themes, commenters became polemic at times; this is ironic because scholars have argued that this way of writing through narrative techniques is meant to be unifying, as in collective memory work.[54] In these forums, *citizens* decide who is hero, who is trickster, what their motivations are, what the setting will be, and how the chronology will play out. Throughout the commenting of the Wisconsin protest anniversary, commenters argued over whether Wisconsin Governor Scott Walker or the unions were the heroes in the original story as well as who was pretending to be something they were not – including journalists, as in this 2012 post: "Another 'objective reporting' article by Spicuzza – she and Barbour, left wing activist posing as journalist [sic]."[55] Consider this comment from the Wisconsin anniversary: "We are entitled to assemble and demonstrate even though you may not like it, that is what democracy is about."[56] Here, "molesaurus" articulated the American democratic ideology championed by traditional journalists and a key news value espoused decades ago by Gans. It strikes me that these texts must be read, as Bourdieu[57] suggested, not only as expressions of an individual's value system, but also as a positioning within the broader field structure. I assert, as Bourdieu might, that commenters pressing a "submit comment" button activate both the opportunity to propose a value system for the field and also an explicit claim of legitimacy for the self. This space suggests competing value systems at times, offering an ambiguity necessary for the forum to be a true boundary object, according to Bailey et al.[58] Using the commenting forum, participants act as interlopers countering the mainstream journalism with stories that, in effect, contest the boundaries of the field.

Historian

Zelizer,[59] Kitch,[60] Robinson,[61] Carlson,[62] and others have shown how reporters produce American society's collective memory of major news events through their articles – both at the time of the event unfolding and on the anniversaries following. As with all news stories, these articles often depict heroes and villains, declare lessons learned, and help restore order out of chaos. Where once reporters wrote "the first draft of history,"[63] now citizens willingly took on that role. They became eyewitnesses with the authority to retell stories because they have been there. In this recounting, "Guest" described the scene of the rallies that commemorated the Wisconsin protests a year prior:

I reluctantly headed downtown with the feeling that I was all rallied out before I even got there, but was instantly energized by the people and the fine weather. We were part of a smaller group listening to folks at an off-the-square location, but when we walked up to the Capitol, we were instantly welcomed by the cheers of thousands of others already encircling the Square. ... This is what working together is all about.[64]

These personal stories, such as the one above, offered a chance for citizens to bear witness to the events at hand for the posterity of history. "Guest" also resurrects the themes from 2011: community, solidarity, and "working together." He or she submits these themes through the authority gained by witnessing. During these moments of remembering, citizens – like reporters[65] – were self reflective about their own role in the event. Here a commenter reflected on his experience during Hurricane Katrina: "Decided things were going to be worse than normal hurricane emergency and evacuated. Today is the real anniversary of our disaster, and it has little to do with hurricanes."[66] In the process, they corrected the story – or at least re-articulated what the meaning of that story should be for posterity as in the above quote.

Finally, during their retelling, citizens used the opportunity in these first drafts of history to politicize and revise historic events in the moment. Much of the commentary referenced the past, resurrecting U.S. Presidents Ronald Reagan or Franklin Roosevelt or similar issues or crises from the nation's past in order to make a present-day point, as in this comment:

Wow! The Left sure loves to rewrite history! Under President Bush, the average unemployment rate for his 8 years was LOWER than the 8 years of President Clinton! I know this because I lived through both terms and it was a heck of a lot easier to get a job under GWB than it was under WJC.[67]

Note again how the comments use reflexivity and testimony as an author-itative ploy to be heard in this public forum. We can see from all three of these comments how Bourdieu's concept of *habitus* plays out as citizens assert themselves into the information streams about these anniversaries. In the comments from my datasets, we see people explaining themselves, creating an argument, and offering up stories to manifest a perspective of the tragedy to a public. In both of my sample sets, citizens linked to evidence to do this, referencing historical figures and events and recalling personal escapades. Though the result was not exactly a "collective memory" agreed to by any "field," it did offer a "relation of knowledge or 'cognitive construction'" of that historic event (which is how Bourdieu and Wacquant[68] described *habitus*): "*Habitus* contributed to constituting the field as a meaningful world." By bringing the past back toward our present lives in these comments, citizens help produce memory within the field. Through their comments, we can see how they are making sense of these events in a public manner – that is, their cognitive framework.[69] The very act of posting constitutes a deliberate field act. And through these ways of doing this – URLs, allegory, argument, witnessing – we can know the underlying principles guiding citizens, demonstrating how the social agent (the commenter) is positioning him or herself in relation to other commenters, journalists, and to the greater community and the event itself. Given that these acts are performed by intruders at the borders of the journalistic field, we can see how the commenting section as an object represents a fluid opportunity to stake claims and undermine the stability of the field even as we see the field's dynamics influence the work being done in these spaces.

Boundary work

A boundary object can symbolize an intersection of social worlds, a place where forays are made and explorations happen perhaps as a way for field actors both old and new (or potential) to "try on" a new role. In the boundary work of a field, agents compete for position while interlopers push their own agendas using similar mechanisms. In-group perspective is celebrated as agents employ the kind of "linguistic ideological" language that Gal and Irvine[70] discussed. Like with Bailey et al. in their study of automotive design engineers' processes as boundary objects, my data over the years has demonstrated a constant jockeying through strategic production of text. Commenters played with the field's borders in the strength of their expressed convictions, often taking pot shots at incumbent field agents – journalists – as well as each other. "Sure you did not answer my questions. Also, if you do not know who George Soros is obviously you cannot be very well informed. You must only get your news from MSNBC and Captimes."[71] In this comment, "HankandDagney" undermined mainstream news organizations while acting to reveal other interlopers' inadequate answers. In terms of boundary work, "HankandDagney" adopt the goal of the journalists – to uncover accurate information and perform as a fact custodian (i.e., "you did not answer my questions"). He presents himself to be worthy of judging someone else's position-taking. These kinds of comments are ubiquitous in the commentary that I have looked at over the years, especially in these two samples. Citizens challenge journalists' (and each other's) authority over the information (not only its veracity but also the disseminator's credibility and agenda). Such constant contestation in these spaces reveals very active and intense boundary work happening within the journalistic field.

The other interesting work occurring in these forums is the relationship-building (and destroying) as part of position-taking around specific information topics. Bourdieu and others have argued that agents earn various kinds of capital (social, cultural, symbolic, economic, political) to maintain and also improve their position in the field. He wrote about the television field in which

> actors struggle for the transformation or perseveration of the field. All the
> individuals in this universe bring to the competition all the (relative)

power at their disposal. It is this power that defines their position in the field and as a result, their strategies.[72]

In these commenting sections, citizens arrive with no known power and so they immediately begin striving to establish capital. They do this through the information they provide, such as links to credible evidence, firsthand "reporting," or bearing witness. In the 2010 ethnographic work in which I could observe the development of commenting policies within a newsroom, one frequent commenter to those forums told the news organization that it had reached a point in time when "comments have become content" and should be considered as such in policy development.[73] Consider a comment from the Wisconsin-protest anniversary:

> The circle of friends and foes I hang out with on a regular basis all agree that in order for this state and country to move forward we need some teamwork from labor and management. We are the ones denouncing what you are doing to divide this community and state. Bratfest WAS a community event. You have made it political.[74]

Commenter "FormerGOP" brings to bear the strength of his community – "all his friends and foes who agree" – to the position-taking of his fellow commenter, as he seeks to marginalize the other commenter. Relational tie-building happened in spurts throughout both of my datasets, as citizens reached out to like-minded actors for a more concerted challenge to the boundaries within the forum as the object of contestation.

Conclusions

From all of this discussion, we can say that the field's boundaries are being challenged by a range of disparate, ad hoc interlopers. Yet, this evidence doesn't answer the question I posed at the beginning of this chapter: Are journalistic field boundaries shifting as a result of commenters within the very field space of the news entity – with the news entity's permission? Recall that Bourdieu asserted that any successful new actor must be "listened to." A field can only be permeated by agents who not only have the ability to produce output that helps maintain the field, but also who will be noticed and granted an authority to do so on a consistent basis. My evidence has shown that within the commenting sections themselves, some citizens carry influence as people cited each other, engaged with one another, and generally paid attention to the thrust of the conversation. They competed over "facts" and tapped into the political and other power structures that have helped journalists attain the positions that they have. Citizens drew upon the linguistic ideologies of reporters to (re)name heroes and villains, create stories, and relate value systems. And they took on traditional journalistic roles such as historian to (re)articulate the meaning of significant events and crises and direct society on what lessons should be learned as well as on how best to move forward. Other studies I have done indicated that even as they consider the commenting sections with intense disdain, citizens inevitably wander over to read the comments. In one small survey that I conducted, 30 percent considered comments to be a part of the journalism, 51 percent said comments helped them understand the news story, and 90 percent wanted to see journalists directly engaging with the commenters in those user spaces. But this finding would need to be more deeply studied. We know that 32 percent of online users actively participate in these realms.[75] This is not an insignificant number.

But commenters lack some key characteristics of longevity in a field, including a consistent presence (though a few of these people showed up over and over) and a solidly defined, cohesive identity. Most of these commenters represent an anonymous version of themselves. They announce themselves in one forum on one news organization in a conversation that typically lasts a few hours. Is it possible to dramatically alter the dynamic of a field with actors who come and go and who are not networked within the field in any significant sense? I infer that Bourdieu would say no, emphatically. And, moreover, until commenting sections become as influential as journalism spaces, they cannot attain true longevity in the field. Thus, we can see some real issues with answering the research question in the affirmative and stating that commenters are shifting boundaries.

But *something* is happening in the spaces which occupy journalistic places. Those who are commenting have entered the field with a show of force. Together, with every ping and post, the users produce voluminous content that exists *alongside the news articles*. I am arguing that the comments themselves generate a spatial actor that the field must contend with. As a boundary object, these forums – their very presence – operate as agents of change. Where perhaps an individual commenter cannot move a border, comments symbolize a foreign presence with a developing set of norms and etiquette that directly challenge those established by journalists. Wenger[76] described a boundary object as a "nexus of perspectives, and that it is often in the meeting of these perspectives that artifacts obtain their meanings."[77] The object must be flexible enough to encompass all of these meanings in addition to those already existing in the space[78] – that is, the journalists. The collection of links, facts, story-telling, memories and witnessing, debate and communal interaction alongside the news articles contain elements of both enduring and emergent field dynamics – from social capital earning to *habitus* development. Online citizen contributors are mirroring the journalistic lexicon and adapting to their assumed reportorial roles (fact custodian, storyteller, historian) even as they are also confronting and disclaiming assumptions made by the reporters in direct challenges. Within these places situated so very essentially at the core of news organization sites, commenting sections *in their aggregate* represent both an internal competition and a meso-level, collaborative positioning for a *collective citizenry* to take advantage of. If comments have indeed become journalistic content – as one citizen remarked – then the field of journalism has a new agential entity, and borders will expand to make room for it.

Notes

1 Kathleen Jamieson and Paul Waldman, *The Press Effect: Politicians, journalists, and the stories that shape the political world* (Oxford: Oxford University Press, 2003); Barbie Zelizer, "Why memory's work on journalism does not reflect journalism's work on memory," *Memory Studies* 1, no. 1 (2008): 79–87.
2 Steve Fuller, "Disciplinary boundaries and the rhetoric of the social sciences," *Poetics Today* 12 (1991): 301–5; Susan Gal and Judith Irvine, "The boundaries of languages and disciplines: how ideologies construct difference," *Sociological Research* 62 (1995): 967–1001; Michele Lamont and Vigar Molnar, "The Study of Boundaries in the Social Sciences," *Annual Review of Sociology* 28 (2002): 167–95.
3 Lamont and Molnar, "The Study of Boundaries in the Social Sciences."
4 Pierre Bourdieu, *Homo Academicus* (Stanford, CA: Stanford University Press, 1984).
5 Susan Fiske, "Stereotyping, prejudice, and discrimination," in *Handbook of Social Psychology*, eds Daniel T. Gilbert, Susan Fiske, Gardner Lindszey (New York: McGraw-Hill, 1998), 357–411.
6 Thomas Gieryn, "Boundary-Work and the Demarcation of Science from Non-Science: Strains and Interests in Professional Ideologies of Scientists," *American Sociological Review* 48 (1983): 781–95; Thomas Gieryn, *Cultural Boundaries of Science: Credibility On the Line* (Chicago: University of Chicago Press, 1999).
7 Gal & Irvine, "The boundaries of languages and disciplines: how ideologies construct difference."
8 Geoffrey Bowker and Susan Star, *Sorting Things Out: Classification and Its Consequences* (Cambridge: MIT Press, 1999).
9 Fuller, "Disciplinary boundaries and the rhetoric of the social sciences."
10 Susan Star and J. Griesemer, "Institutional ecology, 'translations' and boundary objects: Amateurs and professionals in Berkeley's Museum of Vertebrate Zoology, 1907–39," *Social Studies Science* 19, no. 3 (1989): 387–420.
11 Bowker & Star, *Sorting Things Out: Classification and Its Consequences*; Charlotte Lee, "Boundary Negotiating Artifacts: Unbinding the Routine of Boundary Objects and Embracing Chaos in Collaborative Work," *Computer Supported Cooperative Work* 16, no. 3 (2007): 307–39; Etienne Wenger, *Communities of Practice: Learning, Meaning, and Identity* (New York: Cambridge University Press, 1998).
12 Star and Griesemer, "Institutional ecology, 'translations' and boundary objects: Amateurs and professionals in Berkeley's Museum of Vertebrate Zoology, 1907–39," 393.
13 William Barley, Paul Leonardi, and Diane Bailey, "Engineering Objects for Collaboration: Strategies of Ambiguity and Clarity at Knowledge Boundaries," *Human Communication Research* 38, no. 3 (2012): 280–308.
14 Rodney Benson, "News Media as a 'Journalistic Field': What Bourdieu Adds to New Institutionalism, and Vice Versa," *Political Communication* 23, no. 2 (2006): 187–202; Pierre Bourdieu, *The field of cultural production: essays on art and literature* (New York: Columbia University Press, 1993); Pierre Bourdieu, "The Political Field, the Social Science Field and the Journalistic Field," in *Bourdieu and the Journalistic Field*, eds Rodney Benson and Erik Neveu (Cambridge: Polity, 1995), 29–47; Pierre Bourdieu, *On television* (New York: New Press, 1999); Dominique Marchetti, "Subfields of Specialized Journalism," *Bourdieu and the Journalistic Field*, eds Rodney Benson and Erik Neveu (Cambridge: Polity, 2005), 64–82.

15 Dan Berkowitz, "Doing Double Duty Paradigm Repair and the Princess Diana What-a-story," *Journalism* 1, no. 2 (2000): 125–43; David Mindich, *Just the Facts: How "Objectivity" Came to Define American Journalism* (New York: New York University Press, 2000).

16 Ronald Bishop, "From Behind the Walls: Boundary Work by News Organizations in their Coverage of Princess Diana's Death," *Journal of Communication Inquiry* 23, no. 1 (1999): 91–113; Steven D. Reese, "The News Paradigm and the Ideology of Objectivity: A Socialist at the *Wall Street Journal*," *Critical Studies in Mass Communication* 7, no. 4 (1990): 390–409; Barbie Zelizer, "Journalists as interpretive communities," *Critical Studies in Mass Communication* 10, no. 3 (1993): 219–37.

17 Jamieson and Waldman, *The Press Effect: Politicians, journalists, and the stories that shape the political world*; Zelizer, "Why memory's work on journalism does not reflect journalism's work on memory."

18 Robert Entman, *Projections of Power: Framing News, Public Opinion, and U.S. Foreign Policy* (Chicago: University of Chicago Press, 2003); Herbert Gans, *Deciding What's News: A Study of CBS Evening News, NBC Nightly News, Newsweek, and Time* (Chicago: Northwestern Press, 1979); Jack Lule, *Daily News, Eternal Stories: The Mythological Role of Journalism* (New York: The Guilford Press, 2001).

19 Bourdieu, *On television*.

20 Berkowitz, "Doing Double Duty Paradigm Repair and the Princess Diana What-a-story."

21 Berkowitz, "Doing Double Duty Paradigm Repair and the Princess Diana What-a-story"; Bowker & Star, *Sorting Things Out: Classification and Its Consequences*; Zelizer, "Why memory's work on journalism does not reflect journalism's work on memory"; Barbie Zelizer, *Covering the Body: The Kennedy Assassination, the Media, and the Shaping of Collective Memory* (Chicago: University of Chicago Press, 1993).

22 Bourdieu, *On television*, 57.

23 Bourdieu, *The field of cultural production: essays on art and literature*, 43.

24 Dan Gillmor, *We the Media: Grassroots Journalism by the People, for the People* (New York: O'Reilly Media, 2006); Sue Robinson, "Journalism as Process: The Labor Implications of Participatory Content in News Organization," *Journalism & Communication Monographs* 13, no. 3 (2011): 138–210.

25 C.W. Anderson, *Rebuilding the News: Metropolitan Journalism in the Digital Age* (Philadelphia: Temple University Press, 2013).

26 Seth C. Lewis, "From Journalism to Information: The transformation of the Knight Foundation and news innovation," *Mass Communication & Society* 15, no. 3 (2012): 309–34.

27 Emma Hemmingway, *Into the Newsroom: Exploring the Digital Production of Regional Television News* (New York: Routledge, 2008): 208.

28 Wilson Lowrey, "Tendencies Journalism Innovation and the Ecology of News Production: Institutional," *Journalism & Communication Monographs* 14, no. 4 (2012): 214.

29 Ashley Anderson, Dominique Brossard, Dietram Scheufele, Michael Xenos, Peter Ladwig, "The 'Nasty Effect': Online Incivility and Risk Perceptions of Emerging Technologies," *Journal of Computer-Mediated Communication* 19, no. 3 (2013): 373–87; Matthew W. Hughes, "Racist comments at online news sites: a methodological dilemma for discourse analysis," *Media Culture & Society* 35, no. 3 (2013): 332–47; Vincent Price, "Citizens Deliberating Online: Theory and Some Evidence," *Online Deliberation: Design, Research, and Practice* (2009): 1–22; Bill Reader, "Free Press vs. Free Speech? The Rhetoric of 'Civility' in Regard to Anonymous Online Comments," *Journalism & Mass Communication Quarterly* 89, no. 3 (2012): 495–513; Sue Robinson, "Traditionalists vs. Convergers Textual Privilege, Boundary Work,

and the Journalist–Audience Relationship in the Commenting Policies of Online News Sites," *Convergence* 16, no. 1 (2010): 125–43; Jane Singer and Ian Ashman, "Comment Is Free, but Facts Are Sacred: User-generated Content and Ethical Constructs at the *Guardian*," *Journal of Mass Media Ethics* 24, no. 1 (2009): 3–21; Natalie Stroud, Ashley Muddiman, Joshua Scacco, and Alex Curry, "Deliberation in newsroom comment sections," presented at the *American Political Science Association*, Chicago, 2013; Joseph Walther, David DeAndrea, Jinsuk Kim, James Anthony, "The Influence of Online Comments on Perceptions of Anti-marijuana Public Service Announcements on YouTube," *Human Communication Research* 36, no.4 (2010): 469–92

30 Stroud et al., "Deliberation in newsroom comment sections."

31 Walther et al., "The Influence of Online Comments on Perceptions of Anti-marijuana Public Service Announcements on YouTube."

32 Anderson et al., "The 'Nasty Effect': Online Incivility and Risk Perceptions of Emerging Technologies."

33 Robinson, "Traditionalists vs. Convergers Textual Privilege, Boundary Work, and the Journalist–Audience Relationship in the Commenting Policies of Online News Sites."

34 Sue Robinson, "'If you had been with us': Mainstream press and citizen journalists jockey for authority over the collective memory of Hurricane Katrina," *New Media & Society* 11, no. 5 (2009): 794–814.

35 The sample for that 2009 study also included news articles, broadcast transcripts, books and blogs. But I am only revisiting the comments under news stories for this chapter.

36 Sue Robinson, Sandra Knisely, Mitchael Schwartz, "'A news negotiation of a state's history': Collective memory of the 2011 Wisconsin protests," *Journalism: Theory, Practice, Criticism* (2013):1–18.

37 Jamieson and Waldman, *The Press Effect: Politicians, journalists, and the stories that shape the political world*; Bill Kovach and Tom Rosenstiel, *The Elements of Journalism: What Newspeople Should Know and the Public Should Expect* (New York: Three Rivers Press, 2007); Zelizer, "Journalists as interpretive communities"; Zelizer, "Why memory's work on journalism does not reflect journalism's work on memory."

38 Jamieson and Waldman, *The Press Effect: Politicians, journalists, and the stories that shape the political world*; Kovach and Rosenstiel, *The Elements of Journalism: What Newspeople Should Know and the Public Should Expect*; W. Lance Bennett, Regina Lawrence, Steven Livingston, *When the press fails: Political power and the news media from Iraq to Katrina* (Chicago: University of Chicago Press, 2008).

39 Bennett et al., *When the press fails: Political power and the news media from Iraq to Katrina*; 2008; Eric Darras, "Media Consecration of the Political Order," in *Bourdieu and the Journalistic Field*, eds Rodney Benson and Erik Neveu (Cambridge: Polity, 2005), 156–73; Michael Schudson, "Autonomy from what?" in *Bourdieu and the Journalistic Field*, eds Rodney Benson and Erik Neveu, (Cambridge: Polity, 2005), 214–23.

40 Schudson, "Autonomy from what?" 218.

41 BobPacker, "Pro-union rally draws 35000," *Wisconsin State Journal* (2012).

42 Canteen, "JP 17th Street Canal Side Weak," NOLA (2007).

43 Keepingitreal, "Pro-union rally draws 35000," *Wisconsin State Journal* (2012).

44 DontTreadOnMeBro, "State GOP reacts to misinformation," JSOnline (2012).

45 Bourdieu, *On television*, 76.

46 caddyvista1980, "Capitol rally protests," JSOnline (2012).

47 wbennetti, "17th Street Canal," NOLA, (2007).

48 Jamieson and Waldman, *The Press Effect: Politicians, journalists, and the stories that shape the political world*.

49 Gans, *Deciding What's News: A Study of CBS Evening News, NBC Nightly News, Newsweek, and Time*.

50 Lule, *Daily News, Eternal Stories: The Mythological Role of Journalism*.

51 Jamieson and Waldman, *The Press Effect: Politicians, journalists, and the stories that shape the political world*, xvii.

52 Robinson, "'If you had been with us': Mainstream press and citizen journalists jockey for authority over the collective memory of Hurricane Katrina," 794–814; Robinson, "'A news negotiation of a state's history': Collective memory of the 2011 Wisconsin protests," 1–18.

53 Ivy Lee, "Taking nothing for granted," NOLA (2006).

54 Carolyn Kitch, "Anniversary Journalism, Collective Memory, and the Cultural Authority to Tell the Story of the American Past," *The Journal of Popular Culture* 36, no. 1 (2002): 44–67.

55 midwis, "About 500 turn out to mark beginning of fight," *Wisconsin State Journal* (2012).

56 molesaurus, "A year after dividing the state, Walker in fight of his political life," *Wisconsin State Journal* (2012).

57 Bourdieu, *The field of cultural production: Essays on art and literature*.

58 Bailey et al., "Engineering Objects for Collaboration: Strategies of Ambiguity and Clarity at Knowledge Boundaries."

59 Zelizer, "Why memory's work on journalism does not reflect journalism's work on memory"; Zelizer, *Covering the Body: The Kennedy Assassination, the Media, and the Shaping of Collective Memory*.

60 Kitch, "Anniversary Journalism, Collective Memory, and the Cultural Authority to Tell the Story of the American Past."

61 Sue Robinson, "A chronicle of chaos: Tracking the news story of Hurricane Katrina from *The Times-Picayune* to its website," *Journalism: Theory, Practice, Criticism* 10, no. 4 (2009): 431–50; Robinson, "A chronicle of chaos: Tracking the news story of Hurricane Katrina from *The Times-Picayune* to its website."

62 Matt Carlson, "Making Memories Matter: Journalistic Authority and the Memorializing Discourse Around Mary McGrory and David Brinkley," *Journalism* 8, no. 2 (2007):165–83.

63 Zelizer, "Journalists as interpretive communities."

64 Guest, "Madison Politiscope: Tens of Thousands Rally at Capitol," *Capital Times* (2012).

65 Zelizer, *Covering the Body: The Kennedy Assassination, the Media, and the Shaping of Collective Memory*.

66 mccartney, "levee not storm," NOLA (2006).

67 Totalitarian Left, "State GOP reacts to misinformation," JSOnline (2012).

68 Pierre Bourdieu and L. Wacquaint, *An invitation to reflexive sociology* (Cambridge: Polity, 1992), 127.

69 Neil Fligstein, Doug McAdam, *A theory of fields* (New York: Oxford University Press, 2012).

70 Gal and Irvine, "The boundaries of languages and disciplines: how ideologies construct difference."

71 HankandDagney, "Protesters to host annual brat fest," *Wisconsin State Journal* (2012).

72 Bourdieu, *On television*, 40–41.

73 Robinson, "Journalism as Process: The Labor Implications of Participatory Content in News Organization."

74 FormerGop, "MadisoPolitiscope: Tens of Thousands rally," *Capital Times* (2012).
75 Stroud et al., "Deliberation in newsroom comment sections."
76 Wenger, *Communities of Practice: Learning, Meaning, and Identity*, 107.
77 Wenger goes on to suggest that artifacts such as commenting spaces are initially designed to be boundary objects, and I think that is true, given how much angst journalists pour over developing policy for them (Robinson, 2010). My point here is that commenters can assume control over the section as a boundary object that as an entity might move the field.
78 Bailey et al., "Engineering Objects for Collaboration: Strategies of Ambiguity and Clarity at Knowledge Boundaries"; Star and Griesemer, "Institutional ecology, 'translations' and boundary objects: Amateurs and professionals in Berkeley's Museum of Vertebrate Zoology, 1907–39."

Chapter 10

Resisting epistemologies of user-generated content?

Cooptation, segregation and the boundaries of journalism

Karin Wahl-Jorgensen

Introduction

This chapter examines how news organizations are seeking to defend themselves against the incursions of user-generated content through the closely related strategies of cooptation and segregation. In engaging in these strategies, news organizations carry out a form of boundary work to protect the journalistic profession. The chapter takes a closer look at one specific instantiation of cooptation and segregation: the *Guardian* newspaper's GuardianWitness, which provides a platform for user-generated content built into the newspaper's website – just one of many such sites hosted by traditional or "legacy" news media.

I am here deliberately focusing on how a traditional newspaper known for its commitment to, and investment in, the convergent media environment is negotiating tensions between the professional journalistic content produced by legacy news organizations and the amateur content generated by users. I am therefore steering clear of a range of other widely circulating debates, including those around how these same tensions may play out on social media platforms and other web-based sites that operate independently of legacy media.

My interest is in how legacy news media negotiate the challenges implicit in the technological changes brought about by convergence. Specifically, I examine the ways in which the increasing role of user-generated content has been managed. While I investigate the strategies of cooptation and segregation, through which user-generated content is "normalized,"[1] I am also suggesting that far from a simple process of subsuming and absorbing amateur content, the introduction of user-generated content brings about complex, subtle and sustaining challenges to the epistemology of journalism. It both challenges and transforms its ways of knowing, its truth claims, and its forms of storytelling.

When I refer to user-generated content here, I understand it as content generated by the end-user. This is, however, only one of many ways of referring to the blurring of the line between audiences and producers of media content, and the corresponding increase in the role of the audiences in participating in the generation of this content.[2] These developments have variously been referred to as the rise of "participatory journalism," "citizen journalism" or "produsage,"[3] to name just a few of the labels that describe "the act of a citizen, or group of citizens, playing an active role in the process of collecting, reporting, analyzing and disseminating news and information."[4] It also reflects an increasing awareness of the agency of users, often challenging accounts of a passive audience, and emphasizing the potential empowerment of amateurs resulting from the new participatory opportunities afforded by technological change.[5] Here, I am not interested in entering the debates regarding the potential empowerment inherent in the rise of user-generated content, but rather in assessing the potential consequences for journalism's self-understanding and ways of knowing.

Ultimately, the increasing involvement of "The People Formerly Known as the Audience" in news production entails a shift in the paradigm of what constitutes journalism. It also implies an epistemological challenge – or a challenge to the theories of knowledge associated with conventional journalism.[6] Put differently, even if it may oversimplify journalism's historical trajectories to emphasize the long-standing stability of conventional "objective" journalistic story-telling, it is nonetheless true that the affordances of convergent news platforms have ushered in a more diverse set of practices and storytelling forms. These developments challenge the epistemology of conventional journalism. I will examine this idea in more detail in the following section, before considering how GuardianWitness – one specific platform for incorporating user-generated content – addresses these challenges.

The epistemology of journalism

The epistemological implications of journalistic forms have long been discussed by journalism scholars. Ettema and Glasser, who were among the first to develop the idea of the epistemology of journalism, understood and studied it in terms of how "journalists know what they know."[7] Looking at the case of investigative journalism, they sought to trace what "counts as empirical evidence and how that evidence becomes a justified empirical belief – ergo, a knowledge claim about the empirical world."[8] This chapter, however, understands the epistemology of journalism more broadly, in terms of the "rules, routines and institutionalized procedures that operate within a social setting and decide the form of the knowledge produced and the knowledge claims expressed (or implied)."[9] This is particularly important to consider in the light of journalism's epistemological position as the "primary sense-making practice of modernity."[10] The knowledge claims of journalism have broader ideological consequences but are also shaped by sociological forces and prevailing power relations. Here, I am drawing on recent work investigating how knowledge claims are produced by specific forms of journalism, including blogs[11] and broadcast journalism.[12] This approach entails an understanding of how journalists' processes of justification involve the construction of narratives that operate within conventions established by institutional forms of knowing, circumscribed by power relations. As Matheson described it, drawing on a Foucauldian analysis of the relationship between knowledge and power:

> Conventions of newswriting do not simply chronicle the world but ... constitute certain claims to knowledge about such matters as the audiences for news texts, the position of journalists in that world and the relationship between audience and journalist. ... Journalists adhere to these conventions in order to be able to make the kinds of authoritative statements about events and individuals which we are accustomed to hear from them. News discourse can be seen as a particular instance of the more general "will to truth" which motivates and constrains institutional forms of knowing in modern society.[13]

In other words, this approach understands the "will to truth" of journalism as embedded within a larger ideological framework. Examining the epistemology of blogging, Matheson took a closer look at how the *Guardian* responded to the introduction of the new form in its own hosted blogs. He demonstrated that they were characterized by a distinctive way of knowing, premised on the "establishment of a different interpersonal relation, of a different authority and of a journalism focused upon connection rather than fact."[14] To Matheson, the writing represented a "more 'raw', less 'cooked', source of information, allowing users to participate more in constructing knowledge about events in the world."[15] The ways of knowing represented by blogging, then, were made possible by the affordances of the new technology. The suggestion that technological change has a bearing on the ways of knowing in journalism is central to the argument made in this chapter.

Along those lines, Stuart Allan has written compellingly about the epistemological consequences of the increasing place of citizen journalism in the news landscape.[16] To Allan, citizen journalism "may be characterized as a type of first-person reportage in which ordinary individuals temporarily adopt the role of a journalist in order to participate in newsmaking, often spontaneously during a time of crisis, accident, tragedy or disaster when they happen to be present on the scene."[17] Citizen journalism implies a more personal and often subjective stance, free of the constraints of objective journalism. Allan succinctly summarized the main arguments around the epistemological consequences of citizen journalism advanced by critics and its proponents. Its proponents suggest that citizen journalism may serve as a welcome paradigm shift, challenging the "dry, distancing, lecture-like mode of address" of traditional journalism:

> Journalism by the people for the people is to be heralded for its alternative norms, values and priorities. It is raw, immediate, independent and unapologetically subjective, making the most of the resources of web-based initiatives ... to connect, interact and share first-hand, unauthorized forms of journalistic activity promising fresh perspectives.[18]

This positive reading is consistent with research on audience responses to user-generated content, which suggests that audiences tend to value it as more "authentic" than professional content – a view frequently shared by journalists involved in shaping and curating audience contributions. This understanding of authenticity encompasses the idea of an uncensored outpouring of personal storytelling, emotional integrity, realism, immediacy and identification. This is contrasted to the perceived professional distance of journalism, which involves a "cold," "detached," "objective" and "distanced" approach.[19] For example, in describing user-generated content after Hurricane Katrina, Michael Tippett, founder of NowPublic.com, argued that "it's a very powerful thing to have that emotional depth and first-hand experience, rather than the formulaic, distancing approach of the mainstream media."[20]

Nonetheless, for critics of user-generated content (including many journalists and newsroom managers), the dangers of verifying audience content make it a risky proposition for news organisations. Allan summarized the key arguments:

> Citizen journalism may be cheap and popular, hence its not inconsiderable appeal for cash-strapped newsrooms, but in a world where facts matter, ethical codes warrant respect, and audience trust is paramount, it continues to spark intense debate about how best to negotiate its benefits and hazards alike.[21]

Such questions around the verification of user-generated content have always been at the centre of journalistic debates about citizen journalism, and reflect broader anxieties about the growing place of audience contributions in the news landscape, and how journalism should respond to this potential trespass on their professional terrain. Media organizations, which have historically functioned as gatekeepers, have now, according to some accounts, become "gatewatchers" or curators, sorting through and publicizing information available elsewhere on the Internet.[22] As Anderson suggested, this has led to tensions between conventional reporting and the emerging activities of curation and aggregation. Referring to aggregators as "second-level newsworkers," he defines them as "hierarchizers, inter-linkers, bundlers, and illustrators of web content."[23]

Boundary work and journalistic discourses on user-generated content

Journalistic discourses on user-generated content have tended to emphasize the continued need for journalistic skills, upholding the boundary between journalism professionals and audience members as amateurs. For example, a BBC course on user-generated content reflected this broader view, and was titled "Have They Got News for Us?"[24] In researching the role of user-generated content at the BBC in 2007–9, we interviewed Radio Editor Peter Rippon about the public service broadcaster's use of audience materials, and he suggested that if "we apply our journalistic skills, you can just mold these things into really good pieces of journalism."

This statement is typical of the journalistic position on user-generated content, which holds that professional skills are required to turn amateur, unpolished contributions into useable and trustworthy content, or *journalism*. Such a position, which actively asserts the primacy of journalistic skills, represents an active form of "boundary work."[25] Gieryn, in introducing this concept to discuss how scientists demarcate their activity from other intellectual activities, suggested that boundary work is an "ideological style" which contrasts scientific endeavors favorably to other types of activity. One of the situations where boundary work is necessary, according to Gieryn, is "when the goal is protection of autonomy over professional activities."[26] In such situations, "boundary-work exempts members from responsibility for consequences of their work by putting the blame on scapegoats from outside."

To Gieryn, then, boundary work is an ideological strategy for defending the boundaries of the profession. The idea of boundary work has been highly influential for scholars studying the sociology of professions, including journalism (see the Introduction to this volume). In journalism studies, the idea of boundary work has been particularly crucial in understanding perceived incursions on professional turf. As Lewis suggested, journalism "has found digital media and digital culture to be particularly unsettling to its professional paradigm."[27] He therefore argued that it is increasingly urgent to understand "how the complexities of professionalism are embedded in and filtered through the ongoing negotiation of open participation on the part of users."[28] This open participation is frequently viewed as an incursion on journalistic practice. As Carlson and Ben-Porath noted in their analysis of the emergence of a "demotic voice" through a case study of the 2007 CNN/YouTube debates among candidates for the U.S. presidency:

> Voices overlap and compete, which can be witnessed in journalistic reactions to the demotic voice ranging from disdain to fear of displacement. … Given the lack of a codified division separating journalists from non-journalists, the encroachment of a newly amplified public threatens journalists' ability to argue that their cultural value stems from the exclusivity of their position as trained societal narrators.[29]

As other scholars have noted, journalists frequently reference specific professional skills when discussing user-generated content, thus policing the boundaries of their profession. For example, Allan cites crowd-sourcing analyst Eric Taubert:

> Great content captured by smartphone-wielding citizens can die on the vine without ever being seen, unless that content finds its way into the hands of journalists who know how to wrap a story around it, fact-check it and place it into the distribution chain.[30]

This position suggests that even if the smartphone revolution and other technological changes have generated new opportunities for audience contributions,
these would be of little use without the intervention of the professional skills of
storytelling, verification, and distribution. Related journalistic discourses view
user-generated content simply as a resource to be harvested by professionals
for the purposes of integrating it into stories already on the news agenda. For
example, in an interview for our research on user-generated content at the
BBC, Peter Horrocks (then editor of the BBC's integrated newsroom, now
Director of the BBC World Service) framed the importance of audience opinion –
as channeled through the "Have Your Say" comments forums on the BBC
website – as a source for journalistic storytelling. He discussed comments after
the assassination of former Pakistani Prime Minister Benazir Bhutto as follows:

> The top 20 or 30 recommended posts all had variations on the theme,
> attacking Islam in comprehensive terms. ... To be honest it was pretty
> boring wading through them and wouldn't have added much to anyone's
> understanding of the causes or consequences of the assassination. Buried
> amongst the comments however, rarely recommended by others, were
> insights from those who had met Benazir, or knew her. And there were
> valuable eyewitness comments from people who were at the scene in
> Rawalpindi. Our team that deals with user content sifted through the
> chaff to find some excellent wheat.[31]

Horrocks and other high-ranking journalists we interviewed took a top-down
view of user-generated content, viewing its management as a professional task
of sifting the wheat from the chaff – rather than seeing user-generated content as
newsworthy in and of itself, on a par with material produced by professionals.
Such a view puts the audience in its place as a source that can be quoted in
journalistic stories or, more broadly, a source of supplementary (and often
incomplete, low-quality, and emotive) material. Through such discourses,
journalists' privileged status as producers of knowledge and truth is actively
enforced.[32] This observation fits with Singer's argument that news organizations seek to normalize UGC, slotting it into existing structures and practices
rather than fundamentally altering the workings of the newsroom.[33]

Cooptation and segregation as boundary work strategies

Normalization is just one of several strategies engaged by legacy news organizations eager to take advantage of new technologies but concerned about a media
landscape which presents unprecedented challenges as well as opportunities.
More concretely, what I will suggest here is that legacy news organizations
seek to both segregate and coopt user-generated content. By segregation, I here
mean the deliberate separation of audience/amateur content from professional/
journalistic content, signaled by separation physically (as when amateur is

published in different newspaper sections, platforms or webpages) as well as discursively (in terms of how content is described).[34] Historically, such segregation has been central to the maintenance of key professional distinctions, including those between professional and amateur, and between "objective" and "subjective" content.

The received account of journalism history suggests that if the first (and nonprofessional) newspapers made little distinction between "news" and "opinion," professional journalism came to be understood as a "fact-centered discursive practice" premised on ideals of objectivity.[35] Throughout the history of print newspapers, they have clearly – through physical and discursive demarcation – been separated, and this separation has been of fundamental importance to journalism, serving as a structural underpinning of professional practice. This separation, however, is now under fire from the increasing importance of user-generated or amateur content, which is swiftly ushering in new ways of knowing, or new ways of determining what counts as truth within the interpretive communities of journalism, often grounded in more subjective and partial story-telling practices.[36] As Carlson and Ben-Porath put it, "citizen journalism's mix of participatory practices and subjective tone presents a fundamental break from professional journalistic practice."[37]

Here, I suggest that if user-generated content is a perceived threat to such long-standing professional self-understandings and practices, news organizations are generating new strategies for physically and discursively segregating it, thereby highlighting its distinctive and non-professional nature.[38]

Simultaneously, they are engaging in strategies of cooptation by taking on board and actively inviting in contributions. In taking up the concept of cooptation, I am drawing on its meaning within the sociology of organizations literature, as first advanced by Selznick. To Selznick, it refers to the process of absorbing new elements into the structure of an organization as a means of averting threats to its stability or existence.[39] Usually, these "elements" are seen to be representative of the opposition and/or of the views of the broader public. Selznick gives examples of the incorporation of "natives" into the formal mechanisms of colonial governance, and the cooptation of civilians into military courts. For Selznick, such processes of cooptation do not simply involve the appropriation of the outsider. Rather, it is an adaptive response that "is consequential for the character and role of the organization."[40] In a similar way, journalistic organizations could be seen to coopt audience contributions – a process which, at the same time, transforms aspects of journalistic practices and epistemologies.

The idea of cooptation has previously been used in examining news organizations' approaches to citizen journalism. Kperogi drew on theories of hegemony to explore how CNN incorporated user-generated content through its iReport.com citizen journalism platform. He argued that:

> [By] "mainstreaming" it through the iReport.com experiment, CNN is seeking to contain, or at least negotiate, its potentially disruptive effect on

mainstream journalism through a hegemonic cooptation that actively seeks the consent of the practitioners of this fringe, newfangled form of journalism. ... iReport.com does this by democratizing the conception of news – and in fact of journalism as such – in ways that both strategically negate the canons of journalistic orthodoxy and that seem intended to invite the approval and consent of non-professional journalists who dominate the practice of citizen journalism.[41]

Kperogi's contribution is to demonstrate how this citizen journalism experiment sought to negotiate the complex challenges represented by technological change, suggesting that this entailed a strategic negation of "the canons of journalistic orthodoxy" – a move that, in other words, may disrupt conventional journalistic practice through the very effort at maintaining it.[42]

Legacy news organizations and user-generated content

The challenges of managing forms of audience participation and engagement have always occupied news organizations, and raised questions around the boundary between professional and amateur content.[43] However, the growing prominence of user-generated content has made this an increasingly urgent and prominent challenge. As one observer put it in highlighting the growing importance of user-generated content,

> 80% of online content today is user-generated. Social media and self-publishing tools have created a glut of online amateur content while also increasing the overall quality of the material. As a result, we've seen a sea change in the way publishers work with and integrate UGC onto their sites, and the way they sell it as a value-add for brands.[44]

Some of the impetus for the increasing attention paid to user-generated content has to do with its central role in documenting major unfolding news stories over the past decade, starting with the Indian Ocean tsunami in 2004. The centrality of user-generated content, particularly in the form of photographs and video, has only accelerated with the invention of social media. Here, the advent of the 2011 Arab Spring and subsequent revolutions and, in the case of Syria, armed conflict, have been singled out. In several cases, Western news organizations were banned from entering the countries, making news from local sources on the ground indispensable for news reporting.[45] Some scholars have viewed platforms such as Twitter as indispensable in securing information flows in the Arab Spring,[46] even if other accounts question the alleged centrality of social media.[47]

News organizations, anxious to avoid being bypassed by technological developments that may make their products redundant, have developed their own platforms for displaying user-generated content. Most major news media will have some form of user-generated content provision embedded into their websites, and will use social media for both promotional and information-gathering purposes. In the United States, some of the more prominent of user-generated content platforms include *USA Today* YourTake as well as CNN's aforementioned iReport. The *New York Times* has recently launched a new "opinion product" which centrally includes user-generated content selected on the basis of professional curation. As described in a *Digiday* story:

> The product is being quietly billed as "a new, all-day-long opinion experience online and for mobile devices." It will be a mixture of tweets, Facebook updates, original writing and articles aggregated from other websites, and will involve a significant amount of back and forth between readers and contributors to the section, according to two job listings about the developing product.[48]

Furthermore, in a move that signals a significant attempt at incorporating content from users into the offering of mainstream news organizations, the multinational media giant News Corp, owned by the Murdoch family, acquired Storyful, the social news agency that verifies UGC sources, for €18 million in December 2013. The News Corp press release announced the purchase in language representing boundary work, discussing the use of "journalistic sensibility, integrity and creativity to find, authenticate and commercialize user-generated content."[49]

In the U.K., the main national newspapers, including the *Telegraph*, the *Sun* and the *Express*, "host social networks where readers can publish photos and blog posts, and talk on forums."[50] Here, I use the *Guardian* newspaper's GuardianWitness as an example of how an award-winning, high-profile platform for user-generated content uses strategies of cooptation and segregation to normalize audience participation. While this chapter is unable to provide a detailed analysis of the site and its content, the discussion here is intended to signal the usefulness of considering cooptation and segregation as specific strategies of boundary work.

Introducing GuardianWitness

The *Guardian* newspaper, originally founded in 1821 as the *Manchester Guardian*, is a well-known British quality or "broadsheet" newspaper, which is left-leaning in its political orientation. It has a reputation for investigative reporting, and is owned by the Scott Trust, a charitable foundation that aims to secure the paper's editorial independence. It has long been an unprofitable publication, reporting an underlying loss of £30.9m in 2013, compared to £44.2m in 2012.[51] At the same time, since investing heavily in its online presence, it has gained prominence as a global media institution, usually featuring on the lists of the top newspaper sites in the world. For example, in the April

2014 ebizmba rankings (based on Alexa figures), it featured eighth on the list of most visited news websites in the world, with 60,000,000 unique monthly visitors, and behind only the *New York Times* among newspaper sites.[52]

GuardianWitness (https://witness.theguardian.com/) was launched in April 2013 to encourage the contribution of user-generated content and to facilitate its curation for the newspaper and its online platforms. In April 2014, the site won the Digital Innovation of the Year Award at the U.K.'s National Newspaper Awards. The judges were "uniformly impressed with the scope and implementation of this digital newcomer," praising its "innovative implementation of social news gathering which works well across numerous platforms."[53]

According to the site, "GuardianWitness is our new home for content you've created, online and on your mobile. You can contribute your video, pictures and text, and browse all the news, reviews and creations submitted by others. Posts will be reviewed by our team and suitable contributions will be published on GuardianWitness, with the best pieces featured on the Guardian site – you could even help shape the news agenda." This description indicates the ways in which the site seeks to simultaneously encourage and coopt audience contributions, whilst normalizing it through an emphasis on professional editorial control. At the same time, it also suggests that audience members can have a concrete impact through shaping the news agenda – however, this takes place through the mediation and curation of professional practice.

To better understand the ways in which the site discursively constructs the parameters for acceptable content, the call for contributions is worth examining at length, in delineating the types of content elicited, and how this content is discursively framed. First, the site sets "assignments" on specific topics: "Editors will issue call-outs for your input on a wide range of topics – be it a photograph of the first daffodils, your filmed thoughts on the latest cinema release or a witty re-imagination of a sporting event." Here, the idea of "input on a wide range of topics" highlights the active solicitation of audience participation, exemplary of an approach of cooptation, in its clear attempt at incorporating the opposition into the legitimate structure, generating a more easily controllable environment.[54] At the same time, however, the language of the call also performs careful boundary work by segregating audience content. In this case, it is done through the suggestion of particular types of content in the form of "a photograph of the first daffodils, your filmed thoughts on the latest cinema release or a witty re-imagination of a sporting event" – all falling squarely within the category of "soft news." This is more broadly reflected in the site's construction of the nature of audience contributions as "soft news," primarily drawing on personal experience and frequently in the form of visual content, usually photographs. For example, the site typically includes requests for weather photos: "Wherever you are in the world, show us your striking photos of this week's weather." Images of the weather are a long-standing feature of user-generated content sponsored by news organizations, and contribute to a depiction of an audience eager to participate, but largely apolitical and unable to shape the "hard news" agenda.[55] On April 8, 2014, it also requested photos featuring "your attempts to make yourselves look like your favourite Game of Thrones characters," reflecting an emphasis on popular culture in the GuardianWitness agenda which fits the segregation strategy of constructing audience contributions as "soft news."

The boundary work of cooptation and segregation is further evidenced in calls for other types of content. A second category solicited by GuardianWitness includes "Live news tie-ins": "Our editors and reporters will sometimes flag live blogs as suitable for contributions, which will enable you to be part of a breaking or fast-moving story. We'll include the best contributions in the live blog – for instance your experiences of austerity protests around the world or your videos of the latest extreme weather event." In this case, contributions that fit into the "hard news" agenda are solicited from audience members – however, here, the ways of coopting audience content through incorporation takes a particular form: It calls for audience accounts of personal experiences as well as visual imagery, turning the audience into a provider of supplementary emotional and emotive rather than rational and "newsworthy" material.[56] This protects journalists' privileged status as producers of knowledge and truth, thus underpinning a move to defend the epistemology of "hard news" journalism against incursions of audience content. Along those lines, in April 2014, the site requested photographs from voters in India's general election: "We want to see the ink on your fingers to help us tell the story of the size of the vote in India." Here, the emphasis is on securing visual documentation of audience members' personal experience, which can be used as illustrations for stories and live blogs created by professional journalists. This is consistent with a broader construction of citizen journalists as eye-witnesses.[57] The idea of eye-witnessing privileges an ocular metaphor,[58] even if witnessing means far more than "watching" and "seeing."[59] This resonates with longer-standing hierarchies of user-generated content, where images and videos – largely visual material – have tended to be privileged over comments.[60] As such, GuardianWitness strategies of cooptation and segregation, though taking a specific form, could also be viewed as consistent with a longer-standing trajectory in news organizations' approaches to user-generated content.

A final category of content solicited by the site is "open suggestions" – material that hasn't been specifically requested. However, the site provides explicit instructions about what types of "open suggestions" are welcome:

(1) Send us a story: This might be a tip-off or something you may have witnessed in your local area that you think we might want to see. We're always looking for unreported stories, so we would like to hear about things that we might decide to follow up as a story for *The Guardian*.
(2) Send us your assignment ideas: Have you got an idea that your think [sic] other *Guardian* readers would like to participate in? It might be a simple but beautiful idea such as asking everyone to take a picture at a certain

time of day or it might be a way of investigating an issue in more detail. For example asking everyone to share the cost of parking at their local hospital. Or it might simply be an interesting or funny assignment idea which doesn't fit into any of our current assignments.

Of the three types of content solicited, this "open suggestion" category represents the clearest opportunity for audience members to shape the news agenda. Here, it is interesting to note that the two different types of suggestions construct audience contributions very differently. The first suggestion, that of sending story ideas or tip-offs, represents a long-standing practice in news media for broadening their news agendas. Such tip-offs are then potentially picked up by professional journalists who turn them into news stories. The second option is based on soliciting ideas for audience participation – in this case, for ideas that might fit into standard constructions of visual user-generated content ("asking everyone to take a picture at a certain time of day") but also ones that represent novel contributions to the news agenda ("a way of investigating an issue in more detail"). The "open suggestion" category appears to offer more complex and variegated forms of audience contribution, which do not consistently or neatly operate in line with strategies of cooptation and segregation.

Nonetheless, in general terms, the call for content highlights the fact that GuardianWitness contributions are first and foremost understood as content filtered, and rendered legitimate through, professional curation – rather than as newsworthy in their own right. This is further underpinned by the placement of the platform on the newspaper's main website. From the *Guardian* front page, it can be found far down in the third right-hand column, below "Culture" and "Life and Style" sections, rather than as, for example, a header tab. This signals the relatively marginal nature of the site in relation to the *Guardian's* news agenda, and its close conceptual relationship to soft-news categories represented by "Culture" and "Life and Style" stories.

Despite the discursive recognition of the ability of user-generated content to shape the news agenda, the site uses cooptation and segregation strategies to emphasize a view of the audience as a provider of soft-news, experience-based visual materials. This is consistent with broader observations made by scholars studying user-generated content which suggests that despite the rhetoric of empowerment frequently accompanying the launch of user-generated content initiatives, in actual practice news organizations frequently construct audience contributions as distinctly separate from the work of professional journalists, segregating it in sections focused on soft news, and often in the context of consumption and popular culture.[61] Nonetheless, the GuardianWitness approach also entails recognition of a shift in the role of news organizations and the journalists working within them, which acknowledges, in addition to conventional reporting activities, the emerging activities of curation and aggregation.[62] This, then, demonstrates that in journalism, as well as in other organizational types, cooptation is not simply a strategy for incorporation of the opposition, but also leads to changes in the practices of the organization itself. The *Guardian*, in introducing the site, has devoted scarce resources to enhancing audience participation as well as inclusion of audience content – an allocation decision that is in keeping with shifts in the political economy and production routines of news organizations. It makes use of audience contributions on the GuardianWitness site as well as in elements of its news coverage, especially live blogs, and these have the capacity to introduce new storytelling styles at odds with conventional objective journalism, as when a bystander's image of the scene of the Woolwich murder was commended for its "sensitivity and sense of awareness," advancing the interest of "open journalism."[63] These shifts also reflect a real change in the epistemology of journalism itself – a shift in how it produces the knowledge that constitutes our collective truths.

Conclusion

This chapter has argued that the increased prevalence of user-generated content presents a series of unique challenges to the authority of journalists. The affordances of convergent platforms have ushered in a more diverse set of practices and story-telling forms, which shake the foundations of the epistemology of conventional journalism. It is an epistemology which has privileged "objective," unemotional and "hard-news" journalism but now has to contend with the wider range of genres and storytelling forms represented by user-generated or audience content. And whereas in traditional media, audience content was clearly physically and conceptually segregated from professional journalism in forums such as letters to the editor, the advent of convergence and the increasing ease of audience participation online in a variety of formats and on a range of platforms represents a challenge to such segregation. This, in turn, forces journalists carry out boundary work to defend their profession.

In particular, this chapter has suggested that user-generated content is normalized through the closely related strategies of cooptation and segregation. These strategies of boundary work have here been examined by taking a closer look at the *Guardian* newspaper's GuardianWitness, which provides a platform for user-generated content built into the newspaper's website. The chapter suggests that the award-winning site is highly directed in soliciting audience content that is primarily supplementary to professional journalistic storytelling, visual, and based on personal experience. This form of solicitation represents cooptation in its incorporation of audience contributions – all of it filtered through the curatorial practices of journalists. At the same time, it demonstrates the strategy of segregation, as user-generated content becomes supplementary material, clearly demarcated as illustrations for professional accounts, and coming from the partial and personal point of view of audience members. As such, the site, while inviting in the "opposition," keeps it at bay by reasserting journalistic authority through specific forms of boundary work.

GuardianWitness is not unique in this respect, but rather one example of how the epistemology of journalism may be subtly shifting due to technological change. It appears that journalism has located successful strategies for defending its turf and policing its boundaries: professionals consistently make the case for the lasting importance of journalistic skills, and carefully design and delimit participatory opportunities to necessitate the display of these skills, and assert control over the production process. At the same time, it is also the case that new forms of journalistic storytelling (including live blogs), as well as older ones (including conventional news stories) are being shaped and irreversibly changed by the inclusion of user-generated content, which is often more personal, subjective, and experience-based than "objective" journalistic reporting. Ultimately, this chapter has provided just one snapshot of the process by which these changes are taking place, indicating the direction of transformation rather than providing a neat (though not necessarily happy) ending. What is certain, however, is that any claims about breakdowns in distinctions between journalists and their audiences should be taken with a grain of salt, given the careful and consistent strategic work carried out by news organizations to justify their continued relevance.

Notes

1 Jane Singer, "The political j-blogger: 'Normalizing' a new media form to fit old norms and practices," *Journalism: Theory, Practice and Criticism* 6, no. 2 (2005): 173–98.
2 Jane Singer, David Domingo, Ari Heinonen, Alfred Hermida, Steve Paulussen, Thorsten Quandt, Zvi Reich and Marina Vujnovic, *Participatory journalism: Guarding open gates at online newspapers* (Malden, MA and Oxford: Wiley-Blackwell, 2011); Jose Van Dijck, "Users like you? Theorizing agency in user-generated content," *Media, Culture & Society* 31, no. 1 (2009): 41–58.
3 Alfred Hermida, "Mechanisms of participation: How audience options shape the conversation," in *Participatory journalism: Guarding open gates at online newspapers* (Malden, MA and Oxford: Wiley-Blackwell, 2011): 15; Axel Bruns, *Gatewatching: Collaborative online news production* (London and New York: Peter Lang, 2005).
4 Shayne Bowman and Chris Willis, *We media: How audiences are shaping the future of news and information* (Reston, VA: The Media Center at the American Press Institute, 2003); Alfred Hermida, "Mechanisms of participation: How audience options shape the conversation," in *Participatory journalism: Guarding open gates at online newspapers* (Malden, MA and Oxford: Wiley-Blackwell, 2011): 15.
5 Dijck, "Users like you? Theorizing agency in user-generated content," 41; Henry Jenkins, *Convergence culture: Where old and new media collide* (Cambridge, MA: MIT Press, 2006).
6 Jay Rosen, "The people formerly known as the audience," *PressThink*, 2006, http://archive.pressthink.org/2006/06/27/ppl_frmr.html
7 The following section draws on material published in Karin Wahl-Jorgensen, "Changing Technologies, Changing Paradigms of Journalistic Practice: Emotionality, Authenticity and the Challenge to Objectivity," in *Technologies, Media and Journalism*, eds. C. Zimmerman and M. Schreiber (New Haven, CT: Yale University Press, 2014): 264–283.

8 James Ettema and Theodore Glasser, "On the epistemology of investigative journalism," in *Mass communication review yearbook* 6 (Newbury Park, CA: Sage, 1984), 343.

9 Mats Ekstrom, "Epistemologies of TV journalism: A theoretical framework," *Journalism* 3, no. 3 (2002): 259–82.

10 John Hartley, *Popular reality* (London: Arnold, 1996), 32–34.

11 Donald Matheson, "Weblogs and the epistemology of the news: some trends in online journalism," *New Media & Society* 6, no. 4 (2004): 443–68.

12 Ekstrom, "Epistemologies of TV journalism: A theoretical framework," 259–82

13 Matheson, "Weblogs and the epistemology of the news: some trends in online journalism," 445.

14 Matheson, "Weblogs and the epistemology of the news: some trends in online journalism," 453.

15 Matheson, "Weblogs and the epistemology of the news: some trends in online journalism," 455.

16 Stuart Allan, *Citizen witnessing* (New York and Cambridge, England: Polity Press, 2013).

17 Allan, *Citizen witnessing*, 9.

18 Allan, *Citizen witnessing*, 94.

19 Karin Wahl-Jorgenson, Andrew Williams and Claire Wardle, "Audience views on user-generated content: Exploring the value of news from the bottom up," *Northern Lights: Film & Media Studies Yearbook* 8, no. 1 (2010): 177–94.

20 Allan, *Citizen witnessing*, 94.

21 Allan, *Citizen witnessing*, 95.

22 Bruns, *Gatewatching: Collaborative online news production*, 2.

23 Michael Schudson and Chris Anderson, "Objectivity, professionalism, and truth seeking in journalism," in *Handbook of journalism studies* (New York: Routledge, 2009), 70.

24 Williams, Wardle and Wahl-Jorgensen, "'Have they got news for us?': Audience revolution or business as usual at the BBC?"

25 Thomas Gieryn, "Boundary-work and the demarcation of science from non-science: Strains and interests in professional ideologies of scientists," *American Sociological Review* 48, no. 6 (1983): 781–95; Schudson and Anderson, "Objectivity, professionalism, and truth seeking in journalism," 88–101.

26 Gieryn, "Boundary-work and the demarcation of science from non-science: Strains and interests in professional ideologies of scientists," 792.

27 Seth C. Lewis, "The tension between professional control and open participation: Journalism and its boundaries," *Information, Communication & Society* 15, no. 6 (2012): 838.

28 See also Matt Carlson, "Order versus access: news search engines and the challenge to traditional journalistic roles," *Media, Culture & Society* 29, no. 6 (2007): 1014–30.

29 Matt Carlson and E. Ben-Porath, "The people's debate," *Journalism Practice* 6, no. 3 (2012): 307.

30 Allan, *Citizen witnessing*, 19.

31 Claire Wardle and Andrew Williams, "Beyond user-generated content: a production study examining the ways in which UGC is used at the BBC," *Media, Culture & Society* 32, no. 5 (2010): 291.

32 Barbie Zelizer, "Journalists as interpretive communities," *Critical Studies in Media Communication* 10, no. 3 (1993): 219–37; Matt Carlson, "Blogs and journalistic authority: The role of blogs in US election day 2004 coverage," *Journalism Studies* 8, no. 2 (2007): 264–79; Lewis, J., Inthorn, S., and Wahl-Jorgensen, K., "*Citizens or consumers? What the media tell us about political participation*," (Buckingham:

Open University Press, 2005); Williams, Wardle and Wahl-Jorgensen, "'Have they got news for us?': Audience revolution or business as usual at the BBC?"

33 Singer, "The political j-blogger: 'Normalizing' a new media form to fit old norms and practices."

34 See also Coward, R., *Speaking personally: The rise of subjective and confessional journalism* (Houndmills, Basingstoke: Palgrave Macmillan, 2013); Karin Wahl-Jorgensen, "Op-ed pages," in *Pulling newspapers apart*, ed. B. Franklin (London: Routledge, 2008), 70–79; Seth Lewis, "The tension between professional control and open participation: Journalism and its boundaries," *Information, Communication & Society* 15, no. 6 (2012): 836–66.

35 Jean Chalaby, *The invention of journalism* (Basingstoke: Macmillan, 1998).

36 Stanley Fish, *Is there a text in this class?: The authority of interpretive communities* (Cambridge, MA: Harvard University Press, 1980); Zelizer, "Journalists as interpretive communities," 219–237.

37 Carlson and Ben-Porath, "The people's debate," 304.

38 Eg: Williams, Wardle and Wahl-Jorgensen, "'Have they got news for us?': Audience revolution or business as usual at the BBC?"; Lewis, "The tension between professional control and open participation: Journalism and its boundaries."

39 Philip Selznick, "Foundations on the theory of organization," *American Sociological Review* 23, (1948): 34.

40 Selznick, "Foundations on the theory of organization," 35.

41 Farooq Kperogi, "Cooperation with the corporation? CNN and the hegemonic cooptation of citizen journalism through iReport.com," *New Media & Society* 13, no. 2 (2010): 324.

42 Kperogi, "Cooperation with the corporation? CNN and the hegemonic cooptation of citizen journalism through iReport.com," 314–29.

43 Karin Wahl-Jorgensen, "Changing technologies, changing paradigms of journalistic practice: Emotionality, authenticity and the challenge to objectivity," in *Technologies, media and journalism*, eds C. Zimmerman and M. Schreiber (Campus/Yale University Press, 2014), 264–83.

44 Antoine Boulin, "For publishers, user-generated content is the new opportunity: Buzzfeed, Gawker and Forbes are three publishers leading the way with UGC," *Foliomag,* 2013, http://www.foliomag.com/2013/publishers-user-generated-content-new-opportunity/

45 Juliette Harkin, Kevin Anderson, Libby Morgan and Briar Smith, "Deciphering user-generated content in transitional societies," *Report by the Center for Global Communication Studies, Annenberg School for Communication, University of Pennsylvania,* 2012, www.internews.org/sites/default/files/resources/InternewsWP Syria_2012–06-web.pdf

46 Gilad Lotan, Erhardt Graeff, Mike Ananny, Devin Gaffney and Ian Pearce, "The revolutions were tweeted: Information flows during the 2011 Tunisian and Egyptian revolutions," *International Journal of Communication* 5, (2011): 1375–1405.

47 Eg: Fitzgerald, P., "Legitimising dissent: British and American newspaper coverage of the 2011 Egyptian uprising." Thesis (PhD), Cardiff University, 2014.

48 John McDermott, "NYT's opinion section recalibrates for the social web," *Digiday,* 8 January 2014, http://digiday.com/publishers/timess-opinion-section-looking-speed-social-savvy/

49 Jim Kennedy and Ashley Huston, "News Corp acquires social news agency Storyful," *News Corp,* 2013, http://newscorp.com/2013/12/20/news-corp-acquires-social-news-agency-storyful/

50 Paul Bradshaw, "What is user generated content?" 2013, http://onlinejournalismblog.com/tag/user-generated-content/

51 Christopher Williams, "*Guardian* publisher loses £31m," *The Telegraph*, 16 Jul 2013, www.telegraph.co.uk/finance/newsbysector/mediatechnologyandtelecoms/media/10182263/Guardian-publisher-loses-31m.html

52 "Top 15 Most Popular News Websites," *eBizMBA*, July 2014, www.ebizmba.com/articles/news-websites

53 GNM Press Office, "*Observer* wins top prize at 2014 Newspaper Awards," *The Guardian*, 2 April 2014, www.theguardian.com/gnm-press-office/observer-wins-top-prize-at-newspaper-awards

54 Selznick, "Foundations on the theory of organization," 34.

55 Seth C. Lewis, Kelly Kaufhold and Dominic Lasorsa, "Thinking about citizen journalism: The philosophical and practical challenges of user-generated content for community newspapers," *Journalism Practice* 4, no. 2 (2010): 163–79.

56 Williams, Wardle and Wahl-Jorgensen, "'Have they got news for us?': Audience revolution or business as usual at the BBC?"

57 Allan, *Citizen witnessing*; Gilad Lotan, Erhardt Graeff, Mike Ananny, Devin Gaffney and Ian Pearce, "The revolutions were tweeted: Information flows during the 2011 Tunisian and Egyptian revolutions," *International Journal of Communication 5*, (2011): 1375–1405.

58 Allan, *Citizen witnessing*, 100; Paul Frosh and Amit Pinchevski, *Media witnessing: Testimony in the age of mass communication* (Basingstoke, Palgrave Macmillan, 2009).

59 Carrie Rentschler, "Witnessing: US citizenship and the vicarious experience of suffering," *Media, Culture & Society* 26, no. 2 (2004): 296–304.

60 Kari Anden-Papadopoulos, and Mervi Pantii, *Amateur images and global news*, (Bristol: Intellect Books, 2011); Karin Wahl-Jorgenson, Andrew Williams and Claire Wardle, "Audience views on user-generated content: Exploring the value of news from the bottom up," *Northern Lights: Film & Media Studies Yearbook* 8, no. 1 (2010): 177–94.

61 Örnebring, "The consumer as producer – of what? User-generated tabloid content in *The Sun* (UK) and *Aftonbladet* (Sweden)," 771–85; Anna Jonsson, and Henrik Ornebring, "User-generated content and the news: Empowerment of citizens or interactive illusion?" *Journalism Practice 5*, no. 2 (2011): 127–44.

62 Cf. C.W. Anderson, *Rebuilding the news* (Philadelphia, PA: Temple University Press, 2013), p. 70.

63 Abigail Edge, "Woolwich murder image commended at Guardian UGC awards," *Guardian*, 28 March 2014, www.journalism.co.uk/news/woolwich-murder-image-purest-definition-of-witness-at-guardianwitness-awards/s2/a556257/

Chapter 11

NGOs as journalistic entities

The possibilities, promises and limits of boundary crossing

Matthew Powers[1]

For much of the twentieth century, most of the international news reaching American audiences was produced by foreign correspondents stationed in news bureaus scattered across the globe.[2] Whatever that model's merits or shortcomings, there is little doubt it is a model under duress – if it is not entirely broken. The existential crisis facing American journalism has exacted a particularly heavy toll on international news coverage. Foreign news budgets have been slashed: fewer correspondents now staff fewer bureaus in fewer parts of the world.[3] These developments form what Ulf Hannerz calls the "paradox" of contemporary international news: "In an era of intense globalizations, foreign news coverage in many media channels has recently been shrinking."[4]

At the same time as foreign news coverage has been shrinking, non-governmental organizations (NGOs) – groups like Amnesty International, Human Rights Watch and Oxfam – have assumed increasingly prominent roles in the provision of information from abroad. In addition to conducting original research, advocating to public officials and waging public awareness campaigns, NGOs have taken on a number of seemingly "journalistic" functions. Human Rights Watch now assigns photographers and videographers to produce multimedia packages that can accompany research reports; Amnesty International staffs a "news unit" charged with being the online portal for human rights news; and Oxfam sends "firemen" reporters to gather news in the midst of humanitarian emergencies.[5]

What are the possibilities, promises, and limits of NGOs acting as journalistic entities? What factors enable and constrain these possibilities? These are important questions in their own right, and ones with significant implications for thinking about the boundaries of journalism. On the one hand, NGOs may represent an expansion of international news reporting, as their coverage arguably extends news attention to locales and issues that would otherwise go uncovered. On the other hand, such developments may augur a worrisome conflation of the lines separating advocacy from journalism, with deleterious consequences befalling both sides. Discerning between these outcomes thus represents an excellent opportunity for understanding both the nature of contemporary journalistic boundary work and its implications for the changing landscape of foreign news coverage.

In this chapter, I draw on my research examining the information work of humanitarian and human rights NGOs to shed light on these questions.[6] Using a mixture of interviews with NGO professionals, content analysis, and historical research, I make three claims. First, I argue that NGOs can be understood to expand the boundaries of journalism in that they provide diverse information about various parts of the world in a range of accessible formats, both for news organizations and for their own organizational purposes. Second, I contend that what drives this expansion has little to do with journalism itself but resulted instead from a professionalization strategy by NGOs seeking legitimacy vis-à-vis political elites. In this search for legitimacy, the production of timely, credible information became a key resource legitimating the existence of NGOs within elite circles. Third, I suggest that while the factors driving this expansion had little to do with journalism, the norms and practices of journalism still can – and do – exert a force on NGOs in their information efforts by helping to shape what, how, and when stories are told, both in the news and beyond (e.g., in NGOs' own organizational publicity materials).

These findings offer several insights for the study of journalistic boundary work. They suggest that expansions to the boundaries of journalism are sometimes the effect of transformations in domains beyond journalism. At the same time, it suggests that journalists did – and do – *translate* NGO materials into the norms and practices of their profession. As a result, the case of NGOs simultaneously highlights the emergence of a new sort of information provider while underscoring the continued capacity of the news media to define legitimate forms of news – in both content and form – even as their capacity to control and produce that news on their own diminishes.

In what follows, I begin by briefly situating the discussion about NGOs as journalistic entities within existing scholarship on NGOs and journalism. In particular, I pay attention to the various factors that scholars identify as enabling and constraining NGOs to function as journalistic entities – that is, as both news sources and news producers in their own right. I then draw on my research of two leading human rights NGOs – Amnesty International and Human Rights Watch – to argue that NGOs have expanded journalism's boundaries and that this development is driven largely by a desire among NGOs to achieve legitimacy among political elites. Subsequently, I proceed to show how enduring norms and practices within journalism shape the sorts of news that NGOs produce, both when dealing with the news media and when producing materials for their own organizational use. I conclude by discussing some of the ways that the case of NGOs as news makers encourages a rethinking of the factors driving the boundaries of journalism to expand or contract.

NGOs and the boundaries of journalism

NGOs have long been an object of study in both political science and international relations.[7] Yet scholarly analysis of NGOs in journalism is relatively new. The combined uptake in the prominence of NGOs and transformations in the news media have led many scholars to ask what roles NGOs play as information providers and what the implications of these roles might be for the practices of journalism and news making.[8] In this growing literature on NGO news making, scholars have identified four factors that constrain NGOs to function as quasi-journalistic entities.

A first factor is technology. As many have noted, digital technologies make it possible for NGOs (and many other publicity seekers) to produce news packages, either for news outlets or for their own organizational purposes.[9] Reduced production costs – combined with changing patterns of news consumption – enable NGOs to "go direct" to their stakeholders.[10] On this view, NGOs were already acting in journalistic ways – by producing credible research reports, for example – and technology has allowed them to make that work more publicly accessible without their traditional reliance on the news media.

A second factor shaping the capacity of NGOs to act as journalistic entities comes from commercial imperatives shaping news production. As news outlets cut back on their resource commitments to international news coverage, journalists may open up to NGO informational materials, as they provide high quality coverage at little to no cost.[11] From this point of view, the perceived uptake in media receptivity is at least partly a function of journalism's diminished capacity to produce news on its own. Given that commercial imperatives have hit news outlets differently, we might expect those news outlets with the largest international news resource cuts to be those most receptive to NGO messages. By most accounts, it is television news, especially broadcast news, which has cut back on international coverage the most.[12] While newspapers have cut bureaus, most of the national newspapers continue to operate multiple news bureaus internationally.

A third possible factor shaping NGO effects is journalistic professionalism. Several authors have argued that NGO messaging has been shaped – sometimes to the detriment of NGO aims – by the norms and logics of the news media.[13] From this view, commercial cutbacks may have created the opportunity for NGOs to appear more frequently in the news, but professional journalistic norms continue to shape what counts as legitimate news. Cottle and Nolan, for example, argue that subservience to news norms of timeliness and newsworthiness lead NGOs to sensationalize their causes in ways that are meant to appeal to news outlets rather than call attention to the root of the ills addressed. According to these scholars, NGOs have mostly sought to adapt to – rather than challenge – these dominant news values. As Fenton summarizes in her research on NGOs: "We found little evidence of NGOs managing to change news agendas and challenge normative conceptions of news criteria."[14]

A fourth possible factor shaping increased NGO receptivity is transformations within the political field. Communication scholars have long held that news coverage "indexes" the range of debate among political elites.[15] Given that many NGOs have come to occupy key positions at the international level, it follows that increased media receptivity flows from the elites that media index, rather than any changes in journalism per se. From this view, we might expect NGOs to see the greatest uptake in media receptivity in the prestige press and not the broadcast news media, given that the former are most interested in indexing elite debate.[16]

None of the above factors are mutually exclusive, though they do have distinct points of emphasis. It is possible that technology allows NGOs to produce more journalistic materials and that commercial factors make those materials more attractive to resource-constrained news organizations, even as news organizations exert their own influence on what counts as legitimate news. At the same time, technological, professional, and commercial considerations may in fact be subordinate to larger changes in the dynamics of international political debates. In order to assess the impact of these various factors, it is necessary to understand what sorts of information work NGOs are doing. To do this, in the next section I provide data on the variety of information materials NGOs produce as well as an overview on where NGOs appear in the news. I then proceed to contextualize this data by providing a brief historical account – drawn from a close reading of the literature produced by NGO professionals themselves – of the factors driving NGO involvement in the news-making process. Finally, I draw on content analysis and interviews to show how journalists exert a force on the NGO materials with which they are provided by shaping where, when and how such stories are told.

Expanding the boundaries of journalism

In an average week, Amnesty International and Human Rights Watch release one or two research reports (1.9 in 2013).[17] This is more than double the number of reports produced in the mid-1980s (0.7). To give a sense of historical contrast: In 1987, Human Rights Watch published 14 reports, which one writer at the time described as "prodigiously productive."[18] In 2014, the group produced 14 reports in the months of January and February alone. These reports usually run well over 50 pages in length and include eyewitness accounts of human rights issues around the world. The writing style is tailored toward policy makers, not a general audience. Reports include both detailed information about what happened as well as lengthy discussions of what international laws and human rights conventions have been violated.

In addition to these reports, both organizations compose and release approximately 30 press releases and media commentaries per week. This, too, is roughly double the average from the 1980s (12.2). Often, these press releases and media commentaries accompany the newly published reports but many are also released independently in order to address issues and events in the news about which the organizations have something to say.

Both groups also produce a wide variety of information they never could before – including videos, slideshows or interactive maps. For example, both use satellite imagery to create maps showing military movements in conflict zones. These maps provide a bird's eye view, literally, of sites to which neither journalists nor NGOs have access. Finally, staffs in both organizations maintain an active online presence through social media, where they disseminate information and discuss issues among stakeholders and interested publics.

In addition to producing more information (and more varieties of information) NGOs cover a greater number of countries today than ever before – and arguably a much greater number of countries than news organizations do. When Amnesty International became the first NGO to receive a Nobel Peace Prize in 1977, it reported on about 100 countries around the world. Today, that number has increased to 154. A similar development occurred at Human Rights Watch. At the end of the 1980s, the organization reported on about 50 countries. Today, that number has doubled and the organization now monitors about 100 countries per year.

These increases are largely due to substantial staffing increases over time. In itself, this is not a surprising finding. Yet in order to comprehend how NGOs contribute to, and expand, the boundaries of journalism, it is worth reviewing the extent to which the information-gathering capacities of these organizations have grown. In the early 1970s, Amnesty International employed only 14 research staff. Today, it employs about 130 researchers, who are supported by roughly 500 other staff involved in advocacy, public relations, and fundraising. Human Rights Watch had a research staff of about 10 for much of the 1980s. Today, its full-time staff numbers almost 400 (Human Rights Watch does not break down jobs by category in the same way as Amnesty, so more specific data is not readily available). Both organizations employ media professionals – often drawn from the world of journalism – to ensure their information move easily across the news.

Media receptivity has generally reflected NGO developments by citing both organizations more over time. In 1980, the number of combined citations for both organizations in the *New York Times* totaled 80. In 2013, that figure rose to 495 citations. A similar pattern can be seen in the U.K.-based *Guardian*. In 2013, the combined citations for both organizations totaled 332, up from 95 in 1980. On television, a similar pattern holds, even though both organizations receive far less coverage in that format: in the years 1990 and 1995 combined, Amnesty International and Human Rights Watch received 33 citations on broadcast evening news (NBC and ABC). In the years of 2000 and 2005, those figures jump to 78.[19]

Based on these data, it seems that transformation in the news media alone do not provide an adequate explanation for the uptake in NGO media citations. Were that the case, NGO citations should have increased significantly over the last five to ten years as news outlets have shuttered foreign news bureaus. But the last ten years see a rate of change that is constant with the rate of the previous two decades. Between 1980 and 1990, *New York Times* citations of Amnesty and Human Rights Watch doubled from 80 to 146. From 1990 to

2010, citations nearly doubled again (from 146 to 264) and they increased again to about 400 in 2010. A similar pattern obtains in both *The Guardian* and on the broadcast news networks. Data since 2010 suggest a similar pattern continues, as citations have grown steadily year over year at a rate in keeping with previous years.

These data provide an initial overview of the range of information materials NGOs provide and a preliminary glimpse of where these materials go. They suggest NGOs produce more information today than in the past and that media reception – particularly prestige media – expands alongside such developments. They also suggest an interesting twist on discussions about the boundaries of journalism. While most discussions of boundary work concern the specific ways that journalists patrol the boundaries of their field, this data suggests that journalism may expand – in terms of taking in more materials over time – as much as a result of developments outside the field of journalism as any developments inside it.

To be sure, transformations in the news media probably make journalists more open to NGO messaging, but that effect should not be overstated. Were media transformations alone a sufficient explanation for the expanded journalistic roles played by NGOs, one would expect a greater increase in recent years with respect to media citations of NGOs. But this is not what I find. Instead, as I suggest below, there is a more proximate history about NGOs that helps explain how they developed their informational capacities. Only by first understanding this history can we develop a clearer sense of what drives expansions in the boundaries of journalism and, subsequently, what sorts of pressure journalists themselves can exert on these expanding boundaries.

What drives the expansion: NGOs seeking legitimacy vis-à-vis elites

Increases in staff and resources at NGOs are best understood as one element of a professionalization strategy on the part of NGOs in search for legitimacy vis-à-vis political elites. If this point makes intuitive sense today, it is only so in hindsight. When Amnesty began in the early 1960s, governments around the world treated the organization with skepticism and suspicion. Diplomatic reports circulating in the United States suggested the group was "a communist front organization."[20] Conversely, communist countries widely believed Amnesty to be a "front organization for western political interests."[21] Even those not suspicious of the group's motives thought the idea of using public opinion to address human rights violations was hopelessly idealistic. One critic went so far as to call the group "one of the larger lunacies of our time."[22]

Amnesty developed methods for selecting cases and reporting human rights violations as a direct response to these suspicions. The organization's early leaders developed the notion of the "Threes Group," which required the adoption of any political prisoner from one faction in the Cold War (West,

East, Non-Aligned) to be balanced by the adoption of prisoners on each of the other two sides.[23] In their reporting of potential human rights violations, volunteers and staffers strenuously sought to produce a credible empirical account of what happened. One long-time staffer recalled that the organization developed a "quasi-obsessional identification with neutrality" in its quest for legitimacy.[24] To be sure, Amnesty's strategy dovetailed with important journalistic norms: credible reporting, for instance, helped journalists recognize Amnesty as a trusted source, and not just a popular cause. But credible reporting was designed primarily to gain political legitimacy, not journalistic acceptance.

Human Rights Watch followed a similar strategy, even as it developed under different circumstances. Where Amnesty began as a popular movement that needed to earn legitimacy vis-à-vis political elites, Human Rights Watch came into being as a result of intra-elite U.S. foreign policy debates. In the 1970s, American political elites debated how best to manage America's role in a world riven by oil crises, inflation, the crisis of the dollar and claims to sovereignty throughout the Global South.[25] The American right's favored solution would be a turn to the language of the free market. Milton Friedman and his "Chicago Boys" (the all-male group of young conservative economists educated at the University of Chicago) are the most prominent example. In much of Latin America, they established contact with local conservatives and stressed the need for free market economic policies: a strategy that would garner its first victory when Augusto Pinochet came to power in Chile, displacing the socialist regime of Salvador Allende and installing a pro-U.S., free market leader.[26]

The liberal wing of the American foreign policy establishment saw in human rights a tool that could be used to publicly argue that right wing governments needed to be held to the same human rights standards as communist regimes.[27] For liberals, human rights formed the discursive terrain upon which they could do battle with the likes of Friedman. Arthur Goldberg, then an Ambassador-at-Large under President Carter, prevailed upon Ford Foundation President McGeorge Bundy to create Human Rights Watch. Ford's initial grant was $500,000, given to Robert Bernstein (then president of Random House publishing) to "establish liaison" with groups that could be formed following the Helsinki accords. These would form the various "Watch" groups that would ultimately coalesce into Human Rights Watch.

Media coverage was absolutely central to the liberal strategy, even if it was not the driving force behind it. The Ford Foundation initially sought out Robert Bernstein because of his contacts with key figures in the elite echelons of the journalistic and literary worlds. E.L. Doctorow, Toni Morrison and Robert Penn Warren were all involved with Human Rights Watch from the outset.[28] In grounding the group in the upper echelons of the media world, Human Rights Watch sought to position itself as an organization capable of waging a public battle with conservatives over the necessity and implementation of human rights.

As with Amnesty, fact-finding proved crucial to waging this battle. In the organization's earliest years, Aryeh Neier – Human Rights Watch's first executive director – conducted a public campaign against the Reagan admin-istration. In particular, Neier engaged with Elliott Abrams, then Assistant Secretary of State for Human Rights and Humanitarian Affairs, over U.S. foreign policy in Central America.[29] Seizing upon the administration's nominal commitment to human rights, Neier used highly detailed, on-the-ground reporting to demonstrate human rights violations in countries receiving U.S. support. The two debated both on television (Ted Koppel's *Nightline*) and in print (*New York Times* and *New Republic*). "As combatants go," the jour-nalist Morton Kondracke wrote at the time, "you could not ask for a better match ... than Abrams and Neier."[30] Years later, Neier himself would remark on the importance of fact-finding in these publicity duels:

> Abrams and his colleagues made a quarrel over the facts. The style of Human Rights Watch evolved directly out of this. We started producing thick, amply documented reports. ... Our emphasis was on providing the evidentiary bases for the claims we were making.[31]

Both Human Rights Watch and Amnesty ended up committing greater resources to fact-finding as a result of these publicity duels. Initially, the motivation to do this work had very little to do with journalism per se. Instead, it was about using factual reporting as a resource for entering into elite public debates. Amnesty International, for example, doubled its research staff between the mid-1970s and early 1980s: the period before and after the creation of Human Rights Watch.[32] The overall effect was to make reporting more important to NGOs overall. As one close observer at the time noted: "Monitoring groups that used to issue skimpy flyers, designed merely to draw attention to an offending country, now publish lengthy, detailed reports."[33]

As I detail below, NGOs still needed to adapt their work to fit within the logics of the news media. They would time their studies to coincide with important political events and they would regularly update the reports to stay relevant within the evolving conversation. One example: when President Ronald Reagan visited Indonesia for a day in the early 1980s, Human Rights Watch made sure to complete its report about human rights violations in that country just before the president departed. Group representatives handed the report out to journalists as they boarded the plane to accompany the president. As Neier recalls: "The long flight time provided ample time to read the report."[34] On the whole, the effect of these developments was to turn NGOs into quasi-journalistic entities – well before either the Internet or the jour-nalism crisis. What always drove these developments were transformations within elite political circles, which journalism in turned reflected through both its acceptance of NGO materials and its inclusion of them as legitimate actors in the debate. And yet journalism did not *only* reflect these develop-ments, they also – as I show below – refracted it through the norms and practices of their trade.

Journalism's mediating effects

While the boundaries of journalism have expanded to include NGOs as legitimate news providers, it is not the case that journalists mechanically accept and use NGO information materials. Instead, journalists translate political developments into terms of their own: they define what sorts of human rights stories count as news and they demand that specific timing and format considerations be followed. It is here that journalists exert force over the sorts of materials they let pass through their own boundaries – even as those boundaries expand in large part due to developments in the sphere of the political elites.

The most basic effect that journalists exert is a definition of what counts as news. While NGOs produce research from hundreds of countries, it remains the case that only a very small number of countries ever appear in legacy news media. In a content analysis examining geographic patterns of NGO information materials, I found that 60 percent of the stories in which NGOs are mentioned, both in print (*New York Times*) and on television (*NBC Nightly News*), are related to countries that already occupy the media spotlight prominently.[35] This figure contrasts with the fact that the majority of NGO research reports – fully 60 percent – documenting human rights violations are related to countries that *rarely* occupy the media spotlight. In other words, NGOs dedicate more research to countries that are rarely in the news media but achieve publicity primarily for research they do about countries in which the news media already have an established interest.

For the most part, NGO professionals recognize this geographic imbalance and tailor their press releases to adapt to the news media's demands. On average, NGOs spend more of their time sending press releases concerning news occurring in countries already in the media spotlight: 54.1 percent of all press releases are targeted at countries already receiving coverage, with the remainder targeted at countries receiving less attention. This suggests that norms of newsworthiness extend into the decision making of NGOs. When I asked one NGO staffer why they tailored their information materials to the attention patterns of the news media, he replied: "You can't not cover the big places. You can't not cover Israel-Palestine just because nothing's moved on it in how many decades now? ... You just have to be there, be seen there."[36]

In principle, it could be argued that NGOs no longer need journalists as much as they did in the past. Technology makes it possible, for example, for NGOs to target political elites or stakeholders directly, rather than using the news media to reach them. While it is true that NGOs provide a range of online messaging tools, it would be a mistake to see these as strictly bypassing the news media. As the above quotation indicates, media publicity still matters a great deal to NGO professionals: for brand awareness, as well as for public and political legitimacy. In none of my 65 interviews with NGO professionals did I encounter a single person uninterested in media coverage. Instead, most people suggested that online messaging augments, rather than supplants, media coverage. Exactly which *types* of messages are more likely to appear in legacy and emergent media formats is thus a key question that can help further tease out the boundaries of journalism.

Because NGOs still, at least sometimes, want to make the legacy news, they must provide journalists with stories in a manner than suits the temporal needs of the news media. NGOs do not operate on the same production schedule as news organizations: research reports can sometimes take between three and six months to produce. Press releases, too, wind their way through the organizational hierarchy and are often not cleared for publication until the end of the day. "When I came in [to work at the organization]," one NGO press officer explained to me, "a lot of press officers were issuing press releases at five o'clock in the evening" – that is, well after most news deadlines. At the level of the individual journalist, timeliness also means knowing the types of stories that interest a journalist and pitching them at an appropriate time. "Every journalist has their own idiosyncrasies – the types of stories they like, how and when they want to be pitched. ... It's our job to match our asks to their needs."[37]

In a multiplatform world, with a never-ending news cycle, meeting the needs of journalists in real time requires trained staff capable of handling media requests. In addition to employing communication professionals drawn from the worlds of journalism and public relations, NGOs train their research staff to be prepared for media interest whenever it arrives to their country. The head of external relations at Human Rights Watch explained that she coaches researchers to recognize "the moment when the lighthouse light swings around on you. You're the Burundi researcher at Human Rights Watch. The light just doesn't shine on you that much. When you get your moment: be ready."[38]

When producing materials for news organizations, NGOs – like most other publicity seeking organizations – work to ensure their products resemble journalism. As one person puts it:

> We consciously ape the styles of media in our communication [so that] what we produce looks like journalism. [Our media releases] are meant to look like a wire story, so that when it appears in the inbox of a journalist that it moves seamlessly through the media.[39]

Surprisingly, most NGOs report that press releases continue to be the "stock and trade delivery item," even as its format is changing to more closely mimic the conventions of a news article.[40] Here again, while technology in principle affords the opportunity to abandon the press release as an artifact, enduring journalistic routines (e.g., receiving press releases) continue to shape NGO publicity strategies.[41]

NGOs work to ensure that the language in those releases also matches up with journalistic expectations. NGO research generally combines empirical data (e.g., what happened) with prescriptive legalese (e.g., what should be done). The latter typically includes references to international bodies, treaties and laws. When translating their work for news outlets, NGO professionals take into account the type of media outlet they are working with (e.g., prestige press, tabloid, etc.) when shaping their message. An example: In the summer of 2011, a reporter for the *Daily Mail* (a conservative U.K. tabloid), contacted Amnesty International's U.K. section in London for comment on the British government's announcement that it (the U.K. government) was willing to allow Muammar Gadaffi to remain in Libya if it would help bring a more rapid close to hostilities. Amnesty had a defined position on the issue – Gadaffi should be sent to the International Criminal Court. Any deal allowing him to remain in Libya would be illegitimate and unacceptable. "A quick assessment," the person tasked with responding told me, "suggests that it's the *Daily Mail* – they want something simple." Having read the news coverage of Libya extensively, this person was drawn to a phrase he had seen circulating in some blogs, which suggested that Britain was giving the former Libyan ruler a "bolt-hole." The term, British slang for providing a hiding place, was something he thought could nicely encapsulate Amnesty's position. At the start of his response to the *Daily Mail*, he wrote: "There should be no bolt-hole for Gadaffi." When I asked him about his emphasis on the term, he said: "As a media officer, you often tend to use phrases that you know connect with the public and with journalists – they are one in the same quite often."[42]

A final way journalism translates NGO materials is by forcing them to include perspectives alternative to their own organizational viewpoints. This is especially true of audio-visual materials where NGOs try to provide materials that look like something journalists would produce if they were to cover the story on their own. Amnesty International, for example, sent a video team to the Ecuadorian Amazon and worked to ensure that the film had contrasting viewpoints. "We need to take into account interests of broadcasters. ... We can't only give material that gives too much praise to the indigenous group."[43]

In doing this, NGOs also try to ensure that their media output is not only a piece of organizational self-promotion but that it has some news value. Interestingly, this is the case both when NGOs produce content intended for the news media and when they produce it for their own organizational purposes. As one professional at *Médecins Sans Frontières* put it:

> We used to do b-roll with the MSF car, cut to the MSF house, cut to the MSF sign, MSF interview with MSF person with MSF logo on it and obviously people wouldn't take that. So we've had to up our game and provide, roughly, what a news journalist or news cameraman would have shot. Obviously, MSF is still the main interview and we're trying to frame things from our point of view, but we also try to find what they would actually want to shoot. And lots of the time, they will take that. Because it looks like what they would like to use.[44]

These findings point to journalism's continued capacity to define and shape news norms, even as its international news production capacities diminish. Many NGO professionals suggested that such influence may have salutary effects for NGOs, by forcing them to make their materials more accessible, more readily available and, as the above example suggests, even more inclusive of alternative perspectives.

Conclusion

NGOs perform a range of important information tasks, many of which increasingly overlap with the work of journalists. In this chapter, I have argued that NGOs can be said to expand the boundaries of journalism in that they increase the provision of news about parts of the world that otherwise receive little coverage. Yet what drives NGOs to do this has little do with "doing journalism;" instead, NGO information functions have developed as part of their strategies for gaining legitimacy vis-à-vis political elites. At the same time, journalism continues to exert a force in shaping which information materials are most likely to receive news coverage. In fact, even though NGOs provide materials that expand well beyond the usual patterns of media attention, the materials that journalists ultimately use tend to be those that correspond to preexisting attention patterns. Together, these findings highlight the continued capacity of the news media to define legitimate forms of news – in both content and form – even as their capacity to both control and produce that news on their own diminishes.

These findings suggest that the factor most responsible for driving expansions in the boundaries of journalism – at least in the case of human rights NGOs – are changes in the political field. While technology and commercial considerations make possible a range of NGO functions, none is quite as decisive as the political field in shaping the nature and form of NGO information work. Were these latter factors more important, one would expect either a greater uptake in media receptivity to NGO materials over time (instead of steady increases) or less interest from NGOs in receiving news coverage. Neither my content analysis nor my interviews with NGO professionals suggest either factor to be prominent. At the same time, journalistic norms and practices still continue to shape NGO publicity and there is little evidence to suggest that NGOs have any interest in challenging those norms and practices.

Boundary work is often framed in terms of the work that journalists do to protect their autonomy. My findings suggest the importance of seeing how journalistic boundaries can expand even without the consent or active agency of journalists themselves. Instead, boundary expansion can occur – and perhaps often does occur – largely due to changes in the sphere of political elites. Journalists in turn react to these changes and exert important effects on them – but journalists are not themselves the driving force behind the expansion. This suggests that analyses of boundary work require both an understanding of the non-journalistic forces responsible for expanding journalism's boundaries as well as detailed understandings of how journalists translate these changes into their own professional norms and practices.

Contemporary news production is often described in terms of "blurring boundaries" between journalists and non-journalists. On one level, such a metaphor seems apt for describing the roles of NGOs as journalistic entities. NGOs perform a range of information tasks, some of which appear quite similar to the work of journalists. Yet my research largely suggests that the boundaries between journalists and NGOs are well understood by all involved, including and especially NGO professionals. NGOs understand that what they do is different from journalism in that their work aims to get political elites to take action. Media publicity is a key component of that strategy but it is neither the only component nor is it an end in itself.

The promise of NGOs acting as journalistic entities is that they will expand the range of issues and activities to which media consumers are exposed. In many ways, the information work of NGOs has expanded in precisely this way by increasing the amount of news it produces and diversifying the forms that news takes. Furthermore, NGOs' encounters with the boundaries of journalism have produced several salutary effects, as news outlets demand the information to be timely and accessible. And yet the story of NGOs as journalistic entities has its limits. Attempts to expand legacy news coverage beyond the dominant attention patterns of the news media are generally limited. More generally, the news media exert considerable force – for better or worse – in shaping how stories are told. In short, NGOs may expand the boundaries of journalism but the rules within those expanded boundaries remain firmly rooted in the norms of journalism.

Notes

1 Jessica Peragine, a doctoral student in the Department of Communication at the University of Washington, provided research assistance for this chapter.
2 James Maxwell Hamilton, *Journalism's Roving Eye: A History of American Foreign Reporting* (Baton Rouge: Louisiana State University Press, 2009).
3 Pew Research Center Project for Excellence in Journalism, *The State of the News Media: An annual report on American journalism*, www.stateofthemedia.org/2009/index.htm
4 Ulf Hannerz, *Foreign News: Exploring the World of Foreign Correspondents* (Chicago: University of Chicago Press, 2004), 23.
5 On Human Rights Watch, see Carroll Bogert, "Similar Paths, Different Missions," *Nieman Reports* 64, no. 3 (2010): 59–61; on Amnesty International, see Rachel Bartlett, "Amnesty International Launches News Service," https://www.journalism.co.uk/news/-media140–amnesty-international-launches-news-service/s2/a543699/; on Oxfam, see Glenda Cooper, *From Their Own Correspondents? News Media and the Changes in Disaster Coverage* (Oxford: Reuters Institute for the Study of Journalism, 2011), 29.
6 Matthew Powers, "The Structural Organization of NGO Publicity: Explaining Divergent Publicity Strategies at Humanitarian and Human Rights Organizations,"

International Journal of Communication 8, 2014, 90–107; Matthew Powers, *Humanity's Publics: NGOs, Journalism and the International Public Sphere* (unpublished dissertation, 2013).

7 The landmark work in this field is Margaret Keck and Kathryn Sikkink, *Activists Beyond Borders: Advocacy Networks in International Politics* (Ithaca, NY: Cornell University Press, 1998).

8 In a growing literature, see Lilie Chouliaraki, *The Ironic Spectator: Solidarity in the Age of Post-Humanitarianism* (Cambridge: Polity, 2013); Simon Cottle and David Nolan, "Global Humanitarianism and the Changing Aid-Media Field," *Journalism Studies* 8(6) 2007, 862–78; Natalie Fenton, "NGOs, New Media and the Mainstream News," in *New Media, Old News*, ed. Natalie Fenton (London: Sage, 2010), 153–68; Adrienne Russell, "Innovation in Hybrid Spaces: 2011 UN Climate Summit and the Expanding Journalism Landscape," *Journalism: Theory, Practice and Criticism* 14 (7), 2013, 904–20; and Silvio Waisbord, "Can NGOs Change the News?" *International Journal of Communication* 5, (2011): 142–65.

9 Cooper, *From Their Own Correspondents*; Russell, "Innovation in Hybrid Spaces."

10 W. Lance Bennett and Alexandra Segerberg, *The Logic of Connective Action: Digital Media and the Personalization of Contentious Politics* (Cambridge: Cambridge University Press, 2013).

11 Richard Sambrook, *Are Foreign Correspondents Redundant? The Changing Face of International News* (Oxford: Reuters Institute for the Study of Journalism, 2010).

12 Priya Kumar, "Shrinking Foreign Coverage" *American Journalism Review*, www. ajr.org/article.asp?id=4998

13 Cottle and Nolan, "Global Humanitarianism"; Fenton, "NGOs, New Media and the Mainstream News"; Waisbord, "Can NGOs Change the News?"

14 Fenton, "NGOs, New Media and the Mainstream News," 158.

15 W. Lance Bennett, "Toward a Theory of Press-State Relations in the United States," *Journal of Communication*, 40(2) (1990): 103–25.

16 Timothy E. Cook, *Governing with the news* (Chicago: University of Chicago Press, 1998).

17 Data for this section are drawn from my analysis of NGO annual reports and online web sites. Data on the number of countries reported on each year are taken from annual reports for both organizations since 1989. Figures for press releases and media citations are taken from each organization's website and then calculated on a weekly basis. Finally, staff figures were provided to me in interviews at both organizations; historical data on staff figures were found during my historical research.

18 Morton Kondracke, "Broken Watch," *New Republic*, Aug 22, 9.

19 As I demonstrate elsewhere (Powers, "The Structural Organization of NGO Publicity"), different NGOs target different news outlets as a result of economic, political, and organizational variables within the NGO sector.

20 Yves Dezalay and Bryant G. Garth, *The Internationalization of Palace Wars: Lawyers, Economists and the Contest to Transform Latin American States* (Chicago: University of Chicago Press, 2002), 70.

21 Thomas Buchanan, "The Truth Will Set You Free: The Making of Amnesty International," *Journal of Contemporary History* 37(4) (2002): 588.

22 Cited in Jonathan Power, *Like Water on Stone: The Story of Amnesty International* (London: Penguin, 2001).

23 Ann Marie Clark, *Diplomacy of Conscience: Amnesty International and Changing Human Rights Norms* (Princeton: Princeton University Press, 2001).

24 Harry Scoble and Laurie Wiseberg, "Human Rights and Amnesty International," *Annals of the Academy of Political and Social Science* 413 (1974): 25–26.

25 Nicolas Guilhot, *The Democracy Makers: Human Rights and the Politics of Global Order* (New York: Columbia University Press, 2005).
26 Dezalay and Garth, *The Internationalization of Palace Wars*.
27 Dezalay and Garth, *The Internationalization of Palace Wars*, 127–35. See also Barbara J. Keys, *Reclaiming American Virtue: The Human Rights Revolution of the 1970s* (Cambridge, MA: Harvard University Press, 2014).
28 Aryeh Neier, *Taking Liberties: Four Decades in the Struggle for Rights* (New York: Public Affairs, 2003).
29 Tamar Jacoby, "The Reagan Turnaround on Human Rights," *Foreign Affairs* 64 (1986): 1066–86.
30 Kondracke, "Broken Watch," 9.
31 Quoted in David Rieff, "The Precarious Triumph of Human Rights." *New York Times Sunday Magazine* 8 August 1999: 38.
32 Dezalay and Garth, *The Internationalization of Palace Wars*, 133.
33 Jacoby, "The Reagan Turnaround on Human Rights," 1082.
34 Aryeh Neier, *The international human rights movement: A history* (Princeton: Princeton University Press, 2012), 348.
35 Powers, *Humanity's Publics*.
36 Personal communication, communication director, International Crisis Group, 4 July 2011.
37 Personal communication, media officer, Amnesty USA, 14 December 2011.
38 Carroll Bogert, "Look who's talking: Non-Profit Newsmakers in the New Media Age." Online video file: www.media.mit.edu/events/2012/09/10/media-lab-conversations-series-carroll-bogert-look-whos-talking-non-profit-newsmakers-new-media-age
39 Bogert, "Look who's talking."
40 Personal communication, press officer, Amnesty International, 15 July 2011.
41 I thank Seth Lewis for raising this point with me.
42 Personal communication, press officer, Amnesty International, 13 July 2011.
43 Personal communication, audio-visual producer, Amnesty International, 7 July 2011.
44 Personal communication, broadcast relations manager, *Médecins Sans Frontières* U.K., 19 July 2011.

Chapter 12

Drawing boundary lines between journalism and sociology, 1895–2000

C.W. Anderson

Introduction

In 1905, the *American Journal of Sociology* (AJS), the official academic journal of the then-emerging profession of sociology, published a rather remarkable first-person article by George Edgar Vincent. In this article Vincent, who would go on to serve as the sixth president of the American Sociological Association (ASA), described at length how he turned his undergraduate sociology class at the University of Chicago into a full-time news bureau that produced a finished newspaper and gave students "under university auspices, a practical introduction to the technique of newspaper work."[1] Vincent originally conceieved the seminar as consisting in both lectures on sociological theory and actual day-to-day newspaper production; journalists would become versed in the science of society and thus become better reporters. But he found that this was actually a terrible idea – sociology had more to learn from journalistic production techniques, he claimed, than the reverse. "The sum of the whole matter," Vincent concluded, "is to bring practical newspaper men into the lecture and seminar room, not for mere general address on the importance of the press to civilization, but for … clinical, laboratory work."[2] Perhaps even more shocking than this startling conclusion, however, was the basic notion that a leading sociologist would find it a worthy use of his time to have his students produce a popular newspaper as part of a sociology class.

More than a century later, timed to the launch of his wildly anticipated website *Five Thirty Eight*, political journalist and quantitative modeler Nate Silver released a manifesto in which he decried the ad hoc, evidence-free nature of much political reporting. "The problem [with this reporting] is not the failure to cite quantitative evidence. It's doing so in a way that can be anecdotal and ad-hoc, rather than rigorous and empirical, and failing to ask the right questions of the data." And while Silver went on to note that his "methods [were] not meant to replace 'traditional' or conventional journalism," and while he nuanced his data-driven, causality-oriented model in a number of interesting ways, he fundamentally set up a contrast between quantitative and qualitative forms of evidence-gathering, and between what he called anecdotal (read: journalistic) and rigorous (read: social scientific) forms of analysis. In short, Silver made a basic argument that journalism – by embracing data, by seeking to determine causality, by showing more openness to quantitative approaches – should be more like social science, not less.[3]

In the move from a world where a leading sociologist could embrace notions of industrial truth production in the journalistic style to a world where a renegade journalist called on his profession to be more like sociology and political science, much has obviously changed in the fields of both journalism and sociology. One of these things has been the emergence of a boundary between journalism and social science, one that we take for granted today, but one whose contours were far, far less evident at the turn of the twentieth century. In this chapter I want to map the divisions and boundary markers that have driven the knowledge-building occupations of journalism and sociology apart for more than a century, but also trace the threads that still link, however tenuously, George Vincent and Nate Silver's very different professional worlds.

As should be obvious from my introduction, this question – how did different knowledge occupations distinguish themselves during the formative years of standardization and growing occupational coherence – is of more than simply antiquarian interest. One of the many underlying rhetorics of twenty-first century data journalism seems to be an urge to become more "socially scientific," or at least socially scientific without the jargon, the slow production cycles, and the over-reliance on abstract theory. But this rhetoric of data and empiricism is far from new. As far back as the 1960s (and even before, as I hope to show in this chapter), scholars like Philip Meyer were calling for an "application of social and behavioral science research methods to the practice of journalism": what Meyer called precision journalism. There seems to be a half-articulated desire on the part of some in the data journalism world to embrace more contextual, temporally flexible, or explanatory form of knowledge.

To be united, of course, something must have been separate in the first place, but when we examine the history of journalism and sociology in a relational sense we find this sharp division is far from a historical given. From the turn of the twentieth century well into the 1930s and even the 1940s, the line between a journalistic ontology and a sociological one was far from straightforward, particularly when we extend the range of exactly what we consider to be a properly journalistic publication. In this chapter I want to explore the processes of boundary work through which academic sociology and journalism were constructed as separate professions in the period between the 1920s and 1950s, decades that happened to coincide with formative period of professionalization across a wide range of knowledge disciplines.

Journalism, in other words, once included a plethora of material and methods that we would today consider "sociological." Increasingly, it may be integrating this sort of material again. But this chapter hopes to demonstrate that the line between "journalism" and "social science" is not one of unalterable forward progress. It is a line with zigs and zags, moments of embrace and moments of repulsion. In their days of professional infancy, journalists and sociologists were once far more closely aligned than seems possible today – and yet both groups may have had compelling reasons for expelling the other group from their club. Journalism once included sociologists and people like sociologists in their ranks, but they chose to move away from such a position. This boundary-analysis perspective can help us understand journalism and journalistic culture in the digital age as well.

Drawing on theories of knowledge that understand professional expertise as both material and networked, this chapter moves between an analysis of the processes of boundary drawing (in which clear divisions and well-articulated categories and temporalities of evidence are reified) and an analysis of a messy, hybrid world of journalism/sociology (in which clear occupational divisions are both rhetorically unsettled and repeatedly transgressed in practice).[4] I begin by briefly setting out the social-technical context of the early twentieth century, a world in which journalistic and sociological practice were deeply entangled. I then undertake a qualitative discourse analysis of the *American Journal of Sociology*, the *American Sociological Review*, and the *Columbia Journalism Review* in order to examine the techniques through which this entanglement began to be sorted out through the erection of boundaries through rhetoric. I focus, in particular, on the different ways that sociology imagined and represented journalism within its scholarly journals. The chapter concludes with a return to the present and to the world of modern data journalism, asking what we might understand about the knowledge boundaries of our own time in the light of this excavation of past practices.

Hybrid practices, entangled commitments: Journalism and sociology in the early twentieth century

I want to begin by briefly setting out the social-technical context of early twentieth century journalism and sociology, a world in which the evidentiary methods of both groups were deeply entangled. I want to touch on three threads in particular, each of which could amount to a chapter or even book of its own: (1) early forms of religiously inclined "problem sociology," (2) the work of journalists-turned-sociologists like Robert Park and Franklin H. Giddings, and (3) the *Survey Graphic*, which represented an attempt to represent sociological knowledge in a visually sophisticated, publicly appealing format. This is not to say that journalism and sociology were the same thing – far from it. Indeed, from the very earliest days of social science its practitioners took pains to distinguish themselves from their reportorial brethren. Nevertheless, divisions were certainly far murkier than they would eventually become, and we can only understand the process of rhetorical separation outlined in the bulk of this paper if we first understand the earlier phases of a more substantive entanglement.

First, we should note that the earliest forms of sociology were what Andrew Abbott and others have called "problem sociology." A number of reform-oriented groups, often religious in nature and embedded within one of the larger currents of the progressive era, sought to gather empirical data on the conditions of urban and rural neighborhoods for the purposes of social reform. Much of this empirical data collection fell under the rubric of the "social survey," about which Shelby Harrison of the Russell Sage Foundation would write in 1930 that it was "not scientific research alone, nor journalism alone, nor social planning alone, nor any one other type of social or civic endeavor; it is a combination of a number of these."[5] I have chronicled the journalistic linkages to the social survey movement elsewhere; for now I can only mention that the surveyors made extensive use of a combination of *journalistic distribution tactics, empirical evidence gathering,* and a crude form of *data visualization* in order to agitate for a variety of urban reforms.[6]

Second, we should note the links between some of the founding fathers of sociology and the newspaper profession. The key figure here, of course, is Robert Park, and historians of sociology such as Rolf Linder have devoted entire volumes to the thesis that it was Park's background as a city reporter that helped shape his sociological *habitus* and his belief in the academic value of "nosing around."[7] These blurred boundaries apply not simply to Robert Park, however; even early sociologists now known for their statistical approaches, such as Franklin Giddings, began their careers as journalists. As was noted above, one of the presidents of the American Sociological Association not only had an impressive journalistic career before becoming a sociologist but even turned his sociology classroom into a working newspaper production center for a time in 1909.

Finally, social scientific and journalistic practices were entangled on the material level as well. For the first few decades of the twentieth century, a variety of newsletters, magazines, and special reports made use of both journalistic and sociological methods and authors, many of these volumes growing out of the activity of the Social Survey Movement mentioned earlier. While the muckraking magazines are well known, less famous is the work of settlement workers like Jane Addams whose reports and visualizations were replete with both journalistic and sociological language, and of magazines like the *Survey Graphic*, which probably represents the finest flowering of the hybrid techniques of reporting, empirical research, social reform, and data visualization before the 1980s.[8]

In short, while journalism and sociology were always divided by a variety of social and organizational factors, the boundaries between them were less stable and more permeable in the early part of the twentieth century than they would become 50 years later. How that rhetorical boundary work was deployed in practice is the subject of the next section.

Erecting walls: The professional journals (1895–2000)

Dataset and methods

In his introduction to this volume, Carlson invokes Gieryn's understanding of rhetoric as one of the means through which retroactively proper demarcations between different forms of expert knowledge are fixed. "It is through rhetorical means that various groups engage in 'boundary-work' to compete publicly for 'epistemic authority': 'the legitimate power to define, describe, and explain bounded domains of reality.'"[9] One of the strategies of boundary-work is *expulsion*, in which deviant group members, deviant practices, and deviant values are all publicly cast-out and branded as no longer acceptable to the expert group. This chapter also examines a related process of expulsion through rhetorical "othering" – in this case, the changing sociological understanding of journalism between 1895 and 2000. As we have seen, the distinction between journalistic and sociological techniques and values was far from self-evident in the early years of the twentieth century; to build the boundary between them required, among other things, active rhetorical work. In this chapter, I am examining more of a process of historical discourse formulation than I am Gieryn's individuated expulsions, though the two concepts differ more in emphasis and method than they do in their underlying understanding of knowledge practices.[10]

How did sociology come to distinguish itself from journalism, and vice versa? My approach to answering that question involves, first, trying to understand how sociologists talked about journalism in their professional journals, specifically the *American Journal of Sociology* (AJS) and the *American Sociological Review* (ASR), from 1895 until 2000. Using a JSTOR search, I downloaded every article in AJS and ASR containing a major reference to either "journalism" or "newspaper[s]," giving me a total of 564 articles. Each of the articles was categorized according to a set of themes that came to light after each piece had been read and analyzed several times. These themes can be understood as representative of different understandings of sociology's relationship to journalism, and are detailed below. Do particular article types or particular clusters of article themes emerge at different moments in time, and if so, when? Can we point to any provisional patterns in the way that different theme clusters emerged at different moments? And, if so, what does this say about the way journalism came to be understood from the perspective of social science?

The second piece to the puzzle, of course, is to flip the question on its head and examine social science from the journalistic point of view. To accomplish this I undertook a similar exercise, this time using the *Columbia Journalism Review* (CJR) as my data set and searching for all articles that mentioned "social science" or "sociology." Unlike the AJS and ASR dataset, the value of this data is fairly limited, in part because of the small number of results but also because CJR is not the only professional journal within the journalistic field and has only existed since 1963. Nevertheless, there is useful data here as well, and it is important to keep in mind that boundary construction is always, at least in part, a mutual process of exclusion.

The analysis of the *American Journal of Sociology* and the *American Sociological Review* led to a differentiation between three article types and four thematic categories of article.[11] The first category, *a discussion of journalistic methods or a direct comparison of journalism to social science*, is the key one for our analytic purposes insofar as it represents a moment when AJS or ASR authors were specifically reflecting the methodologies of journalistic practice or comparing journalistic methods and values to those embraced by social scientists. This can and does include anything from an offhand in remark in a book review on public opinion that "the present volume, wherein a professor of journalism presents 'a guide for newspaper men and newspaper readers' … will leave most social scientists annoyed"[12] to more extensive but less self-conscious reflections on the relationship between journalism, social science, and the Pittsburgh survey, a touchstone of early sociological and reform-oriented social science.[13]

The second category, *journalism or "the news" as an object of empirical inquiry*, represents what we today would consider part of the sociology of news. Some of the most famous articles in journalism studies are part of this category, including those by Tuchman, Sigelman, and Molotch and Lester.[14] The third category, *news content as empirical evidence for analyzing other social phenomena*, features news content not as an object of analysis in and of itself but as data for investigating other sociological phenomena, such as ecological institutional evolution (using local newspapers as a case study.)[15] One of the most interesting articles in this category actually reflects upon and tests the reliability and validity of using news coverage of urban unrest as a data source.

The final category, *journalism as an object for non-empirical inquiry or moral speculation*, might appear to be the most unusual to our twenty-first century eyes. Suffice it to say that the *American Journal of Sociology* of 1899 resembles today's scientific journal insofar as it has the same title, and little else. Quite often in these articles, journalism is "the object" of rambling, moralistic discourses. These articles include little in the way of empirical evidence and display titles like "Is an Honest and Sane Newspaper Press Possible?"[16] And this very fact helps point to the value of this kind of discursive genealogy: by studying how sociology understood journalism, we are not simply studying the relationship between two professional groups, we are studying how sociology understood itself and how that understanding was transformed over the course of the modern era.

A deeper engagement with a subset of 125 particularly relevant articles highlights the emergence of three key trends in the sociological framing of journalism: a normative concern with the relationship between journalistic and sociological methods and values between 1899 and 1926; a casual or condescending dismissal of "journalistic scholarship" in the 1930s, 40s, 50s and 60s;

and a turn toward journalism and journalistic practice as an object of *empirical* inquiry in the 1970s. While I discuss these trends chronologically, it is important to keep in mind that there are not hard-and-fast lines between the clusters of articles discussed here. There may have been a turn toward the empirical study of journalism as a subject matter in its own right in the 1970s, but even as early as 1910, Frances Fenton would inquire as to the relationship between news framing and crime, and investigate the question "how and to what extent do newspaper presentations of crime ... influence the growth of crime and other types of anti-sociological activity?" using content analysis and adding up newspaper column inches.[17] Nevertheless, there are some real chronological shifts at play here, and all of them are relevant to understanding the boundary between journalism and sociology as it emerged over the course of the twentieth century.

Social science and the moral cohesion of the press (1895–1926)

The most interesting material from the *American Journal of Sociology* in its early years can be characterized by its persistent attempt to understand what sociology itself was – as an intellectual practice and moral commitment – running alongside a series of normative inquiries into the various failings of the press. In addition to the aforementioned article "Is an Honest and Sane Newspaper Press Possible?" other pieces in AJS between 1895 and the mid-1920s complained that "the sociologist would be justified in hailing the modern press as a wonderful moral factor, were it not for that curse and pestilential nuisance, the 'yellow' variety of newspapers"[18] and they praised "attempts at civic publicity represented by the municipal journals of Baltimore."[19] These pieces are not entirely context-free laments, however. Indeed, buried within them, one can see an emerging understanding of journalism not as a system of information provision but rather as a system of social control and cohesion. The spirits of Robert Park and John Dewey, with their ideas of a society that exists in and through communication, is much in evidence here. For example, one article notes:

> The motive, conscious or unconscious, of the writers and of the [urban newspaper] press is to reproduce, as far as possible, in the city the conditions of village life. In the village everyone knew everyone else. Everyone called everyone by his first name. The village was democratic. We are a nation of villagers ... if public opinion is to continue to govern as much in the future as it has in the past, if we propose to maintain a democracy as Jefferson conceived it, the newspaper must continue to tell us about ourselves.[20]

Focusing on the newspaper as a socio-cultural object that fostered community integration (or alienation) and directed "public opinion" would lead these early sociologists, "who themselves marched within the still larger brigades of the charity organization movement and the social gospel," to consider *what kind* of integration and *what kind* of community the newspaper made possible.[21]

It was thus roundly and mercilessly criticized, usually without empirical evidence, for a variety of the failings alluded to above.

There is a connection between this moral trepidation directed toward the social influence of the newspaper and the existence of a number of articles, especially between 1895 and the 1920s, which focused on the relationship between journalistic and sociological methods. This connection is the struggle of a newly professionalizing sociology to define exactly what social science was and what methods it ought to embrace. As we have already noted, sociology in its early years was scarcely distinguishable from the various religious reform and "social gospel" movements of the late progressive era, all of which saw the ills of the industrial era as at least partly attributable to something called "society" rather than to solely individual failings. Given this reform-oriented background, what did it mean to be a sociologist, what were proper sociological methods, and how should college-level instruction in sociology take place? In fact, several articles in the early AJS document nothing more than the composition of sociology programs at different universities, as well as the various departments in which "Introductory Sociology" is taught. The question also arose as to how journalistic instruction and practice might be distinguished from sociological theories and methods.

Several articles before 1926 also discuss the Pittsburgh Survey, inevitably addressing the relationship between the journalistic and sociological aspects of the Survey. In a 1909 article summarizing the survey results, Edward Devine lists the findings and then goes on to lament that, as a surveyor and sociologist, he is "unable to set [our findings free] through yellow journalism methods ... because these are not consistent with our traditions."[22] Park adds that the various urban surveys and reports sponsored by the Carnegie and Russell Sage foundations "are something more than scientific reports. They are rather a high form of journalism, dealing with conditions critically, and seeking through the agency of publicity to bring about radical reforms."[23]

In all the aforementioned examples illustrating the early days of the sociology–journalism relationship, the questions of how to reform the press, what sociology is, how the profession of sociology relates to the problems of moral reform, and how sociology differs procedurally from journalism, remain entangled. While there is a vague notion that a boundary between journalism and social science does indeed exist, we cannot say that there is any boundary work per se. Or perhaps it is more accurate to note that the efforts at boundary work that *did* exist were themselves confused by the inchoate status of sociology itself. Over the next forty years, however, the pace of professional separation would accelerate, and boundary-building would begin in earnest.

Condescension and critique

It is quite obvious, even in the AJS articles from the 1910s and early 1920s, that sociologists were groping toward a dividing line between so-called "higher" forms of journalism (like the social survey and even some kinds of muckraking) and social science. In these early days, however, the division was muddled and the sociological critique of journalism was less methodological and more normative in nature. A distinct change in tone, however, can be seen by the mid-1920s. Following Lannoy,[24] we can see clear signs of this shift in the differences between the original and revised versions of Park's "The City," re-published in 1925. Whereas the first version of "The City" makes reference to the survey movement only briefly, describing it as a form of "high journalism," the revised version injects *both* muckraking journalism *and* the social survey as teleological stopping points along the history of social science, of which sociology is the final and highest stage (Lannoy, 51). "Social interest was first stimulated by polemics against the political and social disorders of urban life [i.e., muckraking journalism] ... [while] sociology sought a surer basis for the solution of the problems from a study of the facts of city life." In this spirit, government statistics provide citizens with data, community surveys gather masses of information and put them in readable form, and settlement writers like Jane Addams have produced "arresting and sympathetic pictures." But only sociology, Park writes later, "yields generalizations of wide or general validity."[25] A later AJS article on the Pittsburgh Survey puts this critique in even more sophisticated and methodologically confident terms. The survey movement is not social science, Hariett Bartlett argues in a 1928 article, insofar as its goal is practical action located at a specific time and place rather than general hypothesis testing. In the articles on journalism, this is perhaps the earliest case in which we see alternate empirical practices contrasted with the scientific method per se. "In the minds of many persons the survey is confused with research," Bartlett writes. "Both are techniques of investigation but should be carefully distinguished ... the survey makes comparisons, but, instead of leading to generalizations, they are intended to bring out more clearly the particular problem."[26] The Pittsburgh Survey, the most famous Survey of all, is tainted even in its origins insofar as it "started out as a journalistic project, undertaken by a committee of a charity organization journal," Bartlett writes dismissively.[27] Bartlett, like Devine in 1909, still draws a connecting line between muckraking journalism and the social survey – but by this time both journalistic and survey techniques are radically differentiated from sociology, rather than being seen as a somewhat uneasy contributors to a larger scholarly tradition of which sociology is also a part. Her concluding sentence is pointed: "most particularly [this article] does eliminate some of the confusion which exists as to the nature of the survey and brings it out as an essentially practical, not scientific, technique."[28]

By the 1940s, barely more than a decade after Bartlett's article and Park's revisions to "The City," the lines are set and references to journalism in the mainstream sociology journals can usually only be found in book reviews. There, it serves as an object of condescension, as a way of "othering" particularly well-written or methodologically unsound sociology books. Reviewing a book which calls for news reporters to be "trained in the social sciences, notably sociology, psychology, and economics, in order to explain and interpret the deeper significance of events and utterances," the ASR reviewer exclaims "God forbid!" and sarcastically notes that such a change would lead to the terrible prospect of newsboys tossing Ph.D. theses on the piazza every morning.[29] In a 1942 review of a collected volume of readings on the newspaper and society, an AJS reviewer notes that the assembled texts are intended "for use by students in classes of journalism."[30] "Selections comprising [Part 1] ... represent primarily contributions of social scientists, and contrast with those other parts of the book which are primarily the work of journalists."[31] For this reason, the book is fairly useless to sociologists as a primer on news but can serve as a primary document for sociologists looking for insights into the journalistic mind-set as defined by journalists themselves.

By the 1950s, this review of a book on public opinion has become typical of the tenor of the (now nearly non-existent) journalism-related discourse in the *American Sociological Review* and the *American Journal of Sociology*:

> almost all of the books recently published on [the] subject [of public opinion] are very uneven, reflecting the competence of the author in his own field and displaying his lack of knowledge in the related fields. Such is the case in the present volume, wherein a professor of journalism presents "a guide for newspaper men and newspaper readers" which equates public opinion with any and all social thought and action and which attempts to explain human behavior by a popular treatment of such topics as "The Nature of Man" (Chapter 2), and "The Nature of Society" (Chapter 3). As in the case of most such attempts, the oversimplification of basic concepts results in a volume which will leave most social scientists annoyed and displeased. While the present text may be useful in schools of journalism, it probably will be of limited value to social scientists. Furthermore, in this reviewer's opinion, the student of journalism would benefit more from a basic text in social psychology than from the present popular translation.[32]

By 1967, these reviews had reached a fairly high level of dismissive dudgeon. A book on a recent development in Boise, Idaho, is called "an extraordinarily commendable work of popular journalism by a professor on that subject at New York University." But

> as social science, the book makes only a minute contribution ... it is, alas, not very coherently written, somewhat hysterical in tone ... and argues "statistically" from an N of twelve – chosen we know not how – about general awareness of deviance in the community. In other words, the book falls sufficiently short of professionally acceptable standards of rigor in the accumulation of data, the marshaling of evidence, and its interplay with relevant theory to disqualify it as a tool of higher education.[33]

Data collection, evidence analysis, and the relationship of empirical work to theory. This is the rhetoric of a mature science, one that has become confident enough in its procedures and its apparatus to denigrate "an extraordinary commendable work of journalism" for its lack of rigor. Boundaries, fortified by the strong professional conception of both journalism and sociology itself, have been erected. The days when a future president of the American Sociological Society would turn his classroom into a working newspaper office, and when a founder of the field would ruminate on the similarities and differences between urban sociology and urban reporting, are long gone.

Journalism as an object of sociological inquiry

From the 1940s until the early 1970s, journalism as an object of sociological inquiry almost entirely vanishes. There was scattered empirical investigation into news reporting in the decades before the 1940s, amid all the moral speculation about the public failings of the press. But, after the 40s, we are limited to the occasional piece such as "Newspaper Circulation from Small Metropolitan Centers."[34] In part, this can be traced to the general sociological abandonment of mass communication research; in part, it should be attributed to the rise of journalism schools and their affiliated "communications" programs.[35] We should keep in mind, however, that many of the articles on journalism in the early years of the AJS would barely be recognized as "sociology" today, even given the relative fondness for the Chicago School in sociology's collective memory. In short, there is virtually no tradition of so-called "mainstream" journalism research in the sociology journals up until the 1970s; the maturation of sociology into a "legitimate" social science and the establishment of academic communications programs run together in history.

In the 1960s and 70s, this would briefly change. As Stonbely puts it in her overview of the U.S. "newsroom studies," "in the 1960s and 1970s, a number of sociologists ventured into newsrooms in American and England to conduct ethnographies on the production of news."[36] Of the four key studies identified by Stonbely in her article, only one of them (by Tuchman) would be originally published in the ASR or AJS;[37] Gans garners a lengthy and praiseworthy review in the AJS,[38] Fishman's original piece on the reporting of crime waves is found in Social Problems,[39] and Epstein's work appears primarily in monograph form.[40] Even outside of the ethnographic work, however, the 1970s and early 80s would see the publication of several other journalism-oriented articles, including two by Molotch and Lester that utilized content analysis and ethnographic research in combination.[41]

Stonbely attributes this (brief) return of a sociology of news to overlapping intellectual and socio-political contexts, including the emergence of organizational theory in sociology, a growing critique of professionalism, the background of Berger and Luckmann's work on the social construction of reality, a broader critique of institutional authority in general, and a liberal call for greater press pluralism. I agree, by and large, with her analysis, and would only add that, even with all these factors working in favor of a sociological embrace of journalism studies, the majority of the work in this vein did not appear in the central sociological journals and acted as something of an outlier even when it did. Now that the boundaries between journalism and sociology are (relatively) secure, sociology can at last turn its analytical gaze upon its exiled cousin, the sense-making profession of news reporting; even here, however, a vague feeling of uncertainty about the ability of a mostly qualitative sociology to pass judgment on other qualitative workers lingers in the background.[42]

By the mid-1980s, this brief resurgence of interest would taper off. If I had to categorize a fourth phase of the sociological understanding of journalism, I would probably label it as an embrace of raw journalistic data and journalistic settings to understand *other* social phenomena (but not the news). But the litera-ture in the 1990s is too scattered to make any broad claims, and perhaps we are too close to that era to fully map the meta-theoretical discourses that lie beneath the placid surface of the academic journal. Suffice it to say that interest in journalism remains low, and I would echo Katz and Pooley and attribute this divide as an "unintended consequence of the handoff to journalism schools."[43] As for these journalism schools, they faced their own internal divisions and arguments about the relationship between the study of the news, social science methods, and journalistic practice. It is to the journalism side of the sociological–journalism boundary work that I now briefly turn.

Through the looking glass: Journalism considers social science

In considering how journalism understood itself in relation to social science, we face the challenge that while sociology is an academic discipline with occasional professional training embedded in its course of study, journalism is both a field of study (usually housed within communication programs) and a professional course of training.[44] Quite often the fields of journalism (profes-sional practice) and communications (the academic discipline) have little or nothing to do with each other, and this makes drawing a line between jour-nalism and sociology more a task of drawing a line between journalism, sociology, *and communications*.[45] Nevertheless, for the purposes of this chap-ter, I will stick to a two-part analysis of the manner through which the pro-fession of journalism discursively framed social science as well as its own relation to that science. To do this, as you will recall, I searched the *Columbia Journalism Review* for all articles that mentioned "social science" or "sociol-ogy," resulting in 36 articles. In general, there are far fewer patterns to be found in the CJR's treatment of sociology and social science than there are in the AJS and ARS. In part this may be because of differences in sample size, and in part may have to do with the fact that CJR was not founded until the 60s (and, as we have already seen, perhaps the most interesting parts of the AJS and ARS come from the 1920s, 40s and 50s).

Still, there are patterns. Most of the relevant articles consist of summarized or excerpted social science research papers in the CJR of the 1960s, or more narrative-driven "research reports" in the 2000s. A few other articles (again, mostly book reviews) directly looked at the relationship between the two empirical domains. And, finally, I discovered a key (perhaps *the* key) paper by Philip Meyer in 1971 called "The Limits of Intuition," as well as two reviews of Meyer's book, *Precision Journalism,* in 1973 and 2002.

Some of the most famous names in media sociology occasionally grace the pages of CJR. Kurt and Gladys Lang discuss the impact of televised hearings in a piece from 1973.[46] Herbert Gans writes about "multi-perspectival news" in 1979,[47] and Michael Schudson and a team of Columbia graduate students contribute a "research report" in the 2000s. Vincent Mosco writes an article on the institutional relationship between minority organizing groups and the FCC,[48] and there is the occasional angry letter from Todd Gitlin. There are less well-known straight academic studies as well, including at least one article adopted from a media sociology doctoral thesis published in CJR's early days.[49]

By and large, however, such articles are rare. Even more rare are articles looking directly or obliquely at the journalism–sociology relationship. One of the few can be found in a review of a collection of essays honoring David Riesman, "Journalism and Social Science: Continuities and Discontinuities," by Gerald Grant. The reviewer notes that Grant attempts to absolve journalism from claims that it is intellectually lightweight, suggesting that it is "to social scientists like Nathan Glazer, Daniel Bell, James Coleman, and David Riesman that [an actually-existing form of] analytical journalism turns to for models." The reviewer, while not entirely dismissive of Grant's claim that journalism can approach the subtlety and sweep of public sociology, does seem to resent "[Grant's] implicit assumption that [journalists] represent a lower link in the great chain of informational being" than public-minded sociologists. The review also begins with a passive aggresive attack on some unnamed writers who wish to make journalism more sociological or analytical, wryly noting that "every once in a while someone discovers an analogy between the practice of journalism and some other discipline – an archaeological dig, say, or a psychoanalytic probe." It seems clear that this swipe is directed against Philip Meyer and his call in the 1970s, in the pages of CJR and elsewhere, for journalism to become more like a social science than the anecdotal, ad hoc collection of more-or-less random data points.[50]

It is here, with Meyer and the first appearance of his notion of precision journalism in the pages of the professional journalism press, that we reach a turning point in the journalism–social science relationship. It is here that we must bring our analysis to a close. Meyer, with his aggressive attempt to fuse journalistic and social science methods, straddles the dividing line between the distant past and the near past of the journalism–social science genealogy that I promised to undertake in this chapter. By the 1980s, sociology had abandoned its concern with journalism (both as an object of empirical inquiry and as grist for methodological speculation), and ceded the field to journalism to more reflexively consider the exact location of its occupational boundary line. It is perhaps not surprising that sociology (as it became increasingly confident in its own theoretical, professional, and analytical moorings), could feel less of a need to inquire more deeply into its epistemological scaffolding than its once-sibling journalism, a profession that has always had far less confidence in its own intellectual underpinnings.

Conclusion

In this chapter I have attempted to outline the process by which a firm, thick boundary was drawn between journalism and social science in the early to mid-twentieth century. We have seen that sociology began by uncertainly engaging with journalism, in part because of its view of journalism as a community-binding social actor and it part because of its own epistemological uncertainty about the exact nature of sociology. There would be a radical shift in this posture after the 1920s, however, as sociology began to find its footing as a legitimate, increasingly professional social science. From the 1940s through the 1960s, references to journalism and the news would be scarce in the most prestigious sociological journals; to the degree these references appeared at all, they were usually in book reviews where they were deployed as a slur to "other" improperly sociological works. Sociology, in short, moved to abandon any interest in attaining the kind of wide, popular accessibility that journalism possessed in exchange for gaining status as a science. Partly this relates to sociology's own understanding of relevant data and the emergence of the "variable revolution,"[51] and partly it relates to sociology's attempt to distance itself from its reformist roots.[52] In the 1970s and early 1980s, this neglect abated somewhat as sociologists turned their attention to the empirical investigation of news practices. Even here, however, journalism was treated more as a specimen on a laboratory bench than as anything resembling a kindred spirit in empirical investigation.

It would be journalism, starting with Philip Meyer in the 1960s, that would attempt to re-bridge the boundary divide that had opened up in the ensuing debates, but it would do so almost entirely on the terms and in the vocabulary of social science. We need to remember that this was a reversal in the epistemological hierarchy, or at the very least a reversal in professional self-confidence. Sociology entered the occupational arena in the 1900s as the little brother to journalism, at least in terms of age and power, and early sociologists adopted an ambiguous attitude toward their reform-minded cousins. By the 1960s, however, the shoe was on the other foot, at least for a vocal minority of empirically minded reporters. The consequences of that turn toward precision journalism and computational journalistic practice, and the role that movement played in the larger history of data journalism, will be the subject of a future work.

Notes

1 George Vincent, "A Laboratory Experiment in Journalism." *American Journal of Sociology* 11, no. 3 (1905): 309.
2 Vincent, "A Laboratory Experiment in Journalism," 311.
3 Nate Silver, "What the Fox Knows," 2014, online at http://fivethirtyeight.com/features/what-the-fox-knows/
4 Gil Eyal and Brenden Hart, "How parents of autistic children became 'experts on their own children': Notes towards a sociology of expertise," Keynote address, BJS Annual Conference. *Berkeley Journal of Sociology,* 54 (2010); Bruno Lator, "The whole is always smaller than its parts: A digital text of Gabriel Tarde's monads," *British Journal of Sociology* 63, no. 4 (2012): 590–615.
5 Shelby Harrison, *The Social Survey* (New York: Russell Sage Foundation, 1931), 21.
6 Christopher Anderson, "Between Public Enlightenment and Public Relations: The Men and Religion Forward Movement and the Ambiguities of Documentary Evidence in Early Modern Journalism," Media Sociology Pre-Conference of the ASA, 9 August 2013.
7 Rolf Linder, *The Reportage of Urban Culture: Robert Park and the Chicago School* (Cambridge, UK: Cambridge University Press, 2006).
8 Cara Finnegan, "Social Welfare and Visual Politics: The Story of Survey Graphic," 2005, online at http://newdeal.feri.org/sg/essay01.htm
9 Carlson, this volume, citing Thomas Gieryn.
10 Michel Foucault, *Power/Knowledge: Selected Interviews and Other Writings, 1972–77* (New York, NY: Vintage, 1980).
11 The article types included traditional research articles, book reviews, and abstracts of articles and biblographies.
12 Edward Suchman, "*Understanding Public Opinion*, by Curtis D. MacDougall [review]," *American Sociological Review* 18, no. 2 (1953): 218–19.
13 E. Devine, "Results of the Pittsburgh Survey." *American Journal of Sociology* 14, no. 5 (1909): 667; H. Bartlett, "The Social Survey and the Charity Organization Movement," *American Journal of Sociology* 34, no. 2 (1928): 331.
14 Harvey Molotch. and Marilyn Lester, "Accidental News: The Great Oil Spill as a Local Occurrence and National Event," *American Journal of Sociology* 81, no. 2 (1975): 235–60; Gaye Tuchman, "Objectivity as Strategic Ritual: An Examination of Newsmen's Notions of Objectivity," *American Journal of Sociology* 77, no. 4 (1972): 660–79; Lee Sigelman "Reporting the News: An Organizational Analysis," *American Journal of Sociology* 79, no. 1 (1973): 132–51.
15 Glen R. Carroll and Yangchung Huo, "Organizational Task and Institutional Environments in Ecological Perspective: Findings From the Local Newspaper Industry," *American Journal of Sociology* 91, no. 4 (1986): 838–73.
16 An Independent Journalist, "Is an Honest and Sane Newspaper Press Possible?" *American Journal of Sociology* 15, no. 3 (1909): 321–34.
17 Frances Fenton, "The Influence of Newspaper Presentations Upon the Growth of Crime and Other Anti-Social Activity," *American Journal of Sociology* 16, no. 3 (1910): 342.
18 Victor S. Yarros, "The Press and Public Opinion," *American Journal of Sociology* 5, no. 3 (1899): 372.
19 A. Weeks, "The Mind of the Citizen III," *American Journal of Sociology* 21, no. 4 (1916): 502.
20 Robert Park, "The Natural History of the Newspaper," *American Journal of Sociology* 29, no. 3 (1923): 278.
21 Andrew Abbott, *Department and Discipline: Chicago Sociology at 100* (Chicago, IL: University of Chicago Press, 1999), 81.

22 E. Devine, "Results of the Pittsburgh Survey," *American Journal of Sociology* 14, no. 5 (1909): 667.

23 Robert Park, "The City: Suggestion for the Investigations of Human Behavior in the City Environment," *American Journal of Sociology* 20, no. 5 (1915): 577–612.

24 P. Lannoy, "When Robert Park Was (Re)Writing 'The City': Biography, the Social Survey, and the Science of Sociology," *The American Sociologist* 35, no. 1 (2004): 34–62.

25 Robert Park, W. Burgess and Roderick McKenzie, *The City* (Chicago: University of Chicago Press, 1925), 331.

26 H. Bartlett, "The Social Survey and the Charity Organization Movement," *American Journal of Sociology* 34, no. 2 (1928): 331.

27 Bartlett, "The Social Survey and the Charity Organization Movement," 343.

28 Bartlett, "The Social Survey and the Charity Organization Movement," 345.

29 S. Shalloo, "*News and the Human Interest Story*, by Helen McGill Hughes. *Backgrounding the News: The Newspaper and the Social Sciences*, by Sidney Kobre." *American Sociological Review* 5, no. 4 (1940): 664.

30 Elizabeth Johns, "*The Newspaper and Society: A Book of Readings*, by George L. Bird; Frederic E. Merwin [review]," *American Journal of Sociology* 48, no. 2 (1942): 274.

31 Johns, "*The Newspaper and Society*," 274.

32 E. Suchman, "*Understanding Public Opinion*, by Curtis D. MacDougall [review]," *American Sociological Review* 18, no. 2 (1953): 218–19.

33 Polsby, N., "*The Boys of Boise: Furor, Vice and Folly in an American City*, by John Gerassi [review]," *American Journal of Sociology* 72, no. 6 (1967): 691.

34 John A. Kinneman, "Newspaper Circulation from Small Metropolitan Centers," *American Sociological Review* 11, no. 2 (1946): 150–55.

35 Jefferson Pooley and Elihu Katz, "Further Notes on Why Sociology Abandoned Mass Communication Research," *Journal of Communication* 58, no. 4 (2008): 767–86.

36 Sarah Stonbely, "The Social and Intellectual Context of the U.S. 'Newsroom Studies,' and the Media Sociology of Today," *Journalism Studies* (2013): 1–17.

37 Gaye Tuchman, "Objectivity as Strategic Ritual: An Examination of Newsmen's Notions of Objectivity," *American Journal of Sociology* 77, no. 4 (1972): 660–79. Gaye Tuchman, "Making News By Doing Work: Routinizing the Unexpected," *American Journal of Sociology* 79, no. 1 (1973): 110–31.

38 J.W.C. Johnstone, "Who Controls the News?" *American Journal of Sociology* 87, no. 5 (1982): 1174–81.

39 M. Fishman, "Crime Waves as Ideology." *Social Problems* 25, no. 5 (1978): 531–43.

40 Edward Jay Epstein (2000 [1973]). *News From Nowhere: Television and the News* (Lanham, MD: Ivan R Dee).

41 H. Molotch and M. Lester, "News as Purposive Behavior," *American Sociological Review* 39, no. 1 (1974): 101–11; H. Molotch and M. Lester, "Accidental News: The Great Oil Spill as a Local Occurrence and National Event," *American Journal of Sociology* 81, no. 2 (1975): 235–60.

42 Gaye Tuchman, "Objectivity as Strategic Ritual: An Examination of Newsmen's Notions of Objectivity," *American Journal of Sociology* 77, no. 4 (1972): 660–79.

43 Jefferson Pooley and Elihu Katz, "Further Notes on Why Sociology Abandoned Mass Communication Research," *Journal of Communication* 58, no. 4 (2008): 767–86.

44 Jefferson Pooley, "Another Plea for the University Tradition: The Institutional Roots of Intellectual Compromise," *International Journal of Communication* 5 (2011): 1442–57.

45 James Carey, "A Plea For the University Tradition," *Journalism Quarterly* (1978): 846–55.

46 Kurt and Gladys Lang, "Television Hearings: The Impact Out There," *Columbia Journalism Review* (1973): 52–57.
47 Herbert Gans, "The Messages Beyond the News," *Columbia Journalism Review* (1979): 40–45.
48 Vincent Mosco, "What's Black and White and Split Down the Middle?" *Columbia Journalism Review* (1980).
49 David Grey, "Supreme Court Headlines: Accuracy vs Precision," *Columbia Journalism Review* (1966): 26–29.
50 Gerald Grant, "Journalism and Social Science: Continuities and Discontinuities," *Columbia Journalism Review* (1979).
51 Theodore Porter, *Trust in Numbers: The Pursuit of Objectivity in Science and Public Life* (Princeton, NJ: Princeton University Press, 1997).
52 Rolf Linder, *The Reportage of Urban Culture: Robert Park and the Chicago School* (Cambridge, UK: Cambridge University Press, 2006).

Epilogue

Studying the boundaries of journalism: Where do we go from here?

Seth C. Lewis

During the revolutionary crisis that rocked Ukraine in 2014, a separatist movement arose. Eastern provinces, dominated by majorities of ethnic Russians, agitated for greater autonomy from Kiev, if not outright allegiance to Moscow. Amid the conflict, Google Maps quietly updated its mapping software, changing its representations of Ukrainian borders. Specifically, the hotly contested Crimean region now would appear differently to different types of users: for Russian visitors to Google Maps'.ru domain, a solid line would divide the Black Sea peninsula from Ukraine, indicating that the region belonged to Russia; meanwhile, for Americans using .com, a dotted line would suggest, in line with the U.S. government's belief, that Crimea is an "occupied territory," its boundaries and governance in dispute. As it turns out, by one account, Google maintains at least 30 versions of its mapping platform for different countries, and other mapmakers, such as National Geographic and Rand-McNally, take their own approaches to distinguishing contested borders through variations in lines and color shading. In its view, Google is trying to be "objective" in adjudicating such matters, in part by honoring the local laws and cultures where its servers are located. But while seemingly subtle, such variations in online mapping don't go without notice, especially by states intent on maintaining their claims over disputed territories. "Historically," as one observer noted, "the most powerful mapmaker in the world was often the most powerful country in the world."[1] Boundaries and the power to determine them, as the British Empire and other sprawling powers no doubt realized, matter a great deal indeed.

One may note that the boundaries of geopolitics are, of course, far different from the boundaries of journalism. Yet the conceptual analogy is no less useful: to understand any phenomenon, in the broadest sense, requires understanding what it *is* relative to what it *is not* – in essence, its boundaries. This relational examination – of insiders vs. outsiders, of acceptable practices vs. deviant ones, of us-vs.-them distinctions made by institutions and individuals alike – is at the heart of inquiry. To chart a particular phenomenon is to chart the boundaries that constitute it as well as the forces that contribute to forging, reinforcing or challenging those boundaries. The determination of boundaries is thus an exercise in power. To set the boundaries of a particular place, process or, in this case, profession is to claim a kind of mapmaking authority: to succeed in marshaling the resources necessary to lay claim to a certain space *and* impose a particular vision about the character, meaning, and distinctiveness of that space. This is not to say that all "boundary work,"[2] in the generic sense, is inherently cynical or calculating; rather, it suggests that boundary struggles are endemic to the human condition, and thus must be understood as key sites through which to examine enduring issues of power, authority, and jurisdiction.[3]

Toward conceptual innovation

But it's not enough simply to acknowledge that boundaries matter and thus should be studied. The better question, as we conclude this volume, is to ask: *How* should boundaries be studied? Or, more specifically yet: What particular elements of boundaries – and boundary work – deserve special consideration as scholars explore the concept generally and in journalism especially?

As the chapters in this book have shown, there is no single protocol for studying the boundaries of journalism, just as there is no single kind of *journalism* to study across the various contexts of media systems, political contexts, institutional forms, occupational norms, pro-am hybrids, and technological arrangements described in these pages. The chapters here have illustrated multiple points of entry: e.g., the shaping of professional values, as older principles such as transparency and verification are re-imagined in light of new digital tools and techniques; the negotiation of journalistic autonomy against the gravitational pull of market forces as business logic assumes greater importance in journalism; and the challenges that certain journalists face in claiming legitimacy and capital – whether externally in relation to state actors or internally in relation to other, higher-status journalists. Moreover, the chapters have shown how boundary contests around actors (who gets to be called a journalist) and activities (what gets to be called journalism) have emerged as defining yet unresolved questions in our present moment of media disruption and "post-industrial journalism."[4] As the "professional logic" of journalistic control confronts an information environment that is seemingly out of control,[5] these chapters demonstrate how certain conditions and considerations – be they economic, political, institutional, sociocultural, or technological in nature – factor into shaping boundaries between journalists and audiences, objectivity and advocacy, facticity and opinion, as well as boundaries around news practices that determine who gets to speak, what gets to be said, and how truth claims are articulated and legitimated in the public arena. The particular role of technology, as a key mediator in journalistic witnessing, storytelling, and commentary, also is highlighted in these chapters – in some cases as the primary object around which and through which boundaries are negotiated, in others as the backdrop against which social actors work through questions of innovation and adaptation.

Such an emphasis on "change" and its connection to "the future of journalism" is quite prevalent in the larger discourse (both scholarly and popular) about boundaries and journalism. Indeed, any mention of journalism's boundaries today seems to presume a changing nature of those boundaries – and no doubt with good evidence, supported by a range of studies into journalism as a professional system, industrial field, and form of practice. There is no shortage of talk about flux, precarity, and even a creeping sense of doom, seasoned with hope for journalistic rebirth.[6] But while it may seem that boundaries everywhere are collapsing, falling in the face of social, economic, and technological stressors, this book shows that such a view is overly simplistic. Yes, some aspects of journalism have been "turned inside-out," as Hermida puts it in his chapter on social media and verification. But in the main, journalism is surprisingly durable. As a professional system, its occupational norms are being subtly revised to "normalize" key attributes associated with digital media culture, thereby allowing concepts like participation from users to become part of the journalistic fold even while keeping the underlying threats associated with such incursion at the margins and thus diluting the potential disruption. As an industrial field, journalism's model – of mass-producing news information mostly through the routinized sourcing of official or traditional institutions to reach mass audiences sold to advertisers – remains quite consistent, even as its business models pivot slightly to make that production more economically viable through the likes of soft news, native advertising, entrepreneurship, and other market-oriented developments. And, as a form of practice, journalism and its epistemological approaches to fact-finding remain mostly enduring, even as the networked information environment presents opportunities and challenges yet to be ironed out. So, is there change in the boundaries of journalism? No doubt. But perhaps what we're seeing is not so much the wholesale collapse of the legacy borders but rather a whole series of disruptions, all varying in scope and source, coalescing into one vast and complicated terrain of contestations – all of it ripe for studying boundaries.

Which brings us again to the question above: With so much that can be considered in the study of boundaries and journalism, and with so much covered in the chapters here, which elements of boundary work deserve particular consideration going forward? Simply put, where do we go from here?

This is a pertinent and pressing question when we consider the fate of some other conceptual approaches applied in communication, media and journalism studies. Let's take "framing," for instance. Framing is at once practically intuitive, provocatively open, and conceptually rich,[7] and so, not surprisingly, it has enjoyed a long and distinguished history in communication research.[8] In fact, framing is often positioned as *the* theoretical approach to unpacking the textual nature of media portrayals, whether from quantitative, qualitative or multi-method perspectives. Yet, the concept is so frequently invoked, and often in a way that simply serves to justify studying "how the news media talks about X or Y topic," that it has lost some of its analytical usefulness, exhausted by overuse and misuse. As Reese has noted:

> I have been sent more manuscripts to review than I care to recall, with many having only the term "framing" in common. Authors often give an obligatory nod to the literature before proceeding to do whatever they were going to do in the first place. ... [Or authors] find in framing a more compelling hook to hang their content analyses on. Often, it is simply a matter of substituting "frame" for what would have been called "topic" or "theme."[9]

How can we avoid a similar fate for "boundaries," even while advocating for its utility? As a concept, it's likewise at once easy to understand, paradigmatically flexible, and analytically deep. It invites us to consider how, why, and under what conditions the contours of a social world and its associated performances and practices are made durable or malleable, and in whose interests and toward what ends such shaping efforts occur. In journalism studies, that expansive view offers all manner of directions for future research. And yet, duplicative research that simply relies on the boundaries concept to justify studying "how journalists negotiate changes in X or Y" would be easy to conduct and yet conceptually vacuous. If journalism studies – and communication and media studies more broadly – is to take boundaries seriously, much like Zelizer has called for "taking journalism seriously,"[10] then we must tread with care in developing this concept and its theoretical implications. In the sections that follow, I would like to suggest two directions in that vein, while acknowledging that these are merely starting points and not the definitive nor the only ways to innovate our study of boundaries of journalism. I will argue for (1) refining our approach to *the social* and *the material*, and the interplay between them, and then (2) building upon that refinement to develop greater sensitivity to the study of emerging conditions of news-making, particularly with regard to technology and the change associated with it.

Refining our approach to the social and the material in boundary work

The social emphasizes those factors of human construction, culture, and rhetoric, or what I might call the "soft" boundary work of *talk that articulates boundaries*. The material emphasizes those factors that are more structural, architectural, and technical in nature, or the "hard" boundary work of *action that actualizes boundaries*. In the first instance boundaries are defined in words or symbols, in the second they are performed in practice or engaged through objects. Notably, the social and the material are not mutually exclusive, but rather are intertwined as partners in the development and deployment of boundaries. To illustrate this, we might draw upon Gieryn's[11] study of science to consider its two-part boundary work: firstly as scientists rhetorically claim the right to conduct research in the public interest, and secondly as they rely on various structural arrangements – from educational requirements to physical resources like lab space to exclusive access to peer-reviewed publishing – to uphold and legitimate those public claims. Journalism does not have the same structural barriers to entry that are typical of professions, such as licensing requirements, but it nevertheless has material delimitations in the form of backstage access via press passes and news conferences, as well as in limited access to built-in audiences via mass media distribution. The news text itself may be seen as a material expression of boundaries: an output, closed to outsiders in its creation, that manifests the parameters of and authority within journalism's professional space.

This social–material delineation draws together and distinguishes the sociological perspectives on boundaries that Carlson outlines in the introduction to this book. In this light, Gieryn[12] generally emphasizes rhetoric and its role in the construction of social recognition in a social space. Abbott likewise emphasizes the social context of claims to cultural legitimacy, or what he describes as "jurisdiction" over a social practice; however, he also notes that "jurisdiction has not only a culture, but also a social *structure*" (my emphasis added)[13] – in effect, both talk and action. This nod to structure aligns with Bourdieu's regard for material forms of capital, such as financial resources, that help determine winners and losers in the relational struggle among social fields.[14] On balance, however, these perspectives on boundaries tend to privilege the rhetorical over the structural even as they acknowledge the importance and interplay of both dimensions.

Perhaps following this bias, studies of journalistic boundaries – particularly in drawing upon Gieryn's framework – have tended to emphasize rhetorical constructions over material ones. We find this in studies of how journalists expel deviant actors or practices from within, and in how they expand their position vis-à-vis external actors such as WikiLeaks and external practices such as social media (again, see Carlson's Introduction). Comparatively few have sought to bring together the social and structural within a single project, perhaps in part because it can be quite difficult to pin down how boundaries shaped in talk are effectuated in action. I speak from some experience, after trying to connect the social and structural in my dissertation study of the nonprofit Knight Foundation and its efforts, rhetorical and otherwise, to shape the nature of what counts as "innovation" in journalism.[15] I found that Knight Foundation, the world's largest private funder of news-related initiatives, sought to alter the boundaries of journalism jurisdiction: moving away from "journalism" and its professional exclusivity, and toward "information" and its openness as a way of seeking the wisdom of the crowd to solve journalism's problems. This happened rhetorically in the way Knight reframed its mission and its conception of journalism,[16] and structurally in the way the Foundation designed a prominent news-innovation contest and selected projects to advance.[17] Ultimately, I argued that, by dropping its patrol of traditional profes-sional boundaries, Knight aimed to make space for external actors (such as software developers) to step in and bring innovation to journalism. Simulta-neously, though, Knight also pushed for concepts on the periphery of journalism, such as user participation, to be embraced as founding doctrines of news innovation leading to the development of an "ethic of participation."[18] Such an ethic provides a hybrid resolution to the tension between professional control and open participation, allowing us to imagine the integration of users and their generative potential as a normative goal – not merely an unfortunate byproduct – of journalism in the digital media environment.

In the years since my 2010 research, I have wondered: To what extent did those boundary reformations *actually* change journalism, as a professional field? It is impossible to know for sure – just as we can't assess the precise shaping "effect" of any particular text, for that matter. But efforts to link the social and structural, even while challenging, are at least a step in the right direction. Indeed, they are a requisite starting point, I would argue, for pursuing a more refined approach to the social and the material in the study of boundaries.

Notably, though, we next need to peel apart "structural" from "material," making a distinction that will help us attend to a more supple representation of *material objects* in general and *technology objects* in particular, as they relate to journalism and its boundaries.

Objects of boundaries, objects of journalism

For the classical accounts of boundaries, the "structural" presumably is more "social" (human) than "material" (nonhuman). Thus Abbott talks of social structure[19] and Starr of social institution-building[20] – the emphasis being on groups of people and the duality of *their* talk/action constructions, rather than on the tools, technologies, and "things" that become enrolled in the work of determining boundaries. This is not to imply, techno-deterministically, that things forge or reinforce boundaries by themselves in some agentic fashion. But nor is it to assume that nonhuman objects do not "matter" in the course of boundary work – for there is good evidence that they do, even the mundane "stuff" through which social activity is accomplished. Geographic maps, after all, are material objects of great import in communicating and reifying boundaries – not to mention the behind-the-scenes technological code, inter-twined with the social decisions, that factors into rendering online maps in certain ways for certain groups, as we saw above.

Represented by an ongoing "material turn" in the social sciences,[21] this paradigmatic shift in emphasis takes the material quality of things seriously. It treats distinct, nonhuman objects as worthy of analysis, not to fetishize them but rather to use them as lenses through which to study social relationships, power dynamics, and, yes, boundary work in broad terms (not often asso-ciated with Gieryn's framework directly). Related to this movement is the rise of conceptual approaches like actor-network theory (ANT), inspired by Bruno Latour, Michael Callon, and John Law.[22] More method than theory, ANT is concerned with tracing relationships among *actants* – be they humans or nonhumans – in networked systems, allowing the determination of agents and their relative influence upon one another in the network to emerge organically and situationally.[23]

In journalism studies, the study of news "objects" has gained great currency of late. This is represented in a growing list of ANT-inspired studies of emerging digital tools, technological practices, and news networks, and is perhaps typified by Anderson and De Maeyer's 2015 *Journalism* special issue on "objects of journalism," which includes studies of objects ranging from content management systems (CMS) to websites to Wikipedia edit boxes to older newspaper artifacts such as pica poles and proportion wheels.[24] Such objects, Kreiss asserts in the issue's coda, "show how often taken-for-granted objects ... shape the organizations, work, and products of journalism through their material and symbolic properties and affordances"[25] – as in the case of a CMS that guided human practices in certain ways according to certain values and relationships encoded into its design. In many such works, ANT is deemed analytically useful because it brings into view the objects, relationships, and dynamics of technological change and innovation, freeing researchers from adhering to old categories that may no longer be relevant to the study of media technologies in their emergent, contingent, and socially situated varieties.[26] For much of journalism studies in this vein, "analyzing 'materiality' essentially means studying (new) technologies," Anderson and De Maeyer note in their special issue – even while they also argue that an ANT or object-aware perspective can be broadened to highlight more historical and social contexts not connected to technologies of the moment.[27] Objects, they contend, matter not in and of themselves, but precisely because of their "deeply *relational* underpinnings," connecting discourses, practices, and cultures (emphasis original). Setting aside ANT and questions about its ultimate necessity in the study of media technologies – and the critiques have serious merit[28] – it's fair to say that, in this technologically saturated environment, it becomes all the more essential to draw relational distinctions between social actors, nonhuman technological actants, and distinct types of media audiences, all enrolled in activities of news-making and news-sharing that are implicated in the boundaries of journalism.[29]

What, then, is the contribution of materiality to the study of boundaries of journalism? For one, it orients us to a study of *boundary objects*, thereby "shift[ing] attention from *discursive* battles over control to *material* connections involved in coordination," as Carlson has noted already (my emphasis added). That is, an emphasis on materiality opens up opportunities not to valorize objects nor lend them agentic qualities but rather to re-orient our gaze in a way that acknowledges the role of *things* in adjudicating and adjusting boundaries – things that often have been "black-boxed"[30] and disregarded because they reside so thoroughly in the background.

Such object-oriented approaches to studying boundaries have migrated from science and technology studies (STS). In their study of Berkeley's Museum of Vertebrate Zoology, Star and Griesemer showed how the museum's development required the collaboration of people from different fields and interests.[31] Boundary objects, they found, were those objects – like maps and diagrams – around which distinct groups with distinct identities could communicate and coordinate, without giving up allegiance to their own fields and their particular ways of seeing those objects. Boundary objects thus are plastic enough to facilitate a variety of meanings across knowledge boundaries yet simultaneously "rigid enough to support particular meanings within them."[32] Another related and important concept to emerge from STS is "trading zone." In his study of the history of physics, Galison shows how different cultures within physics – while possessing their own identities, traditions, and epistemological claims – managed to develop "contact languages" of exchange as they worked in socio-technical spaces such as laboratories – spaces he calls trading zones.[33] He concludes that, in the trading zone, even though different groups ascribe different meanings to words like "mass" and "energy,"

> [t]wo groups can agree on rules of exchange even if they ascribe utterly different significance to the objects being exchanged; they may even disagree on the meaning of the exchange process itself. Nonetheless, the trading partners can hammer out a *local* coordination despite vast *global* differences (emphasis original).[34]

In synthesizing these concepts and applying them to communication, Turner has argued that certain media formations, such as the *Whole Earth Catalog* and its fusion of 1960s counterculture and cyberculture, can function as "network forums" – venues in which dispersed members gather around key "objects," accomplish "trade" together, and ultimately forge new social networks and languages of coordination.[35] Finally, bringing this home to journalism studies, Kreiss and colleagues suggest that the 2012 Democratic National Convention functioned as a "boundary space" – a site through which actors in distinct but related fields seek status and legitimacy by performing for their own fields and for each other, in a single material place, even while also seeking the consent of the wider mediated publics through performances aimed at them.[36] Rather than seeking or accomplishing coordination, groups in boundary spaces – such as the journalists and political actors who Kreiss et al. studied – work to maintain and highlight their differences, even while sharing a space of mutual dependence.

All of these perspectives, borrowed from STS and increasingly adapted to communication, media and journalism studies, allow us to theorize and interrogate the *spatial* as well as the *material* nature of boundaries. In this way, they orient us not only to the human actors and their rhetorical constructions and social structures – important as they are – but also to *where* (in what spaces and places) and *how* (through and around which objects) such boundary work is undertaken. This more holistic view may be hard to maintain in a single project, given limitations of time, resources, human perception, and research methods. But the ideal nonetheless encourages us to take up the study of the boundaries of journalism in a more interdisciplinary fashion, continually cross-checking our findings and frames of reference to see how different perspectives might yield new insights. We might, as it were, need to cross boundaries a bit more readily – certainly beyond the comfortable domain of Gieryn's framework – to make the study of journalistic boundaries a more meaningful, diverse, and conceptually vibrant enterprise.

Particularly as media technologies continue to complicate the journalistic landscape, we'll need an approach to the boundaries of journalism that fully acknowledges the social and the material from multiple perspectives, allowing the range of human actors and nonhuman technological objects, and the interstitial spaces and relationships between them, to come into full view. We need not give technology undue agency in doing so, nor assume that objects are inert, for the boundaries concept is supple enough to help us uncover the social displays of authority, jurisdiction, and power – even as we account for the deeply structural and material factors that are enlisted in making boundaries matter.

Notes

1 Quoted in Bill Chappel, "Google Maps Displays Crimean Border Differently in Russia, U.S.," *NPR*, 12 April 2014, www.npr.org/blogs/thetwo-way/2014/04/12/302337754/google-maps-displays-crimean-border-differently-in-russia-u-s

2 Thomas F. Gieryn, "Boundary-Work and the Demarcation of Science from Non-Science: Strains and Interests in Professional Ideologies of Scientists," *American Sociological Review* 48, no. 6 (1983): 781–95.

3 See Andrew D. Abbott, *The System of Professions: An Essay on the Division of Expert Labor* (Chicago: University of Chicago Press, 1988).

4 Christopher W. Anderson, Emily Bell, and Clay Shirky, *Post-Industrial Journalism: Adapting to the Present* (New York: Tow Center for Digital Journalism, 2012). Available at http://towcenter.org/research/post-industrial-journalism/

5 Seth C. Lewis, "The Tension Between Professional Control and Open Participation: Journalism and its Boundaries," *Information, Communication, & Society* 15, no. 6 (2012): 836–66.

6 Anderson, Bell, and Shirky, *Post-Industrial Journalism*.

7 Stephen D. Reese, "Framing Public Life: A Bridging Model for Media Research," in *Framing Public Life: Perspectives on Media and Our Understanding of the Social World*, eds Stephen D. Reese, Oscar Gandy, and August Grant (Mahwah, NJ: Lawrence Erlbaum, 2001), 7–31.

8 For an overview, see eds Paul D'Angelo and Jim Kuypers, *Doing News Framing Analysis* (New York: Routledge, 2010).

9 Stephen D. Reese, "The Framing Project: A Bridging Model for Media Research Revisited," *Journal of Communication* 57, no. 1 (2007): 151.

10 Barbie Zelizer, *Taking Journalism Seriously: News and the Academy* (New York: Sage, 2004).

11 Gieryn, "Boundary-Work and the Demarcation of Science from Non-Science".
12 Gieryn, "Boundary-Work and the Demarcation of Science from Non-Science"; Thomas F. Gieryn, *Cultural Boundaries of Science: Credibility on the Line* (Chicago: University of Chicago Press, 1999).
13 Abbott, *The System of Professions*, 59.
14 Pierre Bourdieu, *The Field of Cultural Production: Essays on Art and Literature* (New York: Columbia University Press, 1993).
15 Seth C. Lewis, *Journalism Innovation and the Ethic of Participation: A Case Study of the Knight Foundation and its News Challenge*, 2010, unpublished dissertation, University of Texas at Austin.
16 Seth C. Lewis, "From Journalism to Information: The Transformation of the Knight Foundation and News Innovation," *Mass Communication and Society* 15, no. 3 (2012): 309–34.
17 Seth C. Lewis, "Journalism Innovation and Participation: An Analysis of the Knight News Challenge," *International Journal of Communication* 5 (2011): 1623–48. Available at http://ijoc.org/ojs/index.php/ijoc/article/view/1140
18 Lewis, "The Tension Between Professional Control and Open Participation," 851.
19 Abbott, *The System of Professions*.
20 Paul Starr, *The Social Transformation of American Medicine* (New York: Basic Books, 1982).
21 For example, see eds Tony Bennett and Patrick Joyce, *Material Powers: Cultural Studies, History and the Material Turn* (New York: Routledge, 2013).
22 See Bruno Latour, *Reassembling the Social: An Introduction to Actor-Network-Theory* (New York: Oxford University Press, 2005).
23 Ursula Plesner, "An Actor-Network Perspective on Changing Work Practices: Communication Technologies as Actants in Newswork," *Journalism* 10, no. 5 (2009): 604–26.
24 C.W. Anderson and Juliette De Maeyer, "Objects of journalism and the news," *Journalism* 16, no. 1 (2015): 3–9.
25 Daniel Kreiss, "Afterword," *Journalism* 16, no. 1 (2015): 153–6.
26 For example, see Amy Schmitz Weiss and David Domingo, "Innovation Processes in Online Newsrooms as Actor-Networks and Communities of Practice," *New Media & Society* 12, no. 7 (2010): 1156–71.
27 Anderson and De Maeyer, "Objects of journalism and the news."
28 Notably: Rodney Benson, "Challenging the 'New Descriptivism': Restoring Explanation, Evaluation and Theoretical Dialogue to Communication Research," Presentation at Qualitative Political Communication Pre-Conference, International Communication Association, *Seattle*, 22 May 2014, http://qualpolicomm.wordpress.com/2014/06/05/challenging-the-new-descriptivism-rod-bensons-talk-from-qualpolcomm-preconference/
29 Seth C. Lewis and Oscar Westlund, "Actors, Actants, Audiences, and Activities in Cross-Media News Work: A Matrix and a Research Agenda," *Digital Journalism* 3, no. 1 (2015): 19–37.
30 Bruno Latour, *Science in Action* (Cambridge, MA: Harvard University Press, 1987).
31 Susan Leigh Star and James R. Griesemer, "Institutional Ecology, 'Translations' and Boundary Objects: Amateurs and Professionals in Berkeley's Museum of Vertebrate Zoology, 1907–39," *Social Studies of Science* 19, no. 3 (1989): 387–420.
32 William C. Barley, Paul M. Leonardi, and Diane E. Bailey, "Engineering Objects for Collaboration: Strategies of Ambiguity and Clarity at Knowledge Boundaries," *Human Communication Research* 38, no. 3 (2012): 280–308 (281); Star and Griesemer, "Institutional Ecology, 'Translations,' and Boundary Objects," 393.
33 Peter Galison, *Image and Logic: A Material Culture of Microphysics* (Chicago: University of Chicago Press, 1997).

34 Galison, *Image and Logic*, 783.
35 Fred Turner, *From Counterculture to Cyberculture: Stewart Brand, the Whole Earth Network, and the Rise of Digital Utopianism* (Chicago: University of Chicago Press, 2006).
36 Daniel Kreiss, Laura Meadows, John Remensperger, "Political Performance, Boundary Spaces, and Active Spectatorship: Media Production at the 2012 Democratic National Convention," *Journalism* (2014).

Index